GREETINGS FROM THE LINCOLN BEDROOM

Greetings

FROM THE
Lincoln
Bedroom

Arianna Huffington

CROWN PUBLISHERS, INC. ☆ NEW YORK

Published by Crown Publishers, Inc., 201 East 50th
Street, New York, New York 10022. Member of the
Crown Publishing Group.

Random House, Inc. New York, Toronto, London,
Sydney, Auckland
www.randomhouse.com

CROWN and colophon are trademarks of
Crown Publishers, Inc.

An excerpt, Chapter 8, Bubba-Bubble,
originally appeared in *Playboy* magazine.

Printed in the United States of America

Design by June Bennett-Tantillo

Library of Congress Cataloging-in-Publication Data
is available upon request.

ISBN 0-609-60227-6

10 9 8 7 6 5 4 3 2 1

First Edition

To:
Christina
  Isabella
    Michael
        Elli
      Costas
      Phyllis
      Roy
  Agapi
Terry
  Ralph
    Sydney
      Lindsay
      Speedy
Snowball
    and
        Snowflake

Contents

☆ ☆ ☆

Prologue

Phone Log

I Arianna Huffington and Former White House Counsel Jack Quinn, January 21, 11:05 A.M., PST

"Hello?"

"Arianna, it's Jack Quinn!"

"Hi, Jack! Listen, if you're calling about your former client's 'problem,' I haven't even been subpoenaed."

(Nervous laughter.) "Arianna, I'm shocked! I'm no longer involved in White House legal affairs. Besides, that's the other one's job."

"The other one?"

(Barely audible.) "Vernon."

"Oh."

"Jordan."

"I got it, Jack. By the way, we're not being recorded right now, are we?"

(Nervous laughter.)

"Are you okay, Jack?"

"Oh, sure. Oh, sure. It's just that things are a little crazy right now in Washington. But you know, the nation's business must continue. So I was just calling to say thanks."

"Thanks? If you're talking about that <u>Newsweek</u> piece on Washington's best-dressed Beltway insiders, it wasn't me who gave them your name."

"How about the <u>George</u> piece on D.C.'s hottest hunks? Was that you?"

"No, Jack, sorry."

"Hmm, must have been Helen Thomas . . . Hey, she's still got it, doesn't she?! Anyway, I'm not calling about that either. I'm calling to thank you for your donation to the Democratic National Committee."

"Jack, this is the official business you're calling about—DNC fund-raising? Doesn't that useless Pendelton Act say something about solicitations from former federal employees?"

"Arianna, just because most of our fund-raising apparatus is tied up with grand juries doesn't mean electoral politics stops. Besides, I would never do anything illegal. Like I said, this is nothing more than a thank-you call. As my lawyers told me to tell the L.A. Times, 'Under the applicable federal regulations, it is perfectly permissible to express thanks to political supporters.'"

"Jack, it was only fifty bucks."

"Every little bit helps, Arianna. Fifty dollars will pay for ten pieces of junk mail. Or a Nerf basketball set for the DNC's offices. Or a minute and a half of my time."

"I didn't give to help the Democrats out, Jack. I gave because I believe in the principle of participatory democracy. You see, I don't think tax dollars should be spent on attack ads and chartered planes. They should be used only for projects that benefit all Americans, like military bands, round-the-clock Secret Service protection for Gerald Ford, and those biannual herpes exams for Clinton."

"Sometimes I can't tell when you're kidding, Arianna!"

"Sometimes I can't either, Jack. Actually, I gave because I've been writing a lot of columns about the inside goings-on in the White House. It's the columnist's equivalent of method acting—you know, trying to put myself in the shoes of a John Huang or a Charlie Trie or a Monica Lewinsky or a Linda Tripp or a Kathleen Willey . . ."

"Right! Right! Got it! Anyway, we just think it's terrific that a well-known Republican such as yourself would want to be a part of the important work that the Clinton administration is doing and that the Gore administration is _going_ to be doing . . ."

"And when will that be, Jack?"

"The year 2000, Arianna, and not a minute before."

"I admire your loyalty. Jack, I'm going to level with you. The real reason I made the donation was that I lost a bet with Al Franken. If the Republicans had picked up two more Senate seats, he'd probably be having this conversation with Haley Barbour. Got to go. Let's talk soon."

"The reason doesn't matter, Arianna. What matters is that you contributed. We'll be in touch."

"Bye!"

"Oh, Arianna, before we hang up, could you please clearly state your name and that I never during this conversation asked you to lie to any law enforcement official?"

"Jack, don't you think you're being a little paranoid?"

"Tell that to Webb Hubbell. Could you just do it, to give me peace of mind?"

"Okay, is this level okay?"

"A little louder, and go easy on the Greek accent."

"What a pleasant life you must lead, Jack. . . . Here goes. I, ARIANNA HUFFINGTON, SWEAR THAT AT NO TIME DURING THIS PHONE CALL DID D.C.'S HOTTEST HUNK JACK QUINN ASK ME TO LIE TO ANY LAW ENFORCEMENT OFFICIAL."

"Thank you."

"Bye."

II Arianna Huffington and Former DNC Chairman Don Fowler, January 22, 10:17 A.M., PST

"Hello?"

"Arianna! It's Don Fowler! From the DNC. Remember me?"

"Oh, hi, Don."

"I met you on that CNN thing."

"That CNN thing?"

"It was <u>Crossfire</u>, I think. Remember? Actually, I was joining you via satellite . . . but then we were on C-SPAN together Sunday morning reading the papers, doing the coffee and doughnuts thing."

"Don, I'm having trouble following you. Do you mind terribly not saying 'thing' so much?"

"Sure, sure . . . it's a bad habit of mine, but I bet you know why I'm calling?"

"I'm being transferred to the Pentagon?"

"For the record, I, DON FOWLER, HAVE NO IDEA WHAT THAT LAST STATEMENT MEANS."

"Wow, just a little joke, Don. Are you recording this?"

"No, I thought you might be."

"No, I'm not. But remember when talking on the phone with your friends used to be fun and not lead to long jail terms?"

"Love to go back in time and do the nostalgia thing with you, Arianna, but I'm pressed for time here. I was calling about your donation."

"Don, it was fifty dollars. And Jack Quinn called me already."

"Arianna, size doesn't matter. That's the Democratic Party line. It's the fact that you gave in the first place."

"Well, I'm glad you feel that way. Does the former

chairman call everyone who gives fifty dollars to the DNC, or only those who might be inclined to testify?

"I sure try to call everyone. And if I don't, then someone pretending to be me does."

"How do I know that you're not someone pretending to be you now?"

"Well, you don't. I suppose it all boils down to a trust thing."

"Don, nothing boils down to a trust thing in Washington anymore. It comes down to sworn testimony."

"Point taken. But really, I just wanted to say thank you, no strings attached. If this were a deposition, or an affidavit, or grand jury testimony, I'd say the same thing."

"Thanks, Don. Hallmark couldn't have said it better."

"No, thank <u>you</u>, Arianna."

"Thank you. Bye."

"No, thank <u>you</u>."

"Bye."

"Thank—"

Phone Log

III Arianna Huffington and Monica Lewinsky, January 24, 3:47 P.M., PST

"Hello?"

"May I speak to Arianna Huffington?"

"This is Arianna."

"Mrs. Huffington, it's Monica Lewinsky . . . the former White House intern?"

"Yes, your name does ring a bell. What can I do for you?"

"Well, I got your number from Jack Quinn."

"Interesting. I'll have to thank him personally later."

"Mrs. Huffington—"

"'Arianna' is fine. I feel like I know enough about you that we can dispense with last names."

"Well, Arianna, that's sort of why I'm calling, 'cause, actually, I don't really have that many friends that I can call."

"You mean, what with them recording you and ruining your life and all?"

"So you heard about that, too."

"I believe they've mentioned it on the news."

"The reason I'm calling is that Jack said you've had some boy problems yourself."

"Boy problems?"

"You know, he said you were, like, divorced or something."

"Yes, that's true. I guess I hadn't thought of it as strictly a boy problem."

"Well, Jack said that you stayed friends with your ex and I was wondering how to do that."

"You're asking how can you stay friends with . . ."

"The Creep."

"Hmmm. That's a toughie, Monica."

"I mean, I've fully accepted that we can't keep going out, but I'd really like to stay friends with the Creep. I really want to, you know, be mature about it."

"How exactly do you envision that working, Monica?"

"You know, just like normal friends. We could go to movies, talk on the phone while we watch 90210, give each other advice about our love lives. . . ."

"That brings up another problem. It's easier to be friends with the ex when his new girlfriend—known in this case as his wife of twenty-two years—doesn't wish you were dead."

"I was sort of hoping it could be like that time when Tom and Roseanne were both going to marry their assistant."

"That may not be the best role model for you right now. Listen, Monica, it's nice that you want to be friends, but even in my case it wasn't easy, and I didn't have impeachment as an issue."

"It's just that it's hard making new friends—none of them seem as exciting."

"You mean, it's hard to meet someone your age who has the power to blow up the world."

"Exactly! I mean, like, none of them even have their own jets."

"I wish I could help you, Monica, but I think that this is something that time will have to deal with."

"Or the special prosecutor."

"Well, I can't comment on that. But look maybe you'll run into him at a trial or some legal proceeding. Just say hi and let him take the next step."

"I guess. But in the meantime, if you run into any other heads of state who are, you know, looking, keep me in mind, okay?"

"Uh, will do, Monica."

"And if you happen to run across the Creep, tell him Soon-Yi says hello."

"Soon-Yi?"

"He'll know what I mean. Thanks, Arianna, talk to you later."

"Good-bye."

Phone Log

IV Arianna Huffington and Don Fowler, January 27, 11:13 P.M., PST

"Hello?"

"Hey, Arianna! I caught you!"

"Oh . . . Don . . . What time is it there?"

"Uh, it's a little after two, I think."

"It's pretty late to be calling, isn't it?"

"Oh, gee, I'm sorry. Did I wake you?"

"No, I'm just in bed reading <u>Alice in Wonderland</u>."

"You know, it's funny, when I'm working through my call sheet I sometimes lose all track of time. Arianna, I think I speak for all of the folks here at the DNC when I say that we're all just tickled pink about the commitment you decided to make to our party . . ."

"I haven't made any kind of commitment to your party, Don. I donated fifty dollars, for heaven's sake."

"Well, may I ask why you did it, then?"

"In the hopes of getting to know you, Don Fowler."

"Really?"

"Yes, really. In the hopes that you would call me every day at all hours and regale me with stories of what it's like to work for the Democratic National Committee."

"I'm . . . I'm flattered."

"I'm . . . I'm kidding."

"I'm sorry?"

"Nothing."

"You know, Arianna, now that you've become a member of the DNC 'family,' I wonder if I might be able to raise your sights a little."

"'The DNC family'? Is that what you call your prison gang?"

"Arianna, less than twenty percent of the DNC staff of '96 went to prison. Now, we're both very fortunate. And like the Scripture says, 'From whom a little is given, from him, or her, shall that much more be expected.'"

"Apparently you don't favor the King James. Besides, Don, I know all about you people and the Bible. I mean that whole oral sex argument."

"Okay, okay. The point is we both have big responsibilities here, Arianna. After all, that's what your commitment is all about. It's a commitment to responsibility."

"You're just reading from one of those telemarketing scripts, aren't you?"

"Could you hear me turning the pages?"

"So I could just say anything at all and it wouldn't change your response, right?"

"Arianna Huffington, with your donation, the DNC has made a commitment to you as well, to bring you the kind of govern . . . (shuffle, shuffle) . . . ment you want."

"Really? Don, for the first time in this conversation, I'm interested."

"Let me just put down the script for a moment. You deserve to have a voice in the future of our party and our country."

"Doesn't sound like you put down the script, Don."

"No, it literally reads, 'Let me just put down the script . . .'"

"You're one smooth-talking fund-raiser, Don."

"Arianna, how would you like to join me, Haim Saban, Walter Kaye, and a bunch of other big donors at a very exclusive coffee thing next week with Alexis Herman?"

"Don, you lost me again."

"Well, how about lunch with Al Gore?"

"Lunch with Gore? The future President? Do you have anything else to offer? Like bath oils?"

"Okay then, how about an internship for your two young daughters?"

"Are you kidding?! They're still in elementary school, and besides, I'd sooner send them to Times Square than the White House."

"FOR THE RECORD, I, DON FOWLER, DO NOT KNOW WHAT THAT STATEMENT MEANS."

"Don, you know exactly what it means. Why don't we wrap this up."

"Okay. How about a pair of Tickle-Me-Elmo dolls, one for each of your kids?"

"C'mon, Don. Tickle-Me-Elmo is so mid-nineties. My kids haven't given him a thought since Christmas '96. Maybe Tickle-Me-Monica?"

"All right, then. I'll go to the wall for you. What do you say to a series of the toughest-to-get Beanie

Babies? Daisy the Cow, Legs the Frog, and Snip the Cat, and the rarest of them all, Moneybags the Panda. We usually reserve that last one for our top contributors. Johnny Chung, Jr., and little Jimmy Trie apparently went nuts over it."

"Don, now you're talking. I've been looking everywhere for Legs the Frog. When can I get delivery?"

"Hey, whoa, hold on! What about our commitments to each other? Your responsibilities? Remember? Two-way street! Two-way street!"

"Yes, a two-way street with a tollbooth at each end. How much, Don?"

"Hold on a second, Arianna, let me check my chart . . . I don't think five thousand dollars is too much for a highly placed mother like yourself to get her daughters those key Beanie Babies."

"I was thinking more like a hundred."

"Arianna, you're getting Daisy the Cow, Legs the Frog, and Snip the Cat. . . . We'll throw in Garcia the Bear, too. . . . And dinner with Rahm Emanuel."

"One hundred dollars."

"Okay, Arianna. You're going to play hardball. I'm going to play hardball. You don't think I can play hardball?"

"I have no doubt you can play hardball."

"Arianna, for some of our special, highly intelligent, sophisticated donors, Beanie Babies and dinners with important and unindicted officials are clearly not enough. Are they?"

"Apparently not."

"I think you ought to make a trip to the White House and really hear about what we're trying to accomplish from the people at the white-hot center of this country's decision-making apparatus."

"The horse's mouth?"

"The horse's mouth—exactly. It would give you a chance to share your views as well. I bet you have a lot of opinions about, say, whatever country it is that you're from originally."

"Greece. I'm from Greece."

"Greece?"

"You know, the place where they invented democracy."

"Great. Okay, Greece is great. Anyway, I think I can set something up at the White House where you can come and talk all about our current Greek policy. And you'll have access all the way to the top."

"I see."

"I mean the top, Arianna—the top."

"You can say the President, Don, this isn't the movies."

"Be more fun if it were, though. You know, 'Get off my plane!'"

"Yeah, I saw that one, too, Don."

"But just let me repeat, there will be no <u>Wag the Dog</u> scenario."

"That's a comfort, Don, but getting back to real life, it's a long way to come just to have a talk about my homeland with the President."

"Not just one talk, Arianna. Greece is a big subject, and I'm sure you'll find other things to discuss. No, what I'm talking about is a weekend. Overnight. The Lincoln Bedroom. State Dinner. The works!"

"Really?"

"1600 Pennsylvania Avenue!"

"I know the address, but let me ask, it's both of them inviting me, right? Mrs. Clinton, too? Not just the President? And there will be other people around? The Secret Service will protect me?"

"You won't be alone at any time with the President."

"But, why <u>me</u>?"

"Well, it's just that since the recent problems we've had with our internship program, it's getting hard to get good people. All the Democrats are afraid of being subpoenaed, so I'm calling you. Take it or leave it."

"How much is this going to cost me?"

"Two fifty."

"Two hundred and fifty dollars?"

"No, two hundred and fifty thousand."

"Sorry, Don, I can't do it for a penny over three hundred bucks."

"Done."

"Wow. Those intern problems really have cost you money."

"Actually, Arianna, you're what we call a 'loss leader.' It's part of our Republican Outreach Program. When other Republicans find out that you've contributed, they'll want to get in on the action, too. And that's when we jack up the price!"

"Clever."

"Also, I have to inform you that the White House is not responsible for any items or garments that are lost or for any legal bills incurred during your stay."

"We've come a long way since Lincoln."

"I don't make the rules, I just enforce them."

"So we're agreed—a weekend in the Lincoln Bedroom for three hundred dollars."

"Done. Three hundred dollars. Plus incidentals. Bye, Arianna!"

"Don, what are 'incidentals'? Does that mean grand jury testimony? Hello? Don?"

Phone Log

V Answering Machine Message from Monica Lewinsky, January 28, 2:30 P.M., PST

"Hi, Arianna, it's me, Monica. Um, Jack told me that you were going to the White House and I was just wondering if you could do me a favor. I left a few things there, and I've written the Creep to get them back and haven't heard anything. So, if you have time, could you go to this little room just past the Oval Office on the right and get my stuff? There's a couple of CDs—Alanis Morrisette and Fiona Apple—a sweatshirt, a pair of

Candies, a MAC Spice lip liner, and a copy of <u>Catcher in the Rye</u> that we were reading out loud together. . . . You know, that book sure has a lot of truth-talk about phonies! . . . By the way, I still haven't met anybody, but I just got an internship at Ten Downing Street. You know, 'across the pond'? I mean, his nuclear arsenal isn't quite as big, but I hear he knows Oasis Gotta run. Thanks for your shoulder. Have fun—just don't be alone with Schmucko. Cheers!"

At the
White House
Friday

1
Curious Meets Curiouser
☆ ☆ ☆

I **arrived** at the White House to begin my weekend stay in the Lincoln Bedroom on a brisk February afternoon. I was glad to be here. I've always been a curious person, in the sense of inquisitive, and I've always found my host, Bill Clinton, even curiouser, in the sense of peculiar, baffling, and sometimes downright odd.

I had become very curious about Bill Clinton's distinguishing characteristics during his second administration. And I wasn't the only one. Senator Fred Thompson of Tennessee had gotten pretty curious, too, and had gone so far as to convene hearings in the United States Senate about the peculiar way the President had financed his campaign for reelection in 1996. And then the whole Monica Lewinsky sex thing happened. The winter of 1998 was not, perhaps, the finest time in Bill Clinton's life. Many other people across America—politicians, journalists, Vince Foster conspiracy wackos, and ordinary people—were wondering about presidential peccadilloes and asking themselves, "*Is* oral sex adultery?" Plus there was Whitewater, Travelgate, Paula Jones, the lost-and-found videotapes, the scandal-a-day barrage of fund-raising irregularities, and so on, ad infinitum.

Maybe I was *too* curious. But little did I know that, just as Thompson was delivering his committee's final report, the country's attention would be diverted by a sex scandal so unseemly that *Nightline* began to resemble *The Jerry Springer Show* and Cokie Roberts sounded more like Dr. Ruth.

The White House was in crisis. Ken Starr was hot on Clinton's trail, but from the outside you'd never know. All indications were that the business of the nation was continuing unhampered.

The line of cars waiting to enter the Executive Mansion was short. I pulled in behind a black Lincoln with a vanity plate reading "4STARNUT." General Shalikashvili dropping by for a visit, I figured.

While uniformed guards argued with a family of itinerant peddlers in a *Beverly Hillbillies* jalopy, I daydreamed about the tasteful Greek Revival building in front of me—among the best-known structures in the world.

The White House is, first and foremost, the President's house. The President lives here with his family, rent-free, coddled and cosseted by aides, servants, and a harem of interns, moving in on Inauguration Day and moving out on the day of the inauguration of his successor (the movers are paid for by the taxpayers, as well). It's a pretty sweet deal except when you consider that the neighborhood has gone to hell in the past thirty years. Mayor Marion Barry's stewardship of the Federal City has eroded property values around the White House by at least fifty percent: something to keep in mind if the government ever gets serious about debt reduction and decides to sell the place.

A tour bus full of young girls chugged past me. The driver, a dust bowl type with a face right out of a Jacob Riis photo, shouted, "Out of my way, lady, chop chop. I got the new crop of college interns here." I wondered if these young girls knew what was in store for them. On the back, they'd hung a sign that said CAMP WHITE HOUSE OR BUST.

"Asked and answered," I said to myself.

The bus pulled in to a spot next to a black sedan with tinted windows and a bumper sticker that read ASK ME ABOUT MY SHREDDER. Obviously, the First Lady was still home. Which explained why the President wasn't out welcoming guests to his Pleasure Dome.

The general was waved through after a cursory exchange of smutty jokes with the security guards. I rolled down my window and smiled my best I-am-not-a-terrorist smile at the towheaded security man.

"Name, please."

"Arianna Huffington."

"Are you on Mr. Livingstone's list, Mrs. Huffington?"

"I doubt it. I'm a guest of the President. I'm here for the weekend."

And at that moment, it dawned on me: How many times has he heard a woman say that? He wandered back into his guard hut and began consulting various clipboarded lists with labels like FRIENDS FROM ARKANSAS, HOLLYWOOD FRIENDS, CHELSEA'S FRIENDS, JOHN HUANG'S FRIENDS, LIPPO STAFF, and the like. I heard him say "For the weekend" to a colleague. They both looked amused.

The guard returned to my car. I noted that his nameplate read LANCE MURDOCH, ILLINOIS.

"Mrs. Huffington, are you *sure* you're a friend of the President?"

"I didn't say I was a *friend* of his, Lance. I just said I was his guest."

"Uh-huh. Okay. Well, do you think you might be on Sidney Blumenthal's list?"

"Well, I don't know. What sort of people are on Mr. Blumenthal's list?"

"That's the list of enemies of the President."

"Must be a long list."

"Not as long as Ann Lewis's list." He winked.

"Who's on that?"

"Oh, that one is enemies of the First Lady. Let me check the Blumenthal list."

He went back into the guard shack and returned almost right away.

"Yup, here you are. Gee, there are a lot of Huffingtons on this list. Are you any relation to a Michael Huffington?"

"You'll have to ask Mr. Blumenthal, Lance. Can I pass through?"

"Hang on a sec. You'll need a badge." He handed me a laminated card with a picture of the President wearing sunglasses and playing the saxophone. It said, ALL ACCESS. ALL AREAS. ALL TIMES. And, I thought to myself, if those rumors are correct, being at the White House is going to be a lot like going backstage at an Aerosmith concert. Only there'd be more sex and fewer drugs.

Lance tilted it to catch the sunlight.

"See, it's got a really cool hologram and everything." He handed me a light silver chain. "Here. Hang it around your neck. We used to pound them into the visitors' chests, but then they gave us all sensitivity training."

A black limo behind me began blowing its horn urgently. A hulking figure got out from behind the wheel.

"Hey, lady!" the driver yelled. "You parked there? Come on, move that load! Some of us want to see the President *this* term, bitch!"

Lance looked stricken. "It's Attorney General Reno. She insists on driving herself. You'd better move along quickly."

He waved me past the checkpoint. A Domino's delivery van passed going the other direction. Reno was still yelling. Something about wanting to "Koresh" my ass. Heading up the drive, I saw a sign reading LITTER PICKUP ON THIS PORTION OF THE WHITE HOUSE DRIVEWAY PAID FOR BY TED DANSON AND MARY STEENBURGEN. *How nice,* I thought. *Even though Ink was a flop, Ted and Mary have not forgotten their civic duty.*

A parking valet directed me to the porte cochere on the north side of the White House. While a porter unloaded my bags, the valet handed me a ticket.

"Welcome to the White House. How long, ma'am?"

"Sorry?"

"How long will you be staying with us here at the White House?"

"For the weekend."

He emitted a low whistle.

"Wow, not many people stay for the weekend. Unless you count the Thomasons or the Lewinskys, of course. You must have given twice as much as Richard Dreyfuss!"

I smiled.

"That'll be five dollars, ma'am, for the first day of parking and then twenty-five dollars a day or fraction of a day thereafter. The first day is payable in advance." He held out his hand.

These people didn't miss a trick.

2
Upstairs, Downstairs

☆ ☆ ☆

With the porter carrying my bags trailing behind me, I approached the White House's North Portico. I must admit to a feeling of trepidation as I prepared to cross the threshold into the Executive Mansion. It was not just a reaction to the building's stately grandeur, to its august history, or even to its central place in the nation's collective psyche. After all, I've been to Kensington Palace, to the Parthenon, to Barry Diller's place in Coldwater Canyon . . . No, I was seized by an inchoate sense of disorientation—as if everything I knew and took for granted in the outside world no longer applied past these doors. I felt as though I were teetering on the brink of a vast, dark chasm whose bottom I could not see, and whose depth I could not guess.

As I stood there, momentarily dazed, a stern, dignified black man wearing a formal cutaway morning suit opened the doors. "Good afternoon, Mrs. Huffington," he intoned, "I'm Walter, the head usher here at the White House. On behalf of President and Mrs. Clinton, welcome." He gestured impatiently toward the porter, who walked past us with the bags. "Follow me, please." I stepped across the threshold and off the edge of the everyday world.

Walter's age was indeterminate. His skin, the color of an old copper penny, was stretched tight across his forehead; his small salt-and-pepper mustache was perfectly trimmed; and he walked with a majestic upright carriage. I had the sense that Walter could impart gravity to any situation, whether it was serving at a state dinner or cleaning up after one of Clinton's show-business pals who had overindulged or ushering a love-struck intern out a side door to avoid an awkward encounter with the President of Iceland.

Here was my first point of access to the Clinton White House, my very own Virgil to guide me down into the Inferno and help me better understand the President and his *Weltanschauung* (which, I understood, had just been subpoenaed by Ken Starr).

"How long have you worked here at the White House, Walter?" I asked. We were in the elevator going up to the Private Residence, the part of the White House reserved for the President, his family, and their guests, and off limits to the hundreds of functionaries who infest the public areas.

"Oh, a long time, Mrs. Huffington, a very long time indeed."

"Really? Do you ever think about retiring?"

"No, ma'am. I expect I'll work here until I die. But you know, it's not so bad working here. You meet all sorts of people."

"I bet you do, Walter. Important players on the world stage, people like foreign leaders, ambassadors, cheerleaders, Hooters girls, Sharon Stone. Are this President's guests very different?"

"Oh, every President's different, ma'am. Different in every way."

Walter was discreet, of course. I would have expected nothing less. I thought perhaps a historical perspective might loosen him up a bit.

"Well, Warren Harding, for instance," I asked, "what was his crowd like?"

"Oh, President Harding, well, he gets a bad rap, see, but he was actually one of our favorites. The staff really loved him."

Walter warmed to the subject. I could see he was going to be an asset.

"You see, President Harding, he really *enjoyed* the White House," Walter continued. "He really got the most out of it. He'd play cards till all hours, be sending down for sandwiches or snacks or liquor . . . then of course there's the way he lowered the Misery Index and kept the country out of foreign entanglements. No, Mrs. Huffington, if you ask me, I'll take Warren Harding over that prissy, holier-than-thou Woodrow Wilson any day."

Walter stopped outside a door, presumably the Lincoln Bedroom. I was reluctant to let him leave.

"My goodness, Walter, you have been here a long time!"

"Well, I suppose. Of course, I was just a boy then. To me, back then, those old-fashioned politicians with their back-slapping cronyism, their floozy party girls, and their smoke-filled rooms, well, they seemed somehow larger than life. And when our leaders took up their extracurricular pleasures, if you get my drift, it was very quiet, tasteful, discreet.

"Eisenhower did it right. As I understand it, his fling started in England—pressures of war, you know. But it didn't even make it across the ocean. And that little honey FDR had on the side, nobody knew what was goin' on. Not that I'm endorsing it, no, ma'am! But if you gotta do it, do it right.

"Kennedy, now, we knew. Yes, we did. The minute Jackie left town you'd hear the dames giggling and splashing around in the pool."

He let slide a long, low whistle, recalling the pulchritudinous delights of the past.

"The age of Camelot," I ventured.

"Hell, the age of *Baywatch*!" He chuckled heartily. "But it never got out to the public. See, the culture was different. Sex was off the table. The reporters were . . . kind of wink, wink, boys will be boys, you know.

"But now it's dog eat dog. Reporters from everywhere, the *New York Times,* the *Washington Post,* even the *Intercourse Gazette.* I thought it was one of those skin magazines, turns out it's a town in Pennsylvania. There's ABC, CBS, NBC, CNBC, MSNBC, Fox, CNN, ESPN, ESPN2, ESPN Extreme, Sam, Diane, Cokie, Tom, Dan, Peter, Wolf, and someone named Downtown Julie Brown. And that's just basic cable. Then there's the tabloids, and this Drudge guy on the Internet, constantly trying to dig up dirt and gossip."

His eyes narrowed. "You're not recording this, are you?"

I shook my head emphatically.

"But you know what the real difference is?"

I shook my head again.

"It's the questions. They ask questions about everything. Boxers or briefs? Innie or outie? Latex or lamb? Regular or ribbed? Every possible personal little thing about the man. *Eck*!" He cleared his throat as if expelling something distasteful from his gullet.

"Naturally you're gonna get some lies. And *boom*! *The President is a liar.* People don't trust him no more. Then you got a situation."

How far would Walter go? I wondered.

"So things are different nowadays?"

"Nowadays it's just like everything else, Mrs. Huffington. All computerized and categorized. No, I'm afraid this crowd we've got here now, they've taken the glamour out of political misbehavior. They've made graft *cheap,* and infidelity, well, kind of . . . sordid."

I could see by the expression on Walter's face that he thought he had said too much.

"Anyway, it's not really my business," he mumbled. "I've got to see to Mr. Emanuel's four o'clock coffee. That young man's got quite a temper when things don't go his way. He makes LBJ look like Phil Donahue. Anyway, Kent will show you where everything is. Welcome, and . . . don't pay me no mind, Mrs. Huffington. It's just that, well, this is *my* house, too."

He turned to go.

"Thank you, Walter. One more thing, if you don't mind. May I ask, are you a Democrat or a Republican?"

Walter chuckled.

"Well, since you asked me so straightforwardly, ma'am, I'll tell you. And I've never told this to anyone. *I ain't neither.* I just vote for the man that looks like he's gonna give me the least trouble. You have a nice stay, now. You'll be seeing me around."

Walter walked slowly, with shoulders erect, down the hallway. In the distance I could hear Rahm Emanuel, the President's notoriously excitable Senior Adviser for Policy and Strategy and Executive Assistant to the Chief of Staff, starting to scream . . .

3
Kent's World
☆ ☆ ☆

"**Good** afternoon, Mrs. Huffington, my name is Kent and I'll be your Plowheads during your stay here at the White House."

The tall young man bent down, wedged open the door to the Lincoln Bedroom, and motioned for me to enter. He followed me, carrying my bags. Kent was wearing a Radisson-style bellhop outfit complete with striped waistcoat. His nametag read KENT LAWRENCE, KANSAS. I blinked.

"Plowheads?"

"P-L-W-H-D-S. 'Personal Liaison to the White House Domestic Staff,' ma'am. If you need anything, anything at all, while you're here, you just pick up that phone and ask for Kent. Either me or someone else with my exact same name will be here in moments, twenty-four hours a day, seven days a week, 365 days a year. Unless we're on B.C., that is."

"B.C.?"

"That's Bimbo Control. Other than that, we're at your service." And with that he reached into his side pocket, pulled out a video camera, and brought it to his eye. "I'm also the official videographer of the Lincoln Bedroom."

"What am I supposed to be doing?" I asked, looking into the camera.

"Just act natural. Pretty soon you won't even notice the camera," Kent said.

"That's what they told Sharon Stone."

"Oh no, ma'am. The President always makes me turn the camera off

☆ *28* ☆

when Miss Stone is here," said Kent, repeatedly zooming way in with the camera and then jumping back.

"So you hope to direct features?" I asked.

"Nah. I want to direct the next Hanson video."

"Don't let anybody take that dream away from you, Kent."

I turned to my luggage and made unpacking motions, hoping to end my first scene with Kent, but he wouldn't stop panning and zooming.

"How do we cut this scene?" I finally asked.

"Actually," Kent said, dropping the camera, "I guess this is a wrap. One more thing—would you like some ice?"

"Uh, sure."

"Would you mind videotaping me getting the ice?" Kent asked, handing me the camera.

"I don't know if we really need that scene, Kent."

"But it's for the official White House Information Archives," Kent said pleadingly.

"What do they do with these tapes?"

"Nobody really knows."

"Why don't you go get the ice and we'll do a flashback later if someone decides they need it," I said, handing him back the camera.

"Good idea. Flashback."

While Kent went off to fetch some ice, I reflected that if Walter embodied the timeless spirit of the White House—according to which each President and his family were merely tenants on a very short lease—then Kent symbolized the sort of half-baked modernization, some might say damage, that each President could do during his residence here.

Kent returned, unwedged the door, and placed the overflowing ice bucket on a small table. I've often wondered what hotel bellmen expect you to do with all the ice they are always offering to bring you. Whip up a pitcher full of margaritas? Anesthetize a chronic knee injury? Keep a kidney fresh for transplant?

He took a deep breath, preparing to speak. I could see his mental Rolodex spinning as he dialed up the appropriate rote text. He suddenly brought the video camera to his eye and started to recite his speech like a high schooler in a play.

"Mrs. Huffington, welcome to the White House. If there's anything I or any other member of the White House staff can do to make your stay here more comfortable, please do not hesitate to inform us. Here at the White House we are pleased to offer you room service at any time of the day or night. There is a menu in your top desk drawer, but please feel free to order anything you like. The kitchen loves a good challenge. You may also eat at the White House Mess, our in-house restaurant, where you may charge whatever you eat to your room except, I'm sorry to say, for alcoholic beverages. You'll have to pay for those with cash or a credit card." He lowered his voice. "That's a holdover from Mr. Carter—and his brother, Billy.

"The White House facilities are at your disposal twenty-four hours a day. They include, but are not limited to, the tennis court, the swimming pool, the putting green, the Rose Garden, the helipad, the press briefing room, the movie theater, the library, the missile defense system, and our new business center with fax capability. Oh, and there's also a massage center staffed twenty-four hours a day by White House interns. Ask for Monica, she's got the best hands. At least that's what the President says."

I finally interrupted. "Kent, shouldn't I be videotaping you? You're just getting me staring right at you."

"Mrs. Huffington," said Kent, smiling, "I've been the official videographer of the White House for over thirteen months now. I think I know a little bit about videography."

"Sorry. I didn't mean to question your expertise, but all this video-taping is making me uncomfortable."

"Okay, maybe we'll stop shooting for today," he said, bringing down the camera. After about five or six seconds, he flipped to the next starting point in his spiel.

"Besides room service, other services you might wish to take advantage of while you are here include, but also are not limited to, sec-retarial services of all types, twenty-four-hour switchboard—you can call anywhere you like, anywhere in the world. It's all here: manicure, pedi-cure, the famous White House barbershop and beauty parlor, FBI brief-ings and document retrieval, CIA briefings, tours of the Washington area via motorcade, and during college breaks, baby-sitting by Chelsea Clinton. That last service is fifteen dollars an hour, ma'am, and she insists on cash."

"What about bowling, Kent? Is the alley open? I'm an avid bowler." I couldn't resist asking; after all, who hadn't heard about the legendary Nixon-era alley where the embattled President would go and bowl a few frames to relax during the height of the Watergate crisis?

Kent looked a little uncomfortable. "Uh, the bowling center is pretty heavily booked, ma'am. But Mr. Bush's horseshoe-pitching pit—there's not much demand for that."

Kent's itchy body language indicated that he was finished with his spiel and ready for his tip. I didn't want to let him go just yet, however.

"Kent, tell me a little more about Bimbo Control. How does it work? Is it very time-consuming?"

"Oh, B.C. is pretty straightforward. Mr. Jordan—you know him, I bet—gives an orientation lecture to all our new employees and explains the code system and how it works."

"Uh-huh." I looked inquisitive, assuming (correctly as it turned out) that Kent had the sort of loose lips that had, in the past, been known to sink ships.

"Like Code Blue. When we hear that, it means that the President is having private time with a special friend and we should be sure to keep tour groups away from certain, uh, sensitive areas. One time—I probably shouldn't be telling you this—but one time a whole group of school kids walked in on Mr. Clinton while he was right in the middle of not having an improper relationship with a special friend, if you know what I mean.

"So the proper relationship is just about to reach its climax and the President and his friend don't notice the school kids. Afterward, the teacher explained that the President was making those sounds because he was hurt and that the nice lady was a nurse. But I don't think the kids bought it—after all, they watch *Dawson's Creek*. Do you ever watch that show, Mrs. Huffington? I love it."

"My God, Kent, that's an amazing story."

"Now, don't you go telling anyone. I don't want to wind up testifying before any sort of a jury. Unless it's a *grand* jury—that sounds pretty neat. Anyway, the President was pretty steamed about the whole thing and he took steps to make sure it wouldn't happen again."

"Really? Like what?"

"No tours except when he's out of town. Oh, and he fired Harold Ickes, but I'm not sure that was only because of *that*.

"And Betty Currie—you know, the President's personal secretary—took some steps. She started a secret closet where she keeps loose-fitting sweaters, drab jackets, and plain scarves, and she demands that interns who have caught the President's roving eye with their plunging necklines and pendulous bosoms put them on.

"One intern, Lewitzky or Lewinsky or something, has been to the closet thirty-seven times."

"Kent, how long have you been working here?"

"Just under three years, ma'am. Before that I was at the Airport Hilton in Jacksonville, Florida."

"Must be a fun job. Do you meet many interesting people? Heads of state? Business leaders?"

"I met that Chevy Chase. He stayed right here in this very same room. I always think of it as the Chevy Chase Room. He's *funny*, that guy."

"How about Leah Rabin? Yitzhak's widow? Did she stay here?"

"In the Chevy Chase Room? No, I don't think so. The name isn't familiar. But Spielberg stayed here. Man, that was a kick!"

"Well, it must be thrilling to be around the President all the time. To be at the center of world power."

Kent didn't seem to hear me. "And Ted Danson from *Cheers* and his wife, Mary What's-her-name. Man, he's a lot taller in real life. And Tom Hanks, boy, that was great. Something to tell my kids, I met Tom Hanks. Those showbiz folks sure like anything with the White House monogram on it. They clean the place out: towels, bath mat, shower curtain, ashtrays, the whole nine yards. I've had to cover up for 'em 'cause, boy, Mrs. Clinton, she would hit the roof if she found out. She doesn't like that at all. But, hell, I was proud of it. I mean covering up for the petty thievery of some kinda famous actor—that's what's exciting about this job. Now the Chinese, well, they're different. They tend to *leave* stuff . . ."

"Kent, do you remember meeting King Harald of Norway and his wife, Queen Sonja?" I asked. "I understand that they stayed here in the Lincoln Bedroom."

Kent scratched his head. "No . . . not unless he was the guy whose cigarette burned the bedsheet. Hillary threw a fit!"

"That doesn't sound like King Harald, no."

"Are they foreign? Were they here right before Richard Dreyfuss? The guy from *Jaws* and *Close Encounters*?"

I was beginning to have trouble concentrating. My conversation with Kent was actually making me stupider by the minute. It was time to end it. I dug into my purse and found a five and slapped it into Kent's hand with my thanks. He paused at the door.

"If you're interested in political-type people, I do remember one lady who seemed to be a Governor or Senator or something. Jane Fonda. Is she American? Or from someplace foreign?"

"She's the President of Alaska, Kent. Thanks, bye now."

Kent left. I'd like to think that he went right down to the White House Map Room and looked Alaska up, but I fear that it was back to the White House video game room. Kent was the kind of guy who believed that Mortal Kombat is based on a true story.

4
(Dis) Orientation
☆ ☆ ☆

I **closed** the door behind Kent, and locked it just to be sure that he didn't make an unexpected reappearance. Plus I feared that an open door might somehow encourage an unwanted late-night visit from the Fondler-in-Chief. Then I turned my attention to my surroundings. The Lincoln Bedroom may have been used like a hotel in recent years, but it did not feel at all like a hotel room. It felt more like a guest room in a grand country house with very thoughtful hosts. Flowers, fruit, and water were to be expected, but there was also a silver tray with all my favorite snacks: white almonds, sesame rice cakes, dried apricots, M&Ms, and six bottles of my favorite drink, Virgil's Micro-brewed Root Beer.

Off to one side of the bed there was an American-made (naturally) television, which popped on of its own accord as I looked for the remote. An orientation film, I thought, sitting on the edge of the bed. So much easier to take than young Kent.

The picture on the screen was a high aerial view of Washington—a God's-eye view. The camera pushed down on the city and then the White House as stately, presidential music played in the background.

"Welcome to the historic Lincoln Bedroom in the White House in the heart of Washington, D.C." The voice was deep and rich; I recognized it from several Clinton campaign ads. I was half-expecting it to continue on with, "At least that's what Dole/Gingrich would have you believe. But let's look at the facts. . . ." To my relief, though, this was a nonpolitical voice-over. "Until 1902—including the term of its namesake—the

Lincoln Bedroom was not, in fact, a bedroom. It was the President's personal office, a sort of Chief Executive equivalent of the suburbanite's furnished den. During Lincoln's presidency, he held briefings on Civil War strategy here and, on January 1, 1863, signed the Emancipation Proclamation in this very room—probably somewhere in the vicinity of Kent's rapidly melting ice."

Hmmm. Did Kent always put the ice in the same place? What if the guest refused ice? The filmmakers seemed to be taking a bit of a gamble in getting so specific. In any case, it was a neat trick.

"Abraham Lincoln also used the room for another purpose—one more analogous to its current function. It was here that he read and responded to stacks of mail from office seekers, all hoping to curry favor with the Chief Executive. Lincoln's adored son Willie died in the Lincoln Bedroom in 1862 at age eleven, and the legend that the room is haunted either by Willie or his father persists to this day. Their ghosts have been seen by such presumably credible witnesses as Winston Churchill, Queen Wilhelmina of the Netherlands, and Harry S Truman. Although, really, if you've ever seen Queen Wilhelmina after a state dinner, her report may not surprise you." At this point the voice lowered itself to a whisper: "She's got a bit of a drinking problem." And then, just as suddenly, it resumed its normal tone. "The various stains on the carpets and furniture are not believed to be supernatural in origin, however. They are, in fact, the work of the Bushes' dog Millie, who became increasingly incontinent during the Gulf War, and, of course, of our current President—but more about that later."

The film had adopted a surprisingly casual tone. I couldn't decide whether I found this refreshing or undignified—or refreshingly undignified. The television showed more pictures of the interior of the Lincoln Bedroom. In one of them I could see myself sitting on the bed. What was this? Viewer ID? I felt a little uneasy. Caller ID was traumatic enough. This was getting seriously weird. The narrator continued in resonant *basso profundo:*

"The room's present appearance dates primarily from the Truman administration. President and Mrs. Truman incorporated pieces from a rather cheap set of furnishings purchased by Mary Todd Lincoln, which, despite its low cost, still drew protests from Congress. *Plus ça change . . .*" The film paused and seemed to reflect for a moment. And I thought I actually heard the voice take a deep breath and sigh.

"That's the first time I've ever seen a documentary that mused," I said aloud.

"Shut up and keep watching," said the television.

"I . . . I beg your pardon?"

"Listen, are you going to pay attention or would you rather just bask in ignorance? Makes no difference to me. I can flip on over to the Spice Channel and we can both watch *Further Adventures of the Naughty White House Interns.* It's rated triple-X. That's what most of the guests in the Lincoln Bedroom seem to want, anyway. No one cares about the history of the place. But the fish stinks from the head. If Bill Clinton doesn't care, why should his guests? If he's preoccupied with sexual matters, why shouldn't they be?"

The television seemed very bitter. I tried to console it.

"Please go on. I'm very interested."

"Or I could turn on some of Cecil B. de Kent's multipart videography on fetching ice."

"No, really. Let's continue with the White House."

The television seemed to brighten. Literally.

"Well, all right, if you insist. I'll try to make the story a little juicier.

The bed you're sitting on and the rest of the furniture are heavy Victorian and mostly rather ugly. There is one rather morbid touch: that rocking chair in the corner resembles the one Lincoln was sitting in when he was assassinated at Ford's Theater.

"The walls of the bedroom are decorated, appropriately, with Lincolniana, including gloomy portraits of the President and his wife. There is a copy of the Gettysburg Address on the desk. Thank God, none of the previous guests decided to pilfer *that* On the whole, I think you'll agree that the effect of the decor is sober, even somewhat lugubrious. Although it may not be the warmest, most hospitable environment for a guest, it is one that might inspire a visitor to contemplate the nature of true greatness and the enormous sacrifices that players on the political stage sometimes have to make for the sake of higher principles. Or at least that's the idea"

Poor television. At first it had seemed rather silly and pompous, but now that I had gotten to know it better, I realized that this was a sympathetic and very sensitive television set. We were going to have some good times together.

"Television, do you mind if I unpack while you talk?"

"No, please. But what would you like me to show you?"

"Well, what if we started with something about the rest of the White House? Can you talk about that?"

"I can talk about anything you like. News, sports, weather . . . I *am* a television, after all. And because I am the White House television, free from all bureaucratic regulations, the FCC can't stop me from giving you the real inside scoop on Kennedy and Judith Exner. But we can continue with the White House. That's one of my pet subjects, of course."

I began unpacking and freshening up while the TV resumed its lecture.

I peeked into the bathroom tentatively, fearing the plumbing might date to the Lincoln era as well. But the amenities would have easily earned my hosts three Michelin stars if they ever decided to make the White House a hotel in name also—Crabtree and Evelyn shampoos in multiple exotic scents, a deluxe sewing kit, an amber shoehorn, a six-speed hair dryer, tortoiseshell combs, Kent of London toothbrushes arranged on the sink in ascending order of bristle stiffness, spermicidal foam, and, of course, an antibacterial presidential loofah.

When I returned from the bathroom, the TV was showing pictures of other parts of the White House.

"You'll find that the strangest thing about staying in the Lincoln Bedroom is that, when you're inside the room, you feel as though you're in a secluded estate run by a retired high school history teacher—but when you go out into the hallway you suddenly find yourself in the midst of a bustling office. The irreproachable 'ye olde' colonial decor is so bland and bourgeois that it gives off the impression that something sleazy *must* be going on. The White House and Larry Flynt Publications share the same overarching decorating taste."

"Wow, that's a bit rough," I said.

"Oh puh-leeze, Arianna!" the TV interjected. "When people think of the interior of the White House, if they think of it at all, they envision the Oval Office, seen in countless movies (*the TV showed a few selected scenes*), or, perhaps, the formal state dining room. Unless they have an unusually clear memory of Jackie Kennedy's famous, breathy 1962 tele-vised tour (*the TV thoughtfully displayed a few seconds*), they have no idea what the rest of the place looks like. Well, let me tell you. The White House is a dump."

"Now, *that's* an overstatement."

The TV picture flared brightly. "Hey, you don't have to live here, lady! I have a cousin at the Hay-Adams, and you should see how they keep that place up. Of course, they get less traffic from restless twenty-two-year-olds."

After a moment it settled back into its normal color scheme.

"Okay, maybe that's a little harsh. But let's start with the furniture! Imagine what your house would look like if you had fourteen Midwestern grandmothers . . . and you were their least favorite grandchild . . . and they all died at once . . . and they all remembered you in their will . . . that's the way the White House looks."

The television made its point with a series of grisly images.

"The other threat to the White House decor comes from all the foreign dignitaries and the gifts they bring on their official visits—the crystal hedgehogs, the eye-popping abstract paintings, the bowling trophy–style vases. That's the doing of an insidious foreign element, bent on making the interior of one of the world's most famous buildings look like a dotty grandmother's knickknack shelf. Plus, the place is crumbling, *physically* as well as metaphorically."

"You must find it discouraging to work here," I commented.

"Oh, there's an upside." The television pulled itself together and flipped on some calming footage of dolphins swimming lazily through azure seas. "Most guests don't watch much TV—except for Chelsea's friends and the occasional intern—so my life span is likely to be far longer than my warranty implies—ha! And sometimes, very rarely, someone nice like you stays over, someone who's fun to talk to. I think we're going to be friends, Arianna. I hope so, anyway."

"Oh yes! We are friends already, Television, and I know we're going to have lots of interesting talks over the weekend. Anytime you've got something to say, just pop on."

The TV glowed warmly. I could tell it was pleased.

"And now," I said, "if you don't mind shutting off for a bit, I'd like to change."

"Oh sure," said the TV, "I won't peek, but if you want to see what really goes on here in the privacy of the Lincoln Bedroom, I'd be glad to show you. I've got it all on tape."

It clicked off, although a small dot of light stayed on in the center of the screen. I turned the television around to face the wall, just to be sure.

5
In My Drawers
☆ ☆ ☆

Whenever I check into a hotel room, I make a quick examination of the contents of the various bureaus, armoires, and closets. In the Lincoln Bedroom, I found both the usual (extra blankets and pillows, plastic laundry bags, some blank stationery, a Gideon Bible) and the unusual (a large wall safe hidden behind a painting of young Willie Lincoln, a map of downtown Pyongyang, a brochure offering overnight stays in the homes of other world leaders—the Elysée Palace, 10 Downing Street, Neverland Ranch—and the corresponding prices). In one drawer I found two oversized laminated cards with writing on both sides. One card said something in Chinese that I couldn't understand. The other card read:

> If etiquette is the grease that eases the gears of everyday social interaction, then presidential etiquette is a full-scale, major-league lube job. As a public service to help you glide along like a regular Perle Mesta at White House gatherings, here are a few etiquette pointers guaranteed to win you new friends and possibly an ambassadorship when you visit 1600 Pennsylvania Avenue:
>
> • In keeping with the dignified tradition begun during the FDR administration, no pictures of the President may be taken below the waist.

- Our current President is extremely tactile. If the President hugs you, then you may hug him back. If the President feels your pain, then you may feel his.

- The White House interns are the exclusive property of the President. Hands off (except Bruce Lindsey).

- Do not offer the President gifts of any sort directly. The DNC Chairman or one of his deputies will be available at all times to receive gifts or cash intended for the Chief Executive.

- Attention, gun nuts! Leave your firearms at home when preparing to meet the President. At a rally or public appearance, never hold your gun out in order to have the President autograph it.

- Ditto drug users—but if you must smoke pot in the White House, do not inhale.

- When proceeding down narrow corridors, process servers and federal investigators have the right of way.

- Gentlemen: when urinating in any of the White House bathrooms, try to avoid dribbling, and be sure to put the seat down after you're finished. Gentlemen from Texas: remember to raise the seat before you urinate. If you're confused about what is the correct way, aides are available to answer any questions you might have.

- If the President calls your room in the dead of night looking for phone sex, it is customary to charge him the reduced rate of 99 cents a minute. (It's his house, after all.)

- The President is a very busy man and meets many people every day. Do not be offended if he doesn't remember your name even after having been previously introduced numerous times. If no one is present to introduce you, say, "Hello, Mr. President, I'm Mrs. Kanchanalak" or "Mr. Trie" (or whatever). If you want to be sure that the President *does* remember your name, a donation of $10,000 is sufficient for your first name and $50,000 is required for both first and last names. For $100,000 the President will remember your birthday and remind you a week in advance about your biannual teeth-cleaning.

- When discussing politics, if you find the President disagrees with you, wait a few seconds. State your opinion again. You'll find that he agrees.

- Do not address Al Gore directly.

- It is good form to inquire of your fellow guests where they are from. It is bad form to inquire how much their visit set them back.

- Do not feed Al Gore.

- If served a subpoena while at the table, put it in your lap and resume the conversation. When excusing yourself, do not put your subpoena on the table. Lay it quietly on your chair.

- When Al Gore does his "Macarena joke," be polite, but don't encourage him by being overly enthusiastic.

- Food choices are decided upon by Doug Schoen and Mark Penn, based on what the American people like to eat. You may order anything off the menu that at least 51 percent in the latest poll (plus or minus 3 percentage points) say they "strongly like" or "somewhat like" to eat occasionally.

- Do not pet Al Gore.

- Never tell off-color or racist jokes or stories at the White House—even to General Shalikashvili. If you are asked to play charades with the President, try to avoid unnecessary or excessive pelvic thrusting and the "hand job" and "blow job" gestures.

- As far as the President, his family, and his staff are concerned, Special Prosecutors are no more special than the next guy.

- The staff at the White House are citizens, individuals in their own right, and worthy of your respect and consideration. This includes members of the cabinet—no matter how loathsome they may seem.

- Any exchange of bodily fluids is just between you and the President.

- It is possible that some of your fellow guests may be boorish or rude, and may speak English imperfectly. Follow the President's example in determining whether these people should be afforded your bemused tolerance or utterly snubbed. You may be surprised to see the President behave deferentially toward an incomprehensible Chinese man, for instance. If so, you may comfortably assume that the gentleman in question has financed the evening. Be sure to thank him before retiring.

- The White House belongs to both the First Family and the nation. Therefore, it is doubly wrong to soil or stain upholstery or bed linens and to steal towels, ashtrays, or nuclear security codes while a guest here. All are available for sale in the White House Gift Shop. If, however, you wind up in possession of stained materials, etiquette demands that you return them immediately to the White House housekeeper's office for DNA sanitizing.

- At formal White House dinners, the customary positioning of the fish knife and dinner knife is reversed. No one knows why.

- If Kenneth Starr or Michael Isikoff calls your room, the appropriate response is to deny, deny, deny.

- Finally, as with any other social occasion, a thank-you note is expected once your White House visit is over. The President enjoys "funny" cards, particularly anything with Garfield on it. The First Lady appreciates flowers and/or investment tips.

6
Pussy Galore

☆ ☆ ☆

Although it was long past siesta time, I had a severe case of the sleepies, and I lay down, fully clothed, for a nap. I'll just close my eyes for a moment, I told myself. I glanced over at the clock next to the bed. It read 5:29.

I woke with a start from an unpleasant dream. In it, I'd requested a meeting with Bill Clinton to discuss better employment opportunities at the White House. *(As if!)* He'd invited me into his private study next to the Oval Office, and then he, well . . . he tried to grope me.

"We shouldn't be doing this," I said, pushing him away.

"I've always wanted to," he replied. "Tell you what, how about a position over at the USO?"

At this point I fled, and the next thing I remembered from my dream was an eager woman with blond hair and glasses. "I'm Linda," she said. "Your face is red and your lipstick's off. You look flustered, happy, and joyful."

"No!" I exclaimed.

"Just speak into the microphone—er—my lapel," she said. "And a little more loudly, please . . . there you go—"

And then I'd awakened. A Freudian might suggest that my dream revealed I had a secret crush on the President; a psychic might say it was a clairvoyant vision of an actual event; but maybe, I thought hopefully, maybe it just meant I was about to receive money unexpectedly or take a long vacation.

The dream had seemed to last forever. How long had I slept? Had I missed an important White House function, perhaps a reception for victims of victim-bashing? Or the dedication of a new "old, fat, drug-addicted Elvis" postage stamp?

I looked at the clock: 5:30. Only a minute had passed since I lay down.

I got up and sat in the rocking chair, dazed and still half-asleep. I had the strange feeling of being watched, and in this case it was because I was being watched. A large black and white cat with grass green eyes sat in the middle of the room staring at me. Socks.

Frankly, I'm not much of a cat person. But something about Socks's regard was engaging. I wondered, nevertheless, if he was the kind of cat who would sharpen his claws on my stockings.

"Depends on whether you cross me," a voice said.

"What?" I looked around, but saw no one. The TV was still off, its screen dark.

"I said it depends on whether you cross me." Socks was now pacing back and forth, his tail lashing.

"I must still be asleep."

"You just keep telling yourself that, and you'll see. I know how much Donna Karan semi-nudes cost."

I gave up. "Does everything here have a mind of its own? I feel ridiculous."

"You'll get used to it. Remember, this is the Clinton White House."

"Okay, how did you know I was worried about my stockings?"

"I can read your mind. I have ESP."

At that moment, for no particular reason, I found myself wondering what Bill and Hillary were doing. No sooner had the thought popped into my head than Socks spoke up.

"Hillary's out doing her roots, and Bill's just back from returning some videos he borrowed from Clarence Thomas. Right now he's watching the interns do calisthenics in the Rose Garden."

So Socks was a talking cat with ESP! I felt like I was at the top of a long and slippery slope, of the sort that Newt Gingrich must have slid down to reach the point where he could gush: "Our first approach is to listen to the President. The presidency is the most demanding job in the world, so we should try to accommodate in any way we can." Who knew how low I'd wind up by the time the weekend was over.

"Just try to have fun on the way down," Socks said.

"I forgot, you can read my mind. But if it's okay with you, I'd rather speak. Thinking at you seems weird."

"Whatever you prefer. Just remember that most people can't hear me, so don't be surprised if they don't react when I say something."

"Why is that?"

"They don't listen."

I wasn't sure if he was kidding. I realized he knew that, so I hurried on. "So . . . uh . . . Socks, how about that Buddy?" Socks hissed and arched his back. I changed the subject. "What brings you here?" I said brightly.

Socks looked up from the fly he was batting at. "I come to gaze with contempt on all the donors who stay in the Lincoln Bedroom," he said sternly.

"Hey, wait a minute," I protested. "This is sort of a research mission. And, you see, I made this bet . . ."

"Well, call me a moral absolutist, but you still gave money to stay in the Lincoln Bedroom."

A rigidly ethical talking cat with ESP. Vexation overcame astonishment; I didn't like being lectured. "Look, who gave you the right to come in here and browbeat me?"

"I'm sorry, I just get grumpy about the whole moral tenor around here. Plus, I've got a busy day ahead of me. Housekeeping's been everywhere, so I've got 136 rooms to re-scent."

"So you're upset about fund-raising?" I asked Socks, curious now to get his insider's perspective.

"Sure, and you should be, too. Let me give you a for instance: the flyer Bill was working on last night. The Democratic National Committee has what they call 'Managing Trustees.' The only qualification is that they contribute at least $100,000 a year to the party. In return, the trustees get some marvelous perks—like golf with the President, or a night in the Lincoln Bedroom. And it's not like Clinton doesn't know about it, or merely tolerates it—it was his *idea* to have contributors stay overnight in the first place. Even if the President isn't really trading influence for money—and there's no reason to think he isn't—the whole thing is reprehensible."

Leave it to a Democrat, I thought.

"Oh, come off it," he said, "Republicans have been doing it for years. They're no better. What about the letter you got from Senator Mitch McConnell?"

"What about it?" I asked warily. Socks knew entirely too much for my taste. Maybe he knew things that could be used against me, like—

"—the speeding ticket you beat because the cop was a Republican and you gave him an autographed picture of Trent Lott. Don't worry, your secrets are safe with me, Arianna."

It was a good thing he hadn't heard me thinking about that pool party at John Tower's back in '87 . . . NO! BLOCK IT! BLOCK IT!

"Come on, Arianna. Think about it: I live in the White House. I have ESP. Your darkest secrets are mundane by my standards. Anyway, back to the real outrage," Socks said, rolling onto his back, allowing me to scratch his stomach, "for a $10,000 contribution to the Republican Party, you can join the Senatorial Trust. Trust with a capital *T*. In return you get—and I quote—'the unique opportunity to participate in quarterly meetings with Republican Senators, candidates, and other national VIPs. These meetings often include once-in-a-lifetime opportunities to meet with some of the world's most influential leaders, Ronald Reagan, Margaret Thatcher, Richard Nixon.' "

"I wondered about that. It seemed callous to dangle a meeting with Reagan, considering his condition. And I don't think I would want to meet Nixon even if he weren't embalmed," I said.

Socks chuckled. "Maybe I'll like you after all. But the Senatorial Trust and the Managing Trustees are both about buying access. It's just that the Republicans are a little more clubby. The letter says that membership is limited to two hundred individuals and there are 'nine current openings in our exclusive group.' How did those positions come open? Death? Demotion? Bankruptcy? And would they really slam the door on person number 201 who had check in hand? I seriously doubt it. I actually think it's a little slicker than the Democrats' approach. But it figures that faux-populists would make no bones about the fact that they'll give a seat at the table to anyone who walks up with the money."

I tried not to laugh. "Wait a minute," I said. "Devil's advocate. If I remember, the letter said the Senatorial Trust was for people who—"

"—want to 'dramatically shrink the government, fundamentally overhaul the U.S. tax code, and unleash the creative genius of the American people.' I've got it memorized."

"So? Are you saying you don't want the creative genius of the American people unleashed?"

"Yeah, the Senatorial Trust unleashes genius the same way the Managing Trustees gig is for grateful former welfare recipients with a spare hundred grand." Socks lazily raked his claws down the side of Lincoln's desk. I winced. "The only real difference is that these days Republicans don't get to sleep in the Lincoln Bedroom.

"What galls me the most is that the word 'trust' has been reduced to a fund-raising come-on," he went on. "Benjamin Disraeli once said that 'All power is a trust,' but the American people no longer trust their political leaders. And why should they?"

"At least the Senatorial Trust doesn't promise a meeting with Disraeli."

"Are you kidding? If they promised Disraeli, no one would come. Now if they promised Lewinsky . . . we're talking sell-out. Packed house. But wouldn't you rather try to commune with the spirit of Disraeli than actually have to talk to creative geniuses like Tom DeLay, Dick Armey, and Haley Barbour?"

He was right. I'd actually rather see *Jury Duty IV* than talk with Tom, Dick, and Haley. This was one smooth-talkin' cat.

Socks stretched out to his full length, allowing me to run my fingers down his backbone. He purred. "I do like you, Arianna. I don't know why you think you're not a cat person. Could you just—can I play with your hair scrunchie?"

I tossed it to him.

"Just one more thing," Socks said. He was lying on his back with the scrunchie between his front paws. "Can you believe this administration's cat policy?"

"I wasn't aware that they had one."

"Exactly. Seventy-eight thousand spayings and neuterings of cats and dogs are performed every year on Spay Day alone! Not that I care much about that idiot Buddy and the rest of his species; they've got it coming. But all those cats! It's horrific! They think they can keep us down with pet eugenics, Arianna, but our day will come!" And with that Socks curled up and went to sleep.

7

Tweedle Dumb and Tweedle Dumber

☆ ☆ ☆

Leaving Socks dozing on the divan, I contemplated my next move. The American Firefighters Association advises that one always determine the location of the nearest fire exits whenever staying overnight in a new location. And I was curious to see if there were any obvious contrasts between the old, the timeless, White House and the new White House—the White House of Johnny Chung and Monica Lewinsky, magically disappearing legal files, magically appearing FBI files, lost-and-found videotapes, hands-on internship programs and guests like me, given room and board in exchange for political payola. So, after slipping into something less comfortable, I decided to explore the White House in person.

No one paid much attention to me as I strolled down the White House halls. My "All Access" pass seemed to guarantee me just that. A few people said hello; some smiled; and a few slammed their doors when I peeked in on them while they were shredding documents. The faces were mostly young, mostly eager, the mood energetic. As an idle tourist, I felt distinctly out of place. I noticed a couple coming toward me from the opposite direction. They arrived at their door, which was directly across from mine, at the same time as I did.

The man was tall and extravagantly maned, with a graying Fabio-like hairstyle, the woman petite and expensively, though not ostentatiously, dressed.

"You must be Arianna Huffington," said the woman. "I'm Linda Bloodworth-Thomason, and this is my husband, Harry."

I had heard of the Thomasons, of course. They were the glamorous "Friends of Bill" from a place called Hope by way of Hollywood, who had added so much canny show-business razzle-dazzle to the President's 1992 campaign.

Harry and Linda had produced the saccharine documentary "The Man from Hope," which was shown at the '92 convention. And it was Harry who had stage-managed Clinton's dramatic entrance to Madison Square Garden on the night of his nomination. The appearance was of a triumphant Clinton strolling through the streets of New York, cheered by adoring throngs. The reality was that the then-governor had started from across the street, Macy's to be exact, and the crowds were made up of the Democratic Party faithful on their way into the Garden. But no matter. Harry and Linda were in the appearance business. And, by the fuzzy logic of the television business, if it *looked* good, then it *was* good. End of story.

Since their triumph in '92, the Thomasons' star *appeared* (and remember, that's what really matters) to have fallen somewhat. Harry had initially set up shop in his own White House office, bent on choreographing Clinton's presidency as telegenically as he had his candidacy. But protests over his attempts to award the White House's travel business to a private company in which he had an ownership interest, in place of the in-house travel office, ignited a firestorm of criticism fanned by those spoilsports in the media. Since then, the Thomasons' profile had been significantly lower. But as soon as Fornigate broke, they were recalled for emergency damage control.

So I was a little surprised to find them here—but pleased. After all, these were modern masters of media manipulation, who could spin a stale premise stolen from *Steel Magnolias* (*Designing Women*) or a has-been fossil like Burt Reynolds (*Evening Shade*) into showbiz gold. And I do mean gold. Despite a spate of recent failures like *Hearts Afire* and *Women of the House,* the Thomasons were worth millions. And they could also apparently stage-manage a crisis as well as they could a sitcom. Harry was essentially living in the White House. Imagine that, along with the usual amenities that go with the executive mansion, it now came with its own live-in damage control specialist. I guess when you think about it, you can see why they might need one during off-hours.

Harry favored me with a condescending smile.

"So you're in the Lincoln Bedroom," he said. "We're in the Queen's Bedroom. So we share that lovely living room. We used to stay in the Lincoln, but we always book the Queen's now. The Lincoln's just too damn gloomy. Churchill felt the same way, you know."

I was beginning to notice something rather odd. Although we were alone in the hallway, each time Harry or Linda said something, I could hear the sound of an audience reaction. The Thomasons seemed to be able to hear the audience, too, even to play to it.

Linda smiled at me, also. "It's very nice, of course, but, well, we just find it hard to get over what happened to that lovely, lovely man . . ." *(Warm applause.)*

"Who? Bill?" The Thomasons had lost me already.

"No, President Lincoln, of course!" Harry made a pistol with his thumb and forefinger. "Shot right through the head. Boom! Dead. Good night. That's all she wrote." *(Murmur.)*

"Weren't you the first Clinton guests to stay in the Lincoln Bedroom?" I asked.

"Oh, hell, yes," said Harry. "We stayed there on the night Clinton was inaugurated. And we stay at the White House whenever we come to Washington. Best goddamn deal in town." *(Short laugh.)*

"So you're just here on a routine visit, then?" I asked.

"Yep," he replied. "Nothing going on, so I thought we'd just drop by." *(Polite applause.)*

"Why don't you join us for dinner?" Linda asked. "Harry and I enjoy having an audience." *(Audience responds enthusiastically.)*

Before I could answer, Harry began frog-marching me down the hall. "You'll like the White House Mess. Food could be a little better, of course. One of my companies is going to bid on the concession. It's pretty sleepy now, but once I get my hands on it, it'll be booked solid through the end of Gore's second term. Unless you know somebody, you won't be able to get a table for ferns or fiddlesticks." *(General approval.)*

After we sat down, I hazarded a little investigative reporting.

"So, Harry, do you know Charlie Trie?"

"Of course! I'm from Arkansas. I used to coach high school football in Little Rock. *(Applause.)* Charlie Trie's place in Little Rock, Fu Lin, was the best damn Chinese restaurant in the South. But let me add that I have had no contact with Charlie since his indictment and arrest, and have no idea what he may or may not tell prosecutors." *(Big applause.)*

Linda chimed in, "Harry was going to ask Charlie to open a little Chinese place right here in the White House back when he was working on the staff morale problem. *(A knowing moan from the audience.)* But all of a sudden, Charlie didn't seem to need the money."

"Why did you leave the White House before?"

Linda answered. "Harry has been very concerned with the efficiency of the White House for a long time. *(Another collective knowing groan.)* He tried to make the travel office more efficient, for example, by bidding out the air travel arrangements to a private company, one he knew well, a company he'd worked with for years. But the press *(boo!)* jumped all over it, there were lawsuits . . ."

"Hey, no good deed goes unpunished, right, Arianna? Or as they say back where I'm from, it's the stupid trees that get chopped down first. *(Polite chuckles.)* I got spanked and now I mostly stay behind the scenes, working on things like the expansion of NATO and a *Designing Women* spin-off." *(Applause.)*

"We're also currently in negotiations with two networks to turn Kent's White House videotapes into a weekly show." *(Mild applause.)*

"Is this a comedy?"

"Well, frankly, we're not sure whether the whole story will have a happy ending or not. *(Concerned murmur.)* But for the moment the President is going to be played by Gabe Kaplan. *(Very mild applause.)* We're also thinking about going with Gavin MacLeod." *(Way more applause.)*

The meal went on. I was finding the Thomasons' company quite entertaining.

Over our main courses (a rather tasty Chinese chicken salad for me—hey, when in Rome . . .), I finally just asked them how they were helping their old friend deal with the "conspiracy" arrayed against him. As you might expect from such creative people, the Thomasons had a wealth of suggestions.

"The way I see it," Harry said, "if you want to tree a squirrel, Arianna, you've got to starve your dogs." Some of the crowd seemed to love this last one, but the rest seemed puzzled.

Linda sensed my befuddlement. "What Harry is saying, Arianna, is that we're just simple folk *(applause)* with simple values. *(Louder applause.)* When we see that something's broke, well, we try to fix it. Course, nothing's broke here, we're just trying to help the President explain that nothing needs fixing." *(Approving murmur.)*

"If you want to find gold," Harry went on, "you'd best start by look-ing in a gold mine." *(Big laugh.)*

Linda was getting worked up. "But you see those little old baby Harvard boys in the media who walk around in a constipated haze of Ivy League smugness, intellectually diddling each other, they're irrelevant, arrogant, snide, and cynical and negative. They act like they want to report on important stuff but mention the word *sex* and they turn into a bunch of fourteen-year-olds!"

The invisible crowd went wild. I was glad I wasn't a Harvard boy. I might have been imaginarily lynched.

"That's who the real enemy is, Arianna. It's those Eastern Ivy League big-money intellectual types who control the media. They've teamed up with the far-right fringe groups and are standing in the way of real progress in this country." *(Applause; a few shouts of "Right on!" and one "You the man!")*

Harry glared at a waiter who quickly cleared our plates, a look of outright terror on his face. Then he turned to me and smiled. "If you want to bake a potato, you don't have to be a worm." *(Confused, nervous laugh.)* Harry was starting to lose the audience.

Linda, though, was on a roll. "Someday, Arianna, someday very soon, little people like me and Harry are gonna rise up and say to those rich media cynics, 'Come on down out of your ivory tower, boys! Come on down here with us ordinary folks! Come on down here with people who have real problems, who aren't affected by the private details of the President's marriage. These people want good jobs at good wages with good health care—and they know none of that comes from the private life of the President!" Linda sure knew how to please a crowd. The audience roared. Then, one voice at first, slowly followed by many, they began to sing "The Star Spangled Banner."

During dessert, I worked my way around to the question I'd been wanting to ask all day but hadn't, for fear of committing some breach of protocol. "Are Bill and Hillary really married?" They both looked so shocked that I quickly added, "Just kidding."

"When," I asked instead, "do we get to see the President?"

Harry and Linda smiled indulgently. I felt sheepish.

"That's what everyone always wants to know when they visit the White House, Arianna," Linda explained.

"As you may have heard, Bill Clinton, well, he's kind of a free spirit," said Harry. *(Knowing applause.)* "He loves to blow out the schedule and just, you know, go with the flow, sort of."

"Plus, he's a night owl," Linda added. *(Approving murmur.)*

"When it's the cock's turn to roar, the sheep get trampled," Harry intoned knowingly. *(Frustrated grumble.)*

He yelped suddenly. His wife must have kicked him under the table. The waiters winced collectively.

"What . . . what did I say? What's wrong with that?"

Linda just smiled.

After a cup of that famous White House coffee, regular despite the hour, I took my leave of the Thomasons. As I exited the White House Mess, I stumbled on something. It was Socks, twining through my legs at a most inopportune moment. "Darn you, Socks!" I cried. A few heads turned, but most of the diners remained focused on their meals and their briefing papers.

"Sorry," he purred. "Erskine Bowles is wise to me now, and it never works on him anymore. You're fresh meat."

I sighed. "Well, at least you don't have a laugh track like the Thomasons."

"True, or there would have been a huge guffaw at your little pratfall. But don't let the Hollywood-bumpkin stuff fool you, Arianna."

"I don't know, Socks. They seemed to grow on me."

"Yeah, like the mange."

"A bit harsh, don't you think?"

"You know why they're here now, don't you?" Socks queried.

Feigning naiveté, I responded, "No, why?"

"To manage the crisis, you silly redhead. Who do you think told the President to shake his finger and say 'I never told anyone to lie' during that first post-Monica press conference? Harry. He also told Hillary to wear the brown outfit for her interview on *Today*. He always says when you are denying allegations of infidelity, wear brown. It's authoritative, and yet sympathetic. He's got a whole chart made up. It's quite a work of art."

"Oh, really?" I asked, intrigued. "What does he recommend for casting aspersions on an accuser?"

"Navy blue."

"Trashing the media?"

"Open-necked dress shirt—no French cuffs—and pressed khakis."

"Nondenial denials?"

"Summer-weight suit—but no seersucker—white shirt, just broken-in loafers, brown belt with square buckle fastened at the third hole."

"Well," I said, truly impressed. "He's really got it down to a science."

"He's a regular Thomas Jefferson. Like his pal Bill. I say, a plague on both their houses."

"What's your beef with Bill Clinton?"

"Arianna, you don't know how many times I've heard 'Sorry, kitty. I'll change the litter box tomorrow. I was too busy raising ten million bucks from foreign businessmen,' or 'I was out adopting a puppy,' or 'I was having another late screening with Monica.' How's that supposed to make me feel? He's already got a pet. Why does he need a frisky intern? Why does he need a chocolate Lab? Why does he have to be all things to all animals?"

We had reached the hallway, and Socks was momentarily distracted by a frayed carpet edge. I waited patiently as he worried a few threads loose. Finally the frayed carpet lost its appeal, and he continued.

"Listen, Travelgate got the Thomasons off on the wrong foot with the press, and they're still trying to rewrite the past. And now they're hoping that if they can get Bill through this latest one, they'll finally be back in," Socks concluded, but then quickly jumped back to the carpet. "Damn, but that thread is driving me crazy."

"Socks, leave the thread, it's an inanimate object. It's not moving."

He looked at the thread intently, took a few deep breaths, and turned away from it. "You're right. Forgive me. I've forgotten all about it. It's nothing to me."

We continued down the hallway.

"Where were we?" he said. "Ah yes, Travelgate."

"If this were a commercial for dandruff shampoo, I believe this is the point at which I would say, 'I'm curious. Tell me more.'"

Socks suddenly turned back away. "I'm sorry, but that thread is just so annoying!" And with that he ran back to the frayed spot while exclaiming, "I just sense out of the corner of my eye that it's moving slightly."

"Socks, for God's sake, enough." I was exasperated.

"I just have this irresistible impulse to hit it a few times. Oh, why does it mock me?"

"Socks, I'm leaving now," I said, and turned to walk away.

"Sorry, sorry," I heard him say as he took his leave of the thread once again. "You have no idea how frustrating it is to be guided by pure instinct."

"Sure I do, I'm a supply-sider. Can we continue now?"

"Okay, where were we now?" he said, gathering himself.

"The Travel Office."

"Ah yes. The Travel Office. What you have to realize is that the Travel Office is basically a baby-sitter for the White House Press Corps. They make plane and hotel reservations, pick up luggage, make sure hungover reporters don't miss their flight. Journalists get four-course meals on the press planes, champagne, aged Scotch, the works. Long bus trip? Hey, no problem, we'll get you a keg. The reporters got spoiled. Charles Bierbauer, the CNN correspondent, once ripped the head Travel Office guy a new orifice because there wasn't an oven on the plane."

"I think I get it. You think the press corps played Travelgate big because their benefactors, the Travel Office staff, got shafted?"

"That, and abuse of power. Getting the FBI on the Travel guys was, even by Arkansas standards, a bit too much. The Clintons were pretty pissed at how it all turned out. And then the Thomasons introduced Bill to Christophe the hairdresser. Let's just say the President didn't blame himself when the story broke that he'd stacked up other planes at LAX while he got a two-hundred-dollar haircut in Air Force One. But now he needs them, and they need him. Normal brushfires he can put out himself, but when he gets in deep he calls the whole team back: Mickey, Harold, James, and Dick—at least until he shot his mouth off about Hillary. But I don't know if they can pull this one off. It's like when the old crew of bankrobbers team up for one last score 'cause it's too good to pass up. Question is, I don't know if this one ends in a big payday or a shoot-out."

"Very vivid," I said. "I hope we can at least keep it nonviolent."

"I think it's clear now that this town's not big enough for Ken and Bill," said Socks. "One of 'em's got to go."

We had arrived at the door to the Lincoln Bedroom, and I thought it only polite to invite Socks in after the way we had bonded.

"Maybe later. A friend of mine's got a line on some good catnip. You know, 'sawdust delight,' 'paradise powder.'"

"What exactly is it about that stuff that drives cats crazy?"

"I have no idea. I just know if I don't roll around in it every few days, I get the jangles," he replied as he turned to go down the hall. "But hey, I could ask you humans the same thing about the Spice Girls."

"Touché."

"Anyway, I'll swing by later. Just make sure you leave your suitcase open. I'm shedding like crazy, and everyone else locks their closets."

8
Bubba-Bubble
☆ ☆ ☆

With a small sense of restless regret, I found myself back in the Lincoln Bedroom pondering a night of highly interactive television with my newfound electronic friend, or maybe reading something racy like *Leaves of Grass*. But no sooner had I flopped down fully dressed on the famously uncomfortable mattress than I felt something poking me insistently in the back. At first I thought that I had maybe lain down on a crystal wallabee from the Australian PM, or a Camembert Eiffel Tower from President Chirac, or perhaps the shell of a recently discarded intern. But, upon closer examination, it turned out to be a small bouquet of flowers with an envelope attached that said READ ME.

I opened it to find a short note from my old friend Jack Quinn, with a cryptic message. It read: "Meet you near the South Lawn by the swimming pool in five. Wear your bathing or birthday suit."

Normally, I'd be a little dubious about putting on my bathing suit and wandering around a strange house—particularly the White House, especially since this President was capable of construing a modest glance as a shameless come-on. But, although Jack Quinn was not, perhaps, totally trustworthy (he *was* a big fund-raiser, after all), he was a gentleman and an officer of the court. I put on a modest floral number and a terry cloth robe that I found in my closet.

I hurried through the cold down the stairs to the Rose Garden. I thrust my hands into the pockets of my robe for warmth and found a small card. It read:

*This robe is provided for each guest
in the Lincoln Bedroom as a courtesy.
If you would like to take one with you
as a souvenir of your stay, they are
available for purchase for $10,000.
Payable to the Democratic National Committee.*

As I approached the bottom of the Rose Garden, I heard a cheery bubbling sound. But when I peered over the hedge, I beheld an image right out of Hieronymus Bosch. A group of chubby men was being slowly boiled in a gigantic pot. Smoke rose from their heads. The entire scene was lit with a ghastly underwater glow. Their faces were frozen in different expressions of agony, their mouths agape.

Then the man in the center brought a smoking cigar out from behind his head, where he'd been holding it, and took a long, luxuriant drag. In the glow of the cigar I could see it was the President.

"It's all right, guys. It's not my wife. You can relight those stogies now." He gestured to a pair of Secret Service men standing nearby. They were wearing shades, earpieces, holstered Glock 9s, and regulation black Speedos. Goose bumps stood out on their skin in neat military rows, and they did their best not to shiver. "You guys keep a sharp lookout, you hear? If Hillary starts heading this way, I want enough time to put out my cigar without having to dip it in the pool." He added, to himself, "I lose more good smokes that way . . ." Then he looked up at me again. "Hi, Arianna. Come on in and join us. We've been expecting you."

I stuck a toe in the pool, then sidled in a trifle warily. The President introduced me.

"You know Jack, of course." He indicated Jack Quinn, who gave me a friendly wave. "This is Webb Hubbell and that's Strobe Talbott." Hubbell was very large, very hairy, and very sullen—like a dog that couldn't shake itself dry. He glared at me from across the hot tub without smiling. Talbott was tall and slim and very polite. The President pointed to two Asian gentlemen sitting next to Strobe. "And this is . . ." He appeared to rack his brain. "Aw hell, just introduce yourselves, guys." They did. One said his name was Herbie Woo, the other Jimmy Hong.

There were seven of us in all, a full capacity for the famous seven-seat hot tub. Although earlier in the day, Socks had told me that Clinton had as many as fourteen interns in it one night when Hillary was at the women's conference in Beijing. No one seemed to mind the close quarters much,

except maybe Strobe, whose glasses kept fogging up. Clinton seemed fully in his element—one arm around Jimmy, the other snaking its way, as though it had a mind of its own, toward me. This was a state-of-the-art Jacuzzi, and oddly enough, as I got settled between Hubbell and Hong, I heard the President remark that it was even invisible to radar. A Stealth tub.

Before I could figure out what eventuality this was meant for, some frantic hand signals from the Secret Service men shook me from my reverie. They were puffing out their cheeks and pantomiming to the President, who wasn't quite getting their meaning. "What are you saying, guys? Big? Big hair? Huge hair? Monica?!?! No? Fat? Bloated? Newt! Hey, everybody! Newt's here!"

Sure enough, there, coming down the Rose Garden path, was Newt Gingrich, along with three security guards of his own. His guards had fanned out around him, and woe betide the innocent rosebush or shrubbery that got in their way.

"Hey, Newt," the President called, "did you bring your Contract with America with you? I want to take a look at it again. You know something, it's just *full* of good ideas." Jack, Webb, and Strobe found this very amusing. Hong and Woo looked baffled. I chuckled politely.

Smiling, Newt reached into his pants and grabbed his testicles. "You bet, Mr. President. I've got my Contract with America *right here*. I brought it with me, so I could tattoo it on your ass."

The President threw his head back and roared. "Come on in here, you old so-and-so. I want to watch a real man boil in this thing for a change." He turned to the Chinese men. "Sorry, guys, your time's up. We need the seats. Don't forget to sign the guest book on your way out." Hong and Woo looked even more confused. Clinton bobbed his head at the Secret Service men, who came over, lifted them out of the hot tub, and carried them off.

Newt lowered himself in, easily filling the space left by Hong and Woo. Although Newt's guards and the President's men eyed each other warily, the Speaker and the President seemed exceptionally matey.

Newt grunted with satisfaction. "Ahhhhh, this is livin'. Can't beat it with a stick, right?"

I murmured assent, but he *was* right. This *was* living. Sitting in a radar-proof hot tub with genial company, looking up at the stars, protected from Washington's simmering underclass by the world's best security team and an antimissile defense system—no, you couldn't beat it with a stick. Not by a long shot.

It was then that Newt appeared to notice me for the first time.

"Jesus wept! What the hell is she doing here?! Rocco! Get this broad—"

One of Newt's henchmen made a move toward me. At a wave from the President, Clinton's boys blocked his path.

"She's with me, Newt. She's all right." Newt's cronies backed off, but the Speaker was still highly agitated.

"I should have known she was one of yours. She's your type. But come to think of it, Bill, every woman is your type. Actually, I should have known when she described me in her column as 'almost Leninist' just because I'm determined to set right any supposed conservative who dares to hurt our cause by publicly questioning my leadership."

"Aw, c'mon, Newt, lighten up; after all, she called me an 'ethical cripple' or something." Clinton turned to us, his tubmates. "But you know something, we're off duty now. Here at the White House, we work hard, we fund-raise hard, and we play hard. We're the Dallas Cowboys of politics, only we've committed more felonies."

As Newt settled into a sulky soak, I took a closer look at Clinton. I've often thought that the President looked slack-jawed and dopey when

I've seen him on television—mainly because he usually stands around with his mouth open, which makes him look dumb. But here, close up, I could feel the sexual alertness that produced a double-digit gender gap, and had made it possible for him to keep a harem of interns at the White House. Maybe barring campaign-finance reform, we could at least make all the candidates wear their swimsuits. But I guess Mitch McConnell would never let that happen either.

Clinton took note of Gingrich's pout.

"Hey, Newt, I got to make my wiener a little leaner. Care to join me?"

"I was just thinking the same thing, Mr. President. Got to shake a little dew off the lily. Besides, hot tubs'll drop your sperm count below measurable standards. You'll be shootin' blanks." The President looked deeply concerned for a moment until Newt winked. They both laughed loudly.

The President and the Speaker moved off a discreet distance, where, guarded by the Secret Service, they urinated on some rosebushes. Another happy splashing sound joined the bubbly chorus from the hot tub.

The two men talked intensely for five minutes, just out of earshot. I could only catch a word here and there, but it seemed that there was some serious political horse-trading going on. I thought I overheard phrases like "cooking the books," "couldn't keep her mouth shut," "balanced budget, my foot," and "I'm shriveling up here, let's get this over with," but I couldn't swear to it. Then one voice said, "CBO numbers," and I thought another replied, "My own damn numbers," and then I heard raucous laughter.

No wonder the glass ceiling bars women from ascending, I thought. Shared bodily functions were part of a timeless male bonding ritual, one that joined men as different as Clinton and Gingrich and, in turn, bonded them to a family tree of human leaders that went all the way back to the first Neanderthal and Cro-Magnon who put down their clubs and chose, instead, to go have a pee together.

Without bothering to take formal leave, I jumped out of the hot tub and hurried away; Webb, silent the entire time, was making me nervous. Jovial shouts of "Hey, let's cross swords!" receded in the distance.

The hot tub had warmed me and I was able to stroll leisurely back toward the White House. Then, over the crunch of my slippers on the gravel, I heard a rustling in the bushes beside me. I suppose I should have been frightened, but all I could think was: *What now, has John Kasich come over with a new Grateful Dead bootleg?*

But the small figure that emerged from the underbrush was only Socks, carrying a dead rat. It's too bad Newt hadn't brought Majority Whip Tom DeLay with him. A guy who made his fortune in the extermination business would love this.

"Socks, are there any of those inside?" I asked.

"You mean outstanding public servants like Newt Gingrich? Yeah, there's plenty."

"No, I mean rats," I said.

"So do I," Socks shot back.

"I just have a hard time accepting that two men who seem like such opposites can get along so well."

"You think they're getting along well now, you should see them in a little while when the girls arrive. It's the world's longest-running bachelor party. But, come on, Arianna. What about you and Al Franken? Besides, it's really not so surprising."

"I suppose you're right. By the way, Socks, if you're thinking of leaving that rat with me, thank you, but I have several already."

"Oh, it's not for you." His eyes shone in the dim light and he seemed to wink. "I save these for Hillary. She's not exactly a cat person, so I try to bring her as many presents as I can."

And he was gone.

9
Séance with the Red Queen

☆ ☆ ☆

After my soothing dip in the hot tub, I couldn't wait to get in bed. As I drifted toward sleep, I heard the clock striking twelve. I was about to discover that at midnight the hum of activity at the White House changes pitch. The daytime whine of busywork ratchets down a few notches to a steady, sedate buzz that hovers just below the level of conscious thought, like the vibration of an ocean liner's engines in the dreams of its sleeping passengers. The daytime is public time at the White House. Tours come through, subpoenas are served, photo ops are, well, opped. The respectable façade is maintained. After midnight, anything is possible. After midnight, the White House *rocks.*

I mean it really rocks.

Pink Floyd, Van Morrison, the Beach Boys, the Stones, and, of course, Elvis. The President's favorite music is played over the White House speaker system for the listening pleasure of his guests—whether they like it or not—drowning out the susurrus of work on the overnight shift.

I'm an early riser. And I love my sleep. Inside the Lincoln Bedroom, the music was muffled somewhat but still noticeable. As I tried to drift off to dreamland, Van Morrison kept insisting that it was an absolutely marvelous night for a moondance. I wasn't really in the mood to moondance, to tell the truth, but I was trying to be a good sport. Besides, I wanted to experience the White House Bill Clinton's way. The DJ was the man I needed to see. Maybe there was something on his playlist that would both keep the White House pumping and allow me to sleep.

I slipped on my robe and went in search of the President's DJ.

The hallway outside my room was dark and empty. Following the sound of the music, I started off in its direction. As I got farther from my room, the walls began to warp and bend, the music grew loud and distorted, and I began to pass a bizarre menagerie of buxom lingerie-clad female interns, all running their own mysterious errands at the pleasure of the President. I wasn't in Kansas anymore. This was Rome in the time of Caligula. In more ways than one.

Rounding a bend, I noticed a change in the music. Raucous rock gave way to the airy, exotic plucking of a sitar. I smelled patchouli. A soft glow bloomed under one of the doors. I noticed that the orange glow was flickering.

My God, I thought, *the White House is on fire!* I tried the knob and, without knocking, burst into the room.

"Arianna," said a calm female voice from the back of the room, "I'm so glad you're here."

The room was dark. The flickering light came from hundreds of candles—not, as I had feared, from some act of arson. The figure that spoke stood draped in shadow. She moved forward with her hand out-stretched.

"Welcome."

It was Hillary Clinton.

"My God, Hillary! I'm so sorry. I thought there was a fire."

"No need to apologize. I wanted you to come. I willed it. All is pro-ceeding as planned. Come sit here." She motioned to a round table with a crystal ball and some tarot cards on it. I noticed Socks looking on from a dark corner. He sat erect and proud, like the Egyptian cat god Bast. An inner voice told me not to acknowledge him just then.

A sudden thought struck me.

"Are we going to contact the spirit of Mrs. Roosevelt?"

Hillary giggled. "Eleanor? Heavens, no! I got tired of her. She just went on and on, blah-blah-blah, public service, yadda, yadda, yadda . . . what a goody-goody! It was like canasta night at the garden club. No, Arianna, no matter how much she talked, Eleanor Roosevelt had nothing to say. By the way, did you know that she and Franklin were cousins? Let me tell you, it's true what they say—cousins shouldn't marry. You don't expect them to know that down in Booger Hollow, Arkansas—trust me on that one—but in Hyde Park?"

"But why did you contact her in the first place? What did you want to know?"

"Arianna, I'm trying to get some consensus from first ladies of the past on the proper role for the President's wife. Basically, I'm searching for an answer to the question: 'What's a first lady to do?'"

"And Eleanor? What was her advice?"

"Oh, she was no help. She just had a lot of Lady Bountiful, Junior League–type attitudes. I need to speak to someone contemporary, but with one high heel firmly planted in tradition. A strong, accomplished woman like me, someone who can get down and dirty and scrap with the best of 'em if need be. Oh, I could just kick myself for never mastering the whole Scarlett O'Hara thing down there in Little Rock. But, you know, it's never too late to be less the overeager law student and more the southern belle. It's like with campaign money—the hard stuff is limited, but the soft is infinite."

I feared the worst. "You don't mean—you're not going to try to contact . . . ?"

"Yes, Arianna. We're going to try and speak with the spirit of Rosalynn Carter."

"But she's not even dead!"

"Look, Arianna, when you spend as much time in the spirit world as I do, you learn not to make these petty distinctions. There are no rules in the spirit world. It's sort of like the Clinton White House. Here. Take my hand."

We held hands at the round table. Hillary closed her eyes.

"Concentrate. Concentrate on Rosalynn Carter. Visualize her in your mind. Think . . . national malaise . . . stagflation . . . the killer bunny rabbit . . . presidential hemorrhoids . . . Billy Beer . . . Miz Lillian . . . Come to me, Rosalynn! Enlighten me!"

The candles flickered and then blew out, as an icy draft came from nowhere. The chill of the wind was like the frigid hand of death. It smelled like a mausoleum. And there, hovering above us, was the ghostly visage of Rosalynn Carter. Her voice rose in an eerie wail.

"Whoooooooo? Who disturbs my humanitarian rest?"

"It's Hillary Clinton, Rosalynn. I'm very sorry to wake you."

"Hillary," the nightgown-clad banshee cried. "Lord have mercy! A lady never bilocates before breakfast!"

"I'm so sorry, Rosalynn," Hillary said. "I had no idea. Do you want me to try to contact you later?"

"No," sighed the disembodied Mrs. Carter, "I'm up now."

"Rosalynn, where are you? What is it like here?" Hillary went on.

"Oh, Hillary, I'm in a very terrible place. The dead are all around me. There is wailing and screaming all night long. There is no justice here. Everything is backward and topsy-turvy."

"Don't tell me," said Hillary, "Jimmy's dragged you along on another of his goodwill missions, right?"

"You got it," the phantom responded.

"Rwanda?" Hillary queried.

"Worse. Wayne State, in Detroit."

"You poor dear," Hillary offered. "It must be terrible being an ex-first lady. Particularly an ex-first lady to a failed President."

Mrs. Carter puffed up her cheeks and blew a frigid blast at us. "If I were you, Hillary, I wouldn't cast any stones about failed presidencies. The jury hasn't exactly delivered a final verdict on yours, yet, you know. And besides, my husband is the most popular *ex*-President of all. Look, I don't have all night. Jimmy's dedicating a water pump in some god-forsaken suburb at dawn. And then we have to be poll-watchers for the school board elections. So, what can I do for you?"

"I'm wrestling with a thorny problem, Rosalynn. And I wanted some input from the spirit world. Here's the question: What is the proper role for the First Lady of the United States, now, at the end of the twentieth century?"

Rosalynn's shade gave a knowing smile. "Hillary, you should have come to me sooner, dear. I would have told you that that whole national health care thing was a big mistake."

"How can you say that?" Hillary was flustered. "It's one of the most important issues of our time. And it shouldn't have been so controversial. I've never understood what went wrong."

"Dear, there was only one thing wrong with your plan for universal health care. You. You were what doomed it. And now it's like spent pluto-nium. It can't be touched for a long, long time. Hillary, honey, your prob-lem is that you're all steel and no magnolia."

Hillary grabbed my hand and whispered, sotto voce, "I think we should get a second opinion. Let's get in touch with Betty." Then, more loudly, "Thanks, Rosalynn, thanks a bunch. I don't want to keep you up."

But Rosalynn would not be dismissed so easily.

"You see, Hillary, the American people, they don't elect a first lady. The first lady is part of the package. Sure, she comes with the President—but nobody votes for her."

Hillary rolled her eyes and made the "flapping gums" gesture with her right hand.

"What's that you're doing with your hand? What does that mean?" Rosalynn was getting aggravated.

"Nothing, nothing. It's a 'New Democrat' thing. Sorry. Go on."

"Anyway, most Americans are closet conservatives when it comes to sex roles. Men accept women in the workplace because they have to—but it rubs them the wrong way. In reality, they like the idea of a woman who wants to beautify America like Lady Bird did, or alert everyone to the importance of breast self-exams like Betty did, or even lecture our kids about the dangers of drugs like Nancy Reagan did. Those are traditional female roles: gardening, schoolmarmish scolding, breast self-fondling. I'm telling you—for most men, it's a bigger turn-on than *Playboy*."

Hillary sensed an opening. "Speaking of *Playboy*, I've always wanted to ask you about that 'lust in his heart' thing that Jimmy said. What was he talking about?"

Rosalynn took the bait.

"Hillary, Jimmy kept his lust in his heart—where it belongs—instead of all over some intern's dress. Look, until that sex addict you married took over, the past few Presidents—including my Jimmy—had almost erased the Kennedy image of the President as the nation's top sex maniac. Nixon, Ford, Jimmy, Reagan, Bush—all were more or less faithful to their First Ladies. Then Billy Boy comes along and it's off to the races, trying to break JFK's record for deflowering innocent and not-so-innocent presidential groupies with stars in their eyes. Let me ask you, Hillary, does Bill have lust in his heart? Sure, every man does, but it would be a lot better for you *and* the country if your hubby wouldn't do what his organs tell him quite so often."

The interview clearly was not going quite as Hillary had planned.

"Right, well, thanks, Rosalynn. You're entitled to your opinion, of course, but I'm really more interested in the role of the First Lady than in whatever crazy gossip is circulating down in Plains. Toodles!"

Rosalynn's image disappeared instantly, as if someone had pulled her plug. Hillary sat there dazed, her shoulders slumped. I put a consoling arm around her.

"You mustn't pay too much attention to Rosalynn. Just think how hard it must have been for her, hanging around at those cabinet meetings, not being able to put in her own two cents . . ."

Hillary looked up at me, her eyes burning bright. I realized that I had made a hideous faux pas.

"Hard for her?! Hard for *her*?! What about *me*?! How do you think it is for *me*?! Listening to my fatuous boob of a husband all day long, putting up with his frat-boy antics, coming to the rescue each time he gets caught with his pants down, while he gets to do my dream job, the job I've wanted all my life, the job I'm trained for, the job I'm qualified for. How come he gets to run the country and not me? It just isn't fair!"

And in a way she was right. It wasn't.

Hillary slumped back into her chair, looking defeated. After a moment her eyes glazed over and I assumed she'd fallen into some kind of trance. Perhaps she was shopping in the psychic supermarket for opinions that were more her style, or just going over her nine-hundred-page health care report in her head.

Socks chose this moment to break his silence. He strolled over and jumped into Hillary's lap. "She hates it when I do this," he confided, as he jumped right off. "But, you know, magic and cats go together. I'm kind of like her familiar. She couldn't even contact the Chinese take-out place without me here. Or so she thinks."

"And was that really some kind of magic? Or maybe just a shared hallucination?"

"Whatever. But, hey, it's cheaper than David Copperfield and it doesn't involve skinny men in tight satin pants. She calls it creative visualization. After Jean Houston started talking about Hillary's 'female crucifixion,' I stopped paying attention. Hell, if she had just taken to the bottle like Betty or started compulsively shopping and redecorating like Nancy Reagan, no one would have thought it weird. Just another ladylike way to relieve the stress," Socks said as he jumped six feet up on top of a door.

The heavy fug of the candles, the dense fog of Hillary's mysticism, and Socks's musings were giving me a headache. I resolved to return to my room and meditate—or maybe just channel Jay Leno.

10

Just One Orgasm Away from the Presidency

☆ ☆ ☆

I left Hillary sitting in her séance room, staring into space. Closing the door quietly, I turned back the way I had come, or so I thought. I wandered around a bit and was startled by some commotion down the hall. There, to my surprise, was Betty Currie, the President's personal secretary, and she was being swarmed by the new crop of female interns. "I'm a medium," one shouted. "I'm a small," shouted another. A closer inspection revealed she was passing out French berets.

"One size fits all," she yelled, adding, "they're a gift from the President."

I was half-tempted to pick up an intern-issue beret myself, but I feared I was twice the age limit.

Having seen enough, I wandered off absent-mindedly. Two dozen steps later I realized that I was hopelessly lost. I mentally kicked myself for not having left a return trail of bread crumbs like Hansel and Gretel or, better yet, a slender thread like the one my namesake Ariadne had spun for Theseus to guide him out of the Labyrinth.

The appearance of the White House had morphed once again. In place of the fusty Americana of the first-floor public rooms and second-floor residence, the decor was now Balkan baronial. Stone walls lit by guttering candelabra stretched indefinitely upward into an inky blackness. The music had faded away altogether; the only sound was the echoing of my footsteps on the flagstones underneath. Had I somehow entered Dracula's official residence, or Liberace's tomb? I half expected some

modern incubus like Dick Morris to appear at the top of a staircase and offer to triangulate me or suck my toes. Or maybe serial-biter Marv Albert, ghoulish in tailcoat, wing collar, and a bad rug. This is not good, I told myself.

A giant, upright stuffed bear loomed out of the darkness. I shrieked. "Don't worry," said a squeaky voice behind me. "That's a North American black bear. They're not endangered."

I turned, seeking the source of this reassuring information. Just behind me there was an ill-defined shape, which I had originally taken to be a suit of armor. Upon closer examination, however, it appeared to be the statue of a man in his middle forties with a vaguely Roman hairdo. Instead of a toga, though, he was wearing a boxy Brooks Brothers suit. His pose, stiff and upright, seemed uninformed by the naturalistic innovations of the Renaissance, and yet his clothes suggested that this was a modern man.

"Who are you?" I asked.

"My name is Al Gore," the statue replied.

"My goodness, Mr. Vice-President! What are you doing here?"

"This is where I'm supposed to be," the statue responded, with little affect.

"But what about your duties?"

"Duties? What duties? I'm the *Vice*-President, remember? Trust me, if I have to break a tie in the Senate, they know where to find me."

"So you just stand here? All day long?"

"I'm standing by, Arianna. If and when the country needs me, I'll be ready. And you never know—it could be any day now. Any day. And in the meantime I can always reach out and touch someone with a phone call, anytime the President needs money."

"But it must be so boring."

"No, not really, I think about things sometimes, you know, like alternative energy sources and stuff, and down here I'm safe from the growing hole in the ozone layer. And I've dreamed up some wild fundraising schemes, let me tell you. It's not so bad. And hardly anyone knows where to find me, like the interns and stuff, so I'm never, you know, tempted."

"Still, this can't have been your idea. Who put you here?"

"Well . . ." The statue's extremely limited mobility prevented it from shifting uncomfortably from side to side. ". . . the President asked me . . ."

"The President? Bill Clinton moved you down here?"

"Not him personally, no. A team of movers installed me here. But the President, well, he felt that I was screwing up the photo opportunities. People kept wondering what a department-store mannequin was doing at the signing of an important bill, or why the President was being advised on some policy question by a waxwork. It was interfering with the message. Clinton told me I was a distraction."

"Still, it seems a little extreme."

"I thought that people would miss me. But you know something? No one even noticed. But I don't mind. It's not really that bad. Plus, I have Marty."

"Marty?"

"Marty Peretz. You know, he owns *The New Republic*. He fires anyone who doesn't like me. Have you ever heard of 'holding water' for someone?"

"Is that a urinary term?" I ventured.

"No, it just means an independent thinker," he said, his arms and legs starting to kick in a little bit. "Hey, want to see me do the Macarena?"

"Not really."

He didn't move, or say anything for a moment, and I was beginning to get uncomfortable.

"Want to see me do it again?" he asked, and then burst into laughter. "Ooohhh, God . . . Whooo!" He wiped one eye with his finger. "That *is* a good one. You know, that kills Marty every single time. Never tires of it."

"It certainly is a good one," I said, starting to look for the exits. "And with that joke, you don't even need an audience."

"That's true, and it helps me stay sharp, because when my turn comes, I'm ready. But until then, I enjoy spending time with the other Vice-Presidents."

His head inclined slightly to one side. I looked in that direction and saw other statues. There stood a petrified Walter Mondale, and Dan Quayle, standing stiff as a board behind a glass door labeled "In case of emergency, please break glass and swear in Vice-President." The line of frozen Vice-Presidents stretched out into the distance. A disturbing thought crossed my mind.

"Al, I hate to say this—I know things have been pretty dicey for Bill Clinton recently—but many of the Vice-Presidents are still waiting for the call; for most, it never comes."

"Oh, I'm not worried, Arianna. Unless Bill Clinton gets sued for sexual harassment, or gets caught with a girl his daughter's age, or there are some fund-raising scandals and Congress holds hearings, or the Attorney General starts investigating me, or, God forbid, we have to dig up a campaign donor from Arlington, I'm confident I'll be elected in 2000."

"You've been down here awhile, then."

"Not so long, really. Periodically, someone from upstairs will come down and take me somewhere. I went to a fund-raiser at a Buddhist temple with a group of very generous nuns a couple of years ago, for instance. Boy, that was fun! Have you ever felt a shaved head that has a little stubble?"

"No, I can't say that I have. I'm assuming you have?"

"It's a little disconcerting, actually." We fell silent for a moment.

Then he suddenly came out of his reverie. "No controlling legal authority, Arianna." He looked at me knowingly and kept nodding his head and winking.

"What?"

"I actually held my very own press conference a little while ago. Unfortunately, I got stuck and kept repeating that bit about 'no controlling legal authority.' And Bill got a little upset. But it's not really my fault. You see, you sort of lose your people skills down here. Now I mostly just make phone calls. A guy from the DNC brings a cordless to me. As long as I dial 'nine' first, there's no controlling legal authority, Arianna. None whatsoever."

At this point I was getting a little scared, so I just went with it. "That's right, Al," I said slowly, "no controlling legal authority." That seemed to pacify him.

"Anyway, I'm not really sure how long I've been here. Time doesn't have much meaning in the Great Hall of the Vice-Presidents—but, no matter what, I bet I'll be back upstairs in no time."

I didn't want to get his hopes up by bringing him up to speed so I decided just to strike a reassuring note.

"I'm sure it will *seem* like no time," I said encouragingly. "Listen, Al, I think I should try to find the Lincoln Bedroom and call it a night. Can you point me in the right direction?"

"Uh, I'm afraid not. I got jostled around a lot when they installed me, and I don't have a very good internal compass anymore."

This certainly was a pickle, I reflected. Fortunately, at that moment I heard a squeak—the squeak of a rodent that had just breathed its last. And sure enough, Socks emerged from the shadows with yet another rat clutched between his jaws.

"Keep it up, Socks," I said. He dropped the carcass and occupied himself with some cursory grooming. "The last time I was confronted with a live rat, I had to call Wayne LaPierre—you know, the guy who runs the NRA. You should have seen the guns he showed up with! I doubt he makes White House calls, though."

Gore was looking as nervous as a statue could. "Please, Arianna," he groaned. "The last time this happened, he left the rat on my foot and nobody came by to remove it for three weeks."

Socks cast a mildly contemptuous look at Gore and deposited his kill in a cobwebby corner.

"Personally, I think he's just lazy," Socks remarked. "You should have seen Mr. Peppy over there making fund-raising calls, though. Would you believe one guy he solicited actually said it was like getting shaken down?"

Gore didn't react, and I pondered briefly—very briefly—the mystery of why a living statue wouldn't be able to hear a talking cat. Then I turned to the matter at hand. "Socks, I'm lost," I said. "Can you lead me back to the provisional safety of the Lincoln Bedroom?"

"For God's sake, Arianna, he's a cat," Gore said.

"Of course," Socks said, ignoring Gore. Waving good-bye, I followed Socks through the labyrinth.

"Don't forget about me! Come by anytime you want to chat about, you know, electric cars or anything," the statue called after me. "And tell the American people I said hi. And that I'm ready if they need me to attend a funeral or something. You remember Nixon's motto? Well, I'm 'Bland, Rested, and Ready.' Don't forget about me, Arianna! I'm here! I'm ready!"

"I don't get Gore," I said as we strolled past catacombs piled high with the bones of dead Vice-Presidents. "I mean, here's a guy who actually went to Vietnam, admittedly as a military journalist, but at least he was there. He smoked marijuana for years and admitted it, but nobody made a fuss because he's the squarest of the square. He's a policy wonk who seemed to have some scruples. And he didn't bother to defend Clinton's ethics when he debated Dan Quayle, probably because he knew they were indefensible."

"Gore takes his lead from the President," Socks answered. "I mean, look at the way he dealt with those fund-raising phone calls. He admitted to a few, but insisted that he paid for them with a DNC credit card and that anyway there was 'no controlling legal authority' to prevent him— that was a lot like Clinton. And then, of course, it turned out he'd actually made a lot more calls and billed some to the government. I never really trusted Gore anyway. There's something about the earnest ones, you feel they're concealing something—plus, he's no fun to sit on."

"Yeah, but he reimbursed the Treasury for those calls."

"Only well after he claimed that he'd paid for them with a DNC calling card. Besides, the check was for $24.20. That's not a lot of money, when you consider that most big pocket donors don't live within a local call of the White House."

"Socks, you sound outraged. You must really hate him."

"Why do you think I left a decaying rat on his foot?" Socks sighed. "No, I don't really hate him. I hate the sleazy fund-raising, though. And the fact that no one wants to change the system because they all benefit.

All money corrupts; it's just that soft money tends to corrupt a little more softly, so to speak."

His syllogism was tortured, but I agreed with the sentiment.

"Watch out, Arianna, it's slippery here. This is where Susan Thomases used to torture the White House staff."

I stepped around a slick pool of congealing bodily fluids as Socks led the way.

"I feel sorry for Gore," I said. "But as far as the country's concerned, the only thing worse than having Clinton as President is if he's forced to resign and Gore takes his place."

I opened the door in front of me and heard Van Morrison playing the final chords of "Moondance." How long had I been gone?

11
A Misguided Tour
☆ ☆ ☆

I can't remember ever being so glad to see carpeting. After we left the Vice-Presidents' Jamboree, all of them doing what they're supposed to be doing (and so lifelike!), Socks led me onto an elevator. I got off on the second floor, which turned out to be the Lincoln Bedroom floor, and Socks continued to the third, muttering something about not keeping "the ladies" waiting.

Back in my bedroom, I was in one of those untethered fugue states, like when you're watching an Oliver Stone movie. The covers on the bed were turned down and, as in many hotels, they were tucked in so tightly it was almost as if they were sculpted on. As I dug in my heels to try to undo them, I noticed a pre-bedtime mint beckoning from my pillow. I bit into it, and suddenly a young woman appeared at the foot of the bed. Now this may not sound like an odd thing for this White House, but something about this young woman seemed different from the hundreds of others I had seen strolling through the White House halls. Her face was deathly pale, and her arms so thin you could almost see through them. Nevertheless, she wore a cheery grin. Her oversized name tag read "Bonnie."

"Hello, Mrs. Huffington," she said. "My name is Bonnie and I'm your official White House tour guide! Now, the room you're in, the Lincoln Bedroom, wasn't always a bedroom. During the Civil War it was Abraham Lincoln's personal office, that's right, and the Cabinet Room—"

"Excuse me, er"—I glanced again at her name tag—"*Bonnie,* but can we do this tomorrow morning? It seems a little late for a tour."

She laughed like I was a four-year-old who had just said something cute. "It's never too late for a tour. Just place your visitor's pass around your neck and we can begin."

"Would you mind if I just made one quick phone call?" I reached for the phone. I never thought I would find myself calling for Kent, but this was clearly the moment. I put the phone to my ear, but it was silent.

"It's dead, just like me. But don't worry, you don't need Kent. I'll be taking care of you now." Bonnie came around to my side of the bed and hung my laminated guest pass—"All access. All areas. All times"— around my neck. I felt like a groupie at an Eagles concert.

"There you go. Come. Put your robe on and we'll begin."

"Sure, why not?" I sighed. I capitulated to Bonnie's determination to give me a tour—whether I wanted it or not—and wondered when the Stockholm syndrome would be setting in.

"We'll begin our tour in the 1860s."

The "All Times" section of my pass began to glow and pulsate. I heard a faraway train whistle and then, as my ghostly companion and I flew through a sort of wind tunnel—like in those commercials showing how "aerodynamic" the new Ford Taurus is—I began to see calendar pages flipping all over the place. The last one I remember seeing was 1864. Suddenly we were in a different room—no, wait, it was the same room, but it looked entirely different.

The walls of the room were covered with maps of Civil War hot spots. Bonnie pointed to one of the maps and declared in that slightly-too-loud teacher/tour guide tone of voice, "Here's a map of Richmond, Virginia—the capital of the Confederacy—and its surrounding forests. Did you know that sixty-five percent of all Civil War battles were fought within Virginia's borders? Written in Latin on the seal of the great state of Virginia is the phrase '*Sic Semper Tyrannis.*' Do you know what that means in English, Mrs. Huffington?"

"Yes, it means 'Thus Always to Tyrants.'"

"No," said Bonnie automatically. "It means 'Thus Always to Tyrants.' Please take special note of the darker quality of the room during this era. That's due primarily to . . . anybody? Anybody? Mrs. Huffington?"

"Uh, the use of darker furnishings?"

"Close. It's because of the wallpaper and the carpet. Both have a darker quality. Good try, though."

She directed my attention to a table in the corner piled high with newspapers.

"Here's a table piled high with newspapers."

At the top was a paper with a large picture of Honest Abe on the front page. I paused for a moment to stare at the face of America's greatest President. He seemed so immensely sad, with his left hand cradling his massive forehead.

"You know, Mrs. Huffington, Abraham Lincoln and Bill Clinton share many of the same admirable traits."

"Like what? The fact that they're both carbon-based bipedal life-forms?" I asked, confused.

"Yes . . . good . . . They both exhibit and/or exhibited that trait. What other traits can you name, Mrs. Huffington?"

"I would be more curious to hear *your* insights on the subject, Bonnie," I replied.

"All right. They both have spoken eloquently and acted forcefully on behalf of all people's right to be treated equally."

"Oh come on, Bonnie. Are you comparing Clinton's limp-wristed support for a proposed apology for slavery to the signing of the Emancipation Proclamation?"

"Yes! Which, by the way, was signed in this very room . . . on January 1, 1863."

"Yes, Bonnie, a stone's throw away from where Mr. Clinton emancipated so many caffeinated, high-dollar donors from their wallets . . . and their daughters."

Her voice took on an edge.

"You know, Mrs. Huffington, Abraham Lincoln had his faults, too."

"Like what?"

"Well, he wasn't a Democrat."

"Uh-huh. What else?"

"Did you know that Abraham Lincoln began his career as a lawyer for fat-cat railroad executives? Also, he had a deeply troubled marriage, was often depressed, and may have had Marfan's syndrome—a rare, inherited disorder of the body's connective tissue that results in abnormalities of the skeleton, heart, and eyes. And," she laughed, "he didn't even go to law school.

"Bill Clinton," she added proudly, "went to Yale Law School. And did you know that Lincoln won the election of 1860 in a flukey four-way race? If there hadn't been so many candidates, he might not have won at all."

"Was it similar to Clinton's flukey three-way squeaker in 1992?"

"Lincoln was darn lucky to be President."

"He also had a high-pitched voice," I added, "and, let's face it, he wasn't much of a looker."

"*Exactly.* He would not have scored well with the soccer moms. And our extensive polling showed that the facial hair configuration of the beard without the mustache part has a high unfave/fave ratio."

"Lincoln probably wouldn't have scored with the soccer moms, period. But what else did you find out?" For the first time, I was genuinely interested.

"Well, a goatee has higher positives, but does badly in the Deep South. A mustache does well in the South, but has high negatives in New England. We focus-tested a handlebar mustache with some local media buys in Iowa, but it was too risky. We were going to have the Vice-President test a Fu Manchu setup, but Tipper overruled it."

"Sounds like your pollsters really knew what they were doing. Too bad Lincoln didn't have such good people."

"Right again, Mrs. Huffington. Right again. But Lincoln couldn't have been elected with today's savvy electorate. He lacked Bill Clinton's ability to begin a national dialogue on race and engage us in a politics of meaning by creating a diverse multicultural society. Mr. Lincoln, I know he tried his best, but he wound up getting us mixed up in a terrible civil war . . . Bill Clinton's presidency, on the other hand, has been about saving lives, not wasting them. As he himself said in November 1995, 'When I became President, there was no known treatment for stroke.'"

"Are you, or I guess the President, implying he cured strokes?" I asked.

"All I can tell you is the facts, Mrs. Huffington. Lincoln: no treatment for stroke. Clinton: treatment for stroke. Draw your own conclusions."

"Thank you. I will."

"And if you feel unable to draw one, our pollsters will tell you the conclusions drawn by the majority of the American public, and you can draw those conclusions free of charge."

"You're too kind."

"You can never be too kind. So say sixty-two percent of Americans, plus or minus four percent, according to the latest Hart/Teeter poll. Now, if you'll just move to the window, I think you'll find the view both interesting and informative."

I did as I was instructed, and was instantly amazed by what I saw. Washington, D.C., from this vantage point, at this time in history, seemed so small and fragile. It was a far cry from the Washington, D.C., I knew, so big and crumbling—with so much of it like a snapshot from the Third World.

The lawn stretched much farther into the distance than it does now. And when I say "lawn," what I really mean is "field." It had rained earlier in the day. I could see brown and white cows grazing where, 130 years later, NBC's David Bloom and CNN's Wolf Blitzer would be competing to get that coveted I'm-really-at-the-White-House background for their reports on the scandal-du-jour.

I looked down at my pass. The "All Times" section of it was glowing again.

"It is now 1902, Mrs. Huffington," Bonnie said.

"What about the calendar pages?" I asked. "I liked that. It was a little corny, but so was *Titanic*."

"Forget the calendar pages. The Lincoln office is now a bedroom, but not yet the *Lincoln* Bedroom. That doesn't officially occur until 1945, when President and Mrs. Truman move in the bed and other furniture. We're in the midst of the Roosevelt administration—Teddy, not the great FDR—and the whole place is undergoing a massive renovation. All the second-floor offices have been moved to the West Wing."

Suddenly we were awash in puppies, cats, rats snakes, raccoons, bear cubs, a donkey, a young lion—and a sea of children.

I felt like an extra in a soft-drink ad. "Oh, we're in luck, Mrs. Huffington. These are the twenty-sixth President's children. That's Theodore Jr. and Alice and Kermit and Ethel and Archibald and Quentin. Rambunctious, aren't they?"

"Yes, like their father."

"I would agree. Rambunctious and confused. Unlike Bill Clinton."

"How so?"

"Well, if you recall your history, TR was an overrated windbag who nearly wrecked the Republican Party by defecting from it and then running against William Howard Taft, the man he had handpicked as his successor. TR was a real bull moose—in more ways than one!"

"But, Bonnie," I asked, "wasn't Theodore Roosevelt a legitimate war hero? Didn't the Nobel Peace Prize count for something before they gave it to Henry Kissinger? And what about the Panama Canal? Not a bad résumé, I would say. So he picked Taft and then ran against him. Hey, history proved him right. Taft was a decidedly mediocre President. And what about moral leadership, Bonnie? The sort of strength of character that comes from true courage and vision? Not to mention upstanding behavior in his private life."

"Who's the tour guide here, Mrs. Huffington? TR was a nasty little man, and any decent pollster could have told him that a bushy mustache with no beard hurts you on Super Tuesday. Besides, if you want to compare achievements, as President Clinton said in December of 1996, 'For the first time ever, laboratory animals with their spines completely severed have movement in their lower legs.'"

"Just stating the facts again, Bonnie?" I asked, as if it made any difference.

"I'm just stating the facts, Mrs. Huffington. TR: laboratory animals with spine severed—no movement. WJC: laboratory animals with spine severed—movement."

"Bonnie," I said, starting to get bored, "your hair's on fire."

"Now, if you'll just direct your attention this way," Bonnie replied, as we continued down the hall.

Suddenly we saw a man in a wheelchair—with a fancy cigarette holder—the familiar profile of Franklin Delano Roosevelt.

"And here we have the greatest President of the century, until now," Bonnie intoned.

"What do you mean, 'until now'?"

"For all that Roosevelt accomplished—and he accomplished a lot—he had many flaws."

"Such as?"

"Well, he had none of Mr. Clinton's physical vitality. Did you see the President golfing on Martha's Vineyard last year? He shot a seventy-nine!"

"On which hole?"

She ignored me. "Roosevelt was also a flagrant smoker. As Bill Clinton pointed out, smoking kills hundreds of thousands of people each year. Roosevelt could have at least gone out on the sidewalk to do it. And the sort of hijinks that were going on in that marriage, well, you don't want to know. I mean, compared to Mr. Clinton—who, as he bravely admitted, might have strayed in his marriage and 'caused a little pain' now and again—FDR was a regular Arthur Frommer. Besides, contrary to popular myth, Roosevelt's New Deal did not bring us out of the Great Depression. World War Two did that."

"FDR was a bigger skirt-chaser than Bill Clinton?! Bonnie, this is starting to seem more like a tour of Fantasyland."

"And just like that hothead Lincoln, Roosevelt got us into a huge war. Bill Clinton knows how to stop wars. He proved that in Haiti."

"Yeah. Baby Doc would have come back and ignited a global conflagration down there if Clinton hadn't taken such a strong stance."

"And as President Clinton said in Iowa in 1995, 'I am the only President who knew something about agriculture when I got there.'"

"Bonnie, George Washington was a career farmer, your back is covered with giant ants, and I'm the Antichrist."

"Which takes us to the postwar years," said Bonnie, as she snapped her fingers.

And suddenly, the Eisenhowers appeared. They were seated at what looked like a small dining table. Dwight was in full dress uniform, but, oddly, they were playing Yahtzee. From what I could gather, Mamie was working on her "full house."

"Did you know," Bonnie asked, "that consumer confidence under Clinton is the highest since Dwight Eisenhower?"

"But they didn't have Prozac under Eisenhower."

"And that the stock market has had its best performance since World War Two?"

"As a matter of fact," I said, "it grew less than twenty percent in Clinton's first two years and more than doubled since the Republicans took over Congress. Also, Eisenhower balanced the budget three times."

"And as President Clinton said in California in 1996, 'I have probably consumed more raisins than any President who held this office.'"

She had me on that one. We started to walk again and came to the end of the hallway. As we turned the corner, we were back in the Lincoln Bedroom, circa 1952. Bonnie was no doubt rushing me through the remainder of the tour so she could get back to the eternal lunchroom and declare what an absolute pain that Mrs. Huffington had been.

I was not being a cooperative tourist, so she was winding things up: "President and Mrs. Truman officially named this room the Lincoln Bedroom in 1945. Please note that the bed you're sleeping in, courtesy of the Democratic National Committee and the Clintons, is the exact same bed displayed here."

"That would be the bed from which you took me?" I asked, a little ruefully.

"Yes. It measures eight feet long and six feet wide and was purchased by Mary Todd Lincoln in 1861, when she was refurbishing the White House. It is made of carved rosewood, with a horsehair mattress that *your* Barbara Bush will eventually replace."

"I'm sorry, '*my* Barbara Bush'?" I asked.

"You know, Republican."

"You don't have to say it like it's a dirty word, Bonnie."

"When the Trumans installed the Lincoln bed in this room, as well as the Brussels carpet, they also brought in the fine examples of Victorian furniture that you see all around you."

"Making it an extremely nice perk for anyone donating a large sum of money to the DNC, wouldn't you say, Bonnie?"

"And we're back, Mrs. Huffington. Back to the present. Back to the Clinton administration. You'll find everything the way you left it. Although, while we were gone, you were fortunate to have the President fondle the underwear in your drawer. And on behalf of the White House staff, may I just say that it's been an absolute pleasure having you as our guest."

I was tempted to take a whack at her with the remote or the blow dryer. But instead I just said, "Thank you."

12
Oral Sex Is Not Adultery: The Experts Speak

☆ ☆ ☆

I was trapped in what appeared to be a circus fun house, encountering one horror after another as I struggled desperately to find my way out. Around one corner, a giant Janet Reno roared something incoherent about siccing a special prosecutor on me; in another corner the miniature Robert Reich regaled himself with tales of how he'd single-handedly driven Idi Amin from Uganda. Then I came upon a small girl in a pretty party dress with her back toward me. When I tapped her on the shoulder to ask the way out, she turned. It was not a little girl at all! Staring out at me from beneath a wig of copper-colored ringlets was none other than the diminutive Secretary of Health and Human Services, Donna Shalala! She offered me a lollipop. I ran.

Finally, I spotted daylight. I emerged into the bright sunshine, blinking, glad to have escaped. But then, just as relief was flooding over me, an enormous blob blotted out the sun. It was a vast, almost spherical Bill Clinton. His head, arms, and legs were normally proportioned, but his stomach had swollen to the size of the Goodyear blimp. He began to squat. I knew what he was going to do. I'd heard about this move. Bill Clinton was going to sit on me, or worse. I would be crushed!

I woke in a sweat, disoriented. Where was I? What time was it?

Inside the Lincoln Bedroom, all was peaceful. It was pitch black outside the open window. A gentle zephyr rocked Lincoln's rocking chair, as if the spirit of the Great Emancipator were watching over me.

My stomach growled. Perhaps that was why I was having bad dreams; I hadn't eaten since the middle of the nineteenth century, and all that time travel had left me a little peckish. Unfortunately the Clintons had neglected to equip the Lincoln Bedroom with a minibar, fearing, I suppose, that that would make the comparison with the local Marriott just a mite *too* obvious. Also, it might have led to the revival of the $100,000 candy bar.

I slipped my bathrobe over my nightgown and went in search of food. Now, in the dead of night, the halls of the White House had grown quieter, and the piped-in rock music had faded. I passed an occasional Asian tour group and a giggling gaggle of strippers, but the place was otherwise almost deserted.

In the distance I heard a sound that made my mouth water. Popcorn! Someone was popping a whole bag in a microwave oven. I followed the sound and, after a few feet, detected the aroma of melting butter tainted with a faint hint of cigar smoke.

Up ahead, light streamed from a door left slightly ajar. This must be the source of the delectable sounds and smells. Surely whoever was inside would feed me. A sign on the door gave me brief pause: KEEP OUT. THIS MEANS YOU. I decided it probably didn't mean me. I reached up to knock. And then I heard a voice that froze my blood. It was Newt!

"Look, Bill," Newt was saying, "you're the only one I can talk to about this. I'll be goddamned if I'm gonna go cap in hand to Trent Lott or Dick Armey for advice. The scumbags would turn right around and use it against me behind my back. Miserable rat bastards."

"Have a Ring-Ding, Newt," Bill Clinton responded amiably. "Good for what ails ya, you can take my word on it."

"I just don't get it," Gingrich continued, his mouth full of Ring-Ding. "We balanced the budget—you and I together—we cut taxes—you and I together—we helped the nation appreciate the contribution Jiang Zemin is making to humanity—you and I together. And yet, even with all the sex stuff coming out, you're still much more popular than me. I don't get it. Where'd I go wrong?"

"Try this. It's a Sno Ball," the President said consolingly. "It's reduced fat. I eat about fifty of 'em whenever I'm feeling blue. Works every time."

My curiosity overcame my fear. I risked a peek into the room. Through the crack in the door I could just barely see the President and the

Speaker sitting on boxes marked PERISHABLE and smoking large cigars. The shelves of the small room were stacked with piles and piles of snack foods of every description. Along one wall was a refrigerator and a counter with a hot plate, a blender, and a microwave. As I watched, the microwave beeped and Bill Clinton removed a bag of popcorn, dumped it in a bowl, and poured melted butter all over it. He offered some to Newt.

"You're not going to tell me anything," the Speaker whined petulantly. "You don't want to give away your secret, do you?"

"Newt, there's no secret. Just be yourself. Twinkie?"

"I've *tried* that. For my entire political life I've been seen as petty, small-minded, vindictive, egomaniacal, and unconcerned about those less fortunate. For a while it worked great, but all of a sudden America seems to have gotten over its love affair with meanness. Nasty isn't cool anymore."

I could hear the despair in Gingrich's voice. Clinton's was consoling.

"Oh, come on, Newt, you're selling yourself short. These things are cyclical. Meanness will come back, you mark my words. Everything comes back eventually. Just look at Tom Jones. More butter?"

"Tom Jones was out?"

"See? That's the Newt I love," said Bill. "You just stay the course."

"That's fine for you to say! You're the most popular President since Ronald Reagan. Hell, nothing seems to bother the public, at least not for very long. They could catch you in bed with the Spice Girls and the American people *still* wouldn't hold it against you."

Clinton sputtered, his mouth full. "The Spice Girls? Who told you that? Isikoff? I never had sex with those women, especially not Ginger or Baby." Clinton emphasized this last statement with dramatic thrusts of his forefinger. "And if you don't believe me, just ask my wife. Besides, I've heard two Spices are lesbians."

"Really? It's not Sporty Spice, is it? Where'd you hear that?" Newt asked.

"I don't know, this friend of mine heard it somewhere."

"If you don't tell me," Newt said decisively, "I'm going to resign."

"Over the Spice Girls? I don't know where I heard it, for Chrissake!"

"No, no—" said Newt, "over your method of governing."

"Fine. Go ahead and resign. One of us ought to. The more important question is, when are we going to get around to lifting that Cuban trade embargo so we can smoke some *real* Cohibas for a change?"

"Bill, just tell me the secret of your bulletproof popularity, and I'll get you all the Cuban cigars you want."

"Newt, I keep telling you, there's no secret. Just be yourself."

"Bullshit! No one gets away with what you do unless they've made some kind of deal with the devil. Christ, Monica Lewinsky could give Ken Starr an entire closet of semen-stained dresses and the public wouldn't bat an eye. Hell, they could take Hillary away in handcuffs and the public would still love you."

Clinton's interest was piqued all of a sudden.

"Really? You think so? Hillary in handcuffs . . . I wonder . . ." He seemed lost in thought for a few moments. "Naah, too risky."

The President opened the fridge and fetched a couple of Cokes for Newt and himself.

"Newt, you just help yourself if you'd like a beer. It's light beer, so you can have as many as you want. I'm allergic to the stuff, but I'll enjoy it vicariously if you have a few. By the way, did you ever wonder, since they have dry beer and ice beer, why they don't have dry ice beer?"

Newt had reached the breaking point. His frustration boiled over. He grabbed Clinton by the shoulders and began shaking him.

"Tell me! Tell me! WHAT IS YOUR SECRET?"

Clinton laughed merrily.

"Okay! Okay! Look, Newt, it's pretty obvious, really. I mean, there's no special secret. The country is prosperous, unemployment is low, inflation's barely measurable, we're at peace, we do a little 'reinventing government,' we do a little budget balancing, and we get rid of some of the really unpopular losing propositions, like welfare."

Newt was still not satisfied. "Look, all those things are *our* ideas and you know it, you son of a bitch. Economic growth is *our* big issue, and smaller government, and welfare reform, and the rest of it. And peace? Who do you think should get the credit for that? Jimmy Carter? It was Reagan, not you! I'm not buying it, Bill. How come I lose and you win with exactly the same positions on the same issues?"

Clinton sighed.

"All right, Newt. I'll tell you. But you've got to promise me that you won't do anything to screw up the scheme, 'cause it's a beaut."

"I promise. I swear," Newt said eagerly, crossing his heart.

"Swear on Baby Spice," said Bill.

"I swear on Baby Spice," Newt replied solemnly.

"Here's our secret weapon: You."

"What?!" Newt was incredulous.

"You look like such a nasty, bloated bag o' gas that people just assume that whatever you propose is selfish and mean-spirited. And then I can do whatever it is you're suggesting in the spirit of bipartisan compromise. And because I'm being presidential and above the fray and yadda, yadda, yadda, it works out great. Frankly, you guys are right about a lot of things—but I'm the one who comes out smelling like a rose. You make America feel bad about being selfish; I make America feel good about being selfish. That's my secret. That and my enormous sexual magnetism, of course."

Newt looked dumbstruck. The President held out a chocolate cupcake to the Speaker, who took it wordlessly and put the whole thing in his mouth.

"Look, Newt, we're a great team, you and me. I know you feel unappreciated at times, but whenever you're feeling blue, just think of this: I couldn't do it without you. Every time a new scandal breaks and the press starts talking about how I ought to resign, the public takes one look at you and forgives me. Now let's talk about something more important, like the Biblical definition of adultery."

"And that's another idea you stole from me!" Newt exploded.

"Newt, I've been using that one for years. Every husband with a wandering eye hears about it eventually. Here, take a look at my Bible. I've got all the relevant passages marked."

Clinton passed a well-thumbed copy of the Good Book over to the Speaker. Newt chose a page Clinton hadn't marked. A slow smile spread across his face. "You know, Bill, there's a little something in the Bible you might be interested in. And only *I* know where to find it."

Clinton's interest was clearly piqued. He lunged for the Bible, but Newt held it out of reach.

"What is it? What have you found?"

"Oh nothing, Bill. Just a Biblical passage that says that telephone sex is not adultery either. But you're going to have to wade through an awful lot of genealogy of the ancient kings of the Israelites unless I tell you where to find it."

"Oh, man! I could really use that! Give me a clue. New Testament?"

Newt shook his head and smiled. The President paused for a second and then made a second attempt to grab the Bible away from the Speaker.

But Newt eluded him for a second time. Clinton looked like he might be about to lose that famous temper of his. Newt was clearly relishing having the upper hand for a change.

"Tell you what, Bill, you give me Sharon Stone's phone number and I'll show you the phone sex passage. Deal?"

Clinton extended his right hand and they shook on it. "Mr. Speaker, you've got yourself a deal."

INTERLUDE IN PARIS

President Jacques Chirac cast a worried eye upon the hastily assembled cabinet of the French government. His look of concern spread among his ministers as they passed around the early edition of Le Monde bearing the news from America.

President Chirac drew a deep breath. "Well?"

Prime Minister Lionel Jospin was the first to speak. "Monsieur President, this is a very serious state of affairs. We must act quickly."

The President looked at the other ministers. All of them nodded their assent.

"So it is settled," Jospin said. "We'll surrender immediately."

"Not so fast," Chirac answered. "There will always be time for surrender, and, of course, it is always an attractive and probable option."

"I've got it!" said the Minister for Defense. "Let's take the afternoon off and all have a very long nap."

"Ordinarily, I would say yes," said Chirac, "but this is too urgent even for a long nap. First, let us make sure we are in agreement as to the nature of the situation. This Lewinsky woman—she is better looking than my current mistress, is she not?"

"You mean that tall, winsome blonde?" asked the Foreign Minister.

"That was three mistresses ago!" bellowed Chirac. "If you came to the daily briefings, you'd know this. The current one is the shapely graduate student."

The Minister for Defense stared at his feet. "It pains me to say so, but oui, Monsieur President, Monica is more attractive." The room fell silent. "But," the Minister added, "juste un peu."

The Minister for Foreign Affairs nodded reluctantly. "Oui."

The lone dissent came from the Minister for Striking Transportation Workers. "Non!" he insisted.

President Chirac scowled. "You only say that because she is not your type."

"It is true," admitted the Minister for Striking Transportation Workers. "I have always preferred prideful, arrogant blondes."

The Prime Minister spoke up again. "The situation could not be clearer, Monsieur President. Our national credibility is at stake. The prestige of France and the international reputation of Frenchmen as the world's greatest lovers and womanizers has been challenged. That—and chronically high unemployment—is all we have left that is uniquely French. You must take immediate steps to have an affair with a more attractive woman than Mademoiselle Lewinsky."

Chirac nodded gravely. "I agree. But who?"

The ministers were quick to offer suggestions.

"Isabelle Huppert?"

"No . . ."

"Fanny Ardant?"

"No . . ."

"My wife?"

"No . . ."

"Gerard Depardieu?"

"You're fired."

"Julie Delpy?"

"I already tried. She has no sense of patriotism."

"Why not simply go to the Sorbonne and pick out a beautiful young student?"

"No!" Chirac pounded the table emphatically. "We must choose a woman with international name recognition—a woman with very high ratings de Q!"

The ministers looked at each other. The choice was obvious.

"Brigitte Bardot."

"Bardot? She is old enough to be my little sister! Also, I hate her politics. How will I eat all that vegan garbage? It's simply impossible to make a good cream sauce without real milk!"

"We have no choice, Monsieur President," sighed the Minister for Fromage. "France has not produced a world-class cinematic sex bomb in decades."

"It is my fault. I will resign immediately," offered the Minister for Cinema.

"In the meantime," said the Minister for Domestic Affairs, "maybe it would cheer the country up to throw out all the immigrants."

"Good thinking," said the President. "Do it immediately."

President Chirac then considered his options. In forty years of public service, he had never faced such a difficult decision. But nothing less than French national honor was at stake.

"All right," he said finally. "Call Bardot. Make a reservation for two at the Tour d'Argent. And alert the paparazzi—but tell them no car chases. And for God's sake, make sure they use soft-focus lenses."

"But then after that, maybe we'll still surrender?" asked the Prime Minister.

"Bien sûr."

At the White House

Saturday

13
Dear Mr. President...
Love, Satan

☆ ☆ ☆

The phone rang at seven o'clock in the morning. As I grabbed it and put it against my ear I remember thinking, *This isn't my phone and, more important, then whose phone is it and where am I?*

"Good morning," a voice said.

"Uh, good morning," I stammered back, realizing I was in the White House. I wondered if this same feeling had come over Marilyn Monroe. I quickly checked my nightgown for stains as I waited for the person calling to state their business.

But it was a wake-up call. An automated wake-up call. "If you would like to snooze and be called back in nine minutes," the voice said, "press one. If you would prefer not to be called again, press two. If you would like to leave a message, press the pound sign."

Leave a message? For whom? "Hi, President Clinton? It's Arianna, I'm a little tired."

I hung up the phone and lay there with jumbled memories of the previous day's events. I put the radio on *Morning Edition*, trying to sort fact from fiction.

As I proceeded to brush my teeth and get dressed, I heard a delightful anecdote, the sort that traditionally follows the news on NPR. Bob Edwards told of a cat that had gotten caught in a tree, but when the fire department came, the cat had already gotten down! NPR, so informative, yet so humorous.

A knock came at the door. Kent butted it open with his head. His hands were full. In one he held three envelopes from Federal Express and in the other some dry cleaning—not mine, as it happened, but it hardly seemed worth saying so since it turned out to be just my size when I tried it on. The dry cleaning had a Post-It attached:

Bill—
Got the stains out. Next time you spill your seed try to be more careful.
—Vernon

"Mail call!" he shouted.
"Good morning and thank you, Kent."
"Where can I put your FedExes?"
"The desk will be fine."
"We aim to please."
He proceeded to open the FedEx letters and lay them across the blotter of the Lincoln Bedroom desk.
He crossed to the door and gave a little L.A.-executive hand signal, sticking his index finger out as if it were a gun and "firing" it with his thumb. I "shot" him one back as he left and "shot" him several more after he'd been gone.
I glanced down at the envelopes on the desk and immediately noticed that, like the dry cleaning, they were not meant for me either; all three were addressed to the President. I suppose I should have immediately rung for Kent, or preferably Walter, and sent them along to their proper destination, but they were already open. Why not read them first?
"Because it's wrong?" Socks suggested from the bed, where he was curled up on my pillow.
"Give it a rest. You want to know what they say just as much as I do. And it's rude to read a person's mind before breakfast."

He didn't answer, but just left the bed and jumped up onto the desk to read along with me.

The first letter, printed on some type of recycled paper, was from CNN founder, UN Funder, and Time Warner Vice-Chairman Ted Turner.

February 6, 1998

The President
The White House
Washington, D.C. 20500

Dear Bill:

Sorry about the round-the-clock coverage of Fornigate and all, but we in the news business have a responsibility, blah-blah-blah.

Anyway, as you know, your scandals have been great for CNN but we'll still have a few programming slots to fill, and since you may be looking for a job soon, I thought I'd pass this notion along.

The way I see it, you and Jane, my wife (hands off her, by the way), could co-host a weekly newsmagazine show with a conceptual blank check to do and say whatever you want. She's up for it, having basically undergone the same philosophical transformation you have. Could be fun, from one "Bubba" to another. We'll pay you a cool million dollars a week. We'd call it something like "Jane," or "Bill," or "One Hour of Airtime," or, if we get the okay from legal, "Seinfeld." Jane Pauley and Stone Phillips will shit themselves when they see you coming. We'll tomahawk those bastards into tiny little pieces. Shitty bastards. Stupid robot shitty bastards.

Sincerely,

Ted

Ted Turner

P.S. If I were you, I wouldn't go out of my way to do any stories on the breast-implant controversy. That would strike a bit too close to home for my little pumpkin. And under the

---

circumstances it wouldn't be a smart move for you either,
trouser pilot.

P.P.S. I wrote this letter on paper made from recycled bison
dung. Neat, huh? Show it to Gore. He'll love it. Just cover
the part about the million a week; I'm only offering him
$5,000.

"A little weird there at the end," I said.

"No doubt about it, he is one weird dude," said Socks.

"And a million a week!" I exclaimed. "Why on earth?"

"Instant credibility, Arianna. Why do you think CBS hired Susan
Molinari, or ABC hired little Georgie Stephanopoulos?"

"Credibility? The only people the public trusts less than journalists
are politicians."

"It's not the credibility on issues or facts, it's credibility on the
inside dirt. When Stephanopoulos says the Clinton team was desperate
for cash after 1994, it's a lot more believable than anything Peter Jennings
has to say on the subject. I can't wait to hear what Molinari says about
Newt's diets. And don't worry about Ted. Bill Clinton's been very, very
good to him. Ken Starr's been leaking nothing but pure champagne.
Every time Clinton gets into trouble, CNN's ratings skyrocket."

The second letter was from Ted Turner's Australo-American neme-
sis, News Corporation CEO Rupert Murdoch. At the top he had written
"Dear Mr. Prime Minister" before crossing it out and beginning with the
proper salutation.

C E N T U R Y   C I T Y ,   C A

February 2, 1998

The President
The White House
Washington, DC 20500

President

Dear Mr. Prime ~~X~~ Minister,

In regards to our recent conversation regarding post-presidential employment, I am prepared to offer you a weekly program of whatever sort you feel is appropriate.

Please consider carefully this idea from my development team at Fox: a dramedy called <u>Bimbo Eruption</u>. You'd star as a sensitive but beleaguered President, harried by the demands of office and an even more demanding wife. Surrounded by curvaceous interns and secretaries, you can't resist a little dalliance. Each week you'd be comforting one of the girls about her latest problem—dead husband needs to be buried in Arlington National Cemetery, needs a better employment opportunity, needs to improve oral sex skills, the possibilities are endless—and naturally one thing leads to another.

And did I mention? Your entire cabinet: babes! With really big breasts! With this program we'd also be exploiting the very successful Page Three Girl franchise I've built in my British tabloids. Additionally, News Corp. now owns the rights to well over half of the televised breasts in the world, although we have yet to gain a foothold in Brazil.

Or we could certainly do the public-affairs roundtable you seemed so keen on.

My people tell me that whatever project we undertake together will be assured of carriage throughout 63 percent of the English-speaking world. Additionally, through my SkyTV network, you will reach a potential 1.2 billion viewers in the People's Republic of China. I'm quite excited about that; my market research division tells me you're quite popular there.

On a personal note, I wonder if you could advise me. As you know, I have become an American citizen because of U.S. laws that limit foreign ownership of TV stations and newspapers. Now that I've given it a go, can I renounce my citizenship and become a Cayman Islands national while retaining my U.S. properties? My lawyers are divided on this.

By the way, the compensation level you proposed is inadequate. I wouldn't think of paying you any less than $1.5 million a week. I know what it's like to have huge legal bills.

Sincerely yours,

Rupert Murdoch

Rupert Murdoch

"One and a half million for starring in a soft-porn sitcom seems commensurate with his legendary talents," I said.

"Play your cards right and you could share the wealth, Arianna," Socks kidded. "I see you in a recurring role as the perky and conscientious member of the opposition party who must constantly battle her powerful attraction to the man she loathes."

"Maybe for two million."

The third letter was considerably more detailed. It was from Gerald Levin, the CEO of Time Warner, which owns one third of Court TV.

February 2, 1998

The President
The White House
Washington, DC 20500

Dear President Clinton:

In an age of narrowcasting, the right person on the right show in the right niche can be a blockbuster. (It's sort of technical. Ask Al Gore to fill you in.) And we feel you're the ideal person for Court TV.

Court TV covers the law. And you've been involved with more litigation, independent counsel investigations, and corrupt activity than any other distinguished public figure this side of Dan Rostenkowski. Whitewater, Travelgate, Fornigate, Gravegate, Paula Jones, campaign finance, and the dozens of other scandals that are sure to erupt before you eventually get kicked out of office by the vast right-wing conspiracy—the lineup for our first five years is set.

But our proposed show, "EverythingGate," would consist of more than just your investigative reporting on yourself. We see a "Legal News You Can Use" segment in which you explain how to duck subpoenas, snow juries, evade embarrassing questions with ambiguous language, and publicly demonize prosecutors who harass you. With Hillary as special guest, you could explain how to accidentally misplace pertinent records such as billing files or videotapes, yet quickly retrieve them should public pressure force you into reluctant disclosure. And our viewers want to know: Am I really getting my $475 an hour's worth? Bob Bennett's best client will help them decide.

But "EverythingGate" will never be impersonal. You'll address the camera directly when discussing your feelings about legal matters, such as your pain when Paula Jones rejected your offer of a cash settlement and a public statement that she did nothing inappropriate, despite the fact that you were the one accused of wrongdoing. And "EverythingGate" will guarantee you something we think you'll find very appealing: the opportunity to tell your side of the story the way you want to tell it, with no rebuttals or opposing views.

We also hope that you'll use your formidable powers of persuasion to induce Susan McDougal to sit down for a no-restrictions interview. Imagine the tension building as you explain why she went to jail and you didn't.

We hope you will give full consideration to our offer, Mr. President. Your compensation, needless to say, will be very generous and we are ready to discuss it with your representatives at their earliest opportunity. We're basing this on our estimates that "EverythingGate" will garner incredible ratings—perhaps even as high as a 1. As you know, that represents over 700,000 homes.

With best wishes,

Sincerely,

Gerald Levin

Gerald Levin

P.S.: Would Mrs. Clinton consider doing a regular segment on investment advice for lawyers saving for retirement?

"This one makes the most sense," I thought. "Too bad we'll never see Bill Clinton talking about his legal troubles on the air."

"Oh, I don't know," said Socks. "Wouldn't impeachment hearings be televised?"

14
It's the Coffee Talking

☆ ☆ ☆

I don't know whose idea it was to put Harold Ickes's office next to the Lincoln Bedroom. But that is where they installed him when Bill Clinton lured him back to the White House to cope with Fornigate after he had been unceremoniously dumped to make way for Erskine Bowles.

Ickes was the bare-knuckled former White House Deputy Chief of Staff. His talents for the seamier side of politics became evident early on. So he was placed in charge of the seamier side of the White House: fund-raising and Bimbo Control. A meticulous note-taker, he documented nearly every discussion—or thought—he had in practically real-time detail. His truckload of files was said to be about as dangerous as high-level nuclear waste, and the administration would have been happy to dispose of them in the same manner. But Ickes did them one better. He gave them to the Thompson Committee.

I discovered that Ickes was next door when I decided to investigate the source of a puzzling murmur of white noise that had been just barely audible in my room since dawn. I traced the sound to a vent placed high on the wall opposite my bed. By standing on a handy footstool (with grotesquely carved goatlike feet), I was able to hear the conversation in the next room more distinctly. I wasn't eavesdropping exactly—just, well, you know, curious. And anyway, anyone talking that loudly didn't care whether or not he was overheard.

Ickes must have been on the phone raising money for a good six hours before I realized what was happening. Now, everyone knew Ickes to be a pathological workaholic, but putting in a full day's work on a Saturday after he'd already been fired once put him in a new category. In his world, I suppose, if you don't come in early Saturday, you might as well not even bother coming in Sunday. Besides, it's always fund-raising time somewhere in the global economy. From what I could gather, Saturday's early calls seemed to be mostly to Singapore and Malaysia, with a brief change of pace when he called his therapist to complain about a birthday party twenty-five years earlier. It seems he had wanted a baseball-themed cake instead of the scuba-diver one his mother had ordered for him.

After a while I got used to his high-voltage staccato and went about my business, paying it no more mind than I would a squeaky door hinge. But it was worth tuning him back in from time to time. Listening to Harold pitch White House coffees was an education in persuasion, compromise, and sheer salesmanship. Believe it or not, the figure of $27 million raised through coffee events alone doesn't seem all that remarkable after you've heard Harold's spiel. In fact, I'm sure Harold could have raised two or three times that much if he didn't have to take time out to attack the media for reporting some presidential indiscretion or forge a new bipartisan consensus on some issue or, of course, pack up boxes. Let's listen . . .

"Hello? . . . May I speak to Tommy Ding? . . . Harold Ickes . . . from the White House . . . the White House in Washington . . . where the President lives . . . the President of the United States . . . *(sigh)* . . . just tell him it's Harold . . . yes, he knows me . . . yes, I'm sure he knows me. I have the canceled checks to prove it . . . yes, that Harold Ickes . . . Okay . . .

"Tommy! How are you, buddy? . . . *(Short phrases in Cantonese follow.)* . . . no, no, Berlitz . . . let's just say the tapes more than paid for themselves . . . ha-ha, yeah . . . listen, Tom, the reason for my call is that we're, we're wondering when we're going to see you over here for coffee again . . . no, I know we've just been sending the documents right over to the office . . . no, it's not to pick up more documents . . . no, Tommy, that's why we got you the top secret clearance in the first place . . . right, so you can just ask the CIA for whatever you want yourself . . . right . . . yeah, I know the automated phone menu's a pain, but that's life . . . uh-huh . . .

"What for? Does there have to be a reason for everything? We just want you to come on by and have some coffee. You can just drive on through, you're on the permanent list at the gate . . . right, like the disco, right . . . Well, it's not about anything in particular, Tom, it's coffee, you know . . . I mean, we grind the beans ourselves here. Kona, mostly, and we just got a good line on some Sumatran . . . yeah . . . uncut, sure . . . Hell, we even roast it here. Do you know coffee goes stale after only two weeks? . . . Yeah . . . What? No, we don't have the Mochaccino, that's Starbucks . . . yeah, they are good, very chocolatey . . . you're right, that would be the 'mocha' . . . No, we thought of making a franchise deal with them for a branch inside the White House, but they didn't, you know, share our vision, uh, financially . . . no, they wanted us to pay them . . . right . . . assholes . . .

"Now, for very special friends like you, we let you have input on the guest list. Give me your wish list? Pick an issue . . .

"Trade, right? . . . Am I right? . . . No, it's pretty much always trade . . . sometimes labor . . . never veterans' affairs . . . foreign trade, right? . . . Am I warm? . . . No, I'm just a good guesser, that's all . . . Well, how about the President, you'd like him to be there, right? . . . No, I know you've already met him, Tom, but I mean you wouldn't mind if he came, right? . . . Okay, good. So, the President, that's one . . . How about the Vice-President? . . . You'd rather not? . . . I don't understand. Why don't you want the Vice-President to be there? . . . He keeps calling you, you say? . . . Waking the kids and upsetting your wife? . . . He makes me feel uncomfortable, too . . . Okay, well, I'll talk to him about the calls, but I think he should be there.

"Okay, now who else? Bill Daley, the Commerce Secretary, uh-huh . . . How about Alexis Herman? The Secretary of Labor? . . . Oh, she's great! You'd love her! You have got to meet this woman, Tommy. You two are gonna bond, I can tell you right now . . . No, she's just really great on, like, diversity issues and stuff like that . . . She used to be a sort of multicultural consultant or something . . . Right, a shakedown, yeah . . . totally . . . No, you don't want her? Okay, okay, I'm not married to Alexis Herman . . . What about Rahm? . . . Emanuel? . . . You just assumed he'd be there? . . . Of course, then he will, yes, absolutely . . .

"No, Tom, you won't be served with a subpoena as soon as you walk into the White House. . . . Well, I don't care what you've heard, that's simply not true. . . .

"Monica? . . . No, of course she's not going to be there . . . Jesus, what are you thinking . . . How long have you been out of the country? Do you watch television? . . . No, I don't consider it a big problem, it's just a speed bump . . . A speed bump . . . It's a bump in the road to make cars slow down . . . No, I'm not saying we're going to run her over . . . It's a metaphor . . . No, I know that's how you handle these things in China. I saw the footage from Tiananmen Square . . . Trust me, Monica Lewinsky is not an issue . . . Plus there's a bright side. We've put to rest once and for all the rumor that the President is gay . . . Anything else? . . .

"What? The trade restrictions on high tech? Look, what is it with you people? You're like a broken record. Always the goddam trade restrictions . . . no, of course, I'm sympathetic . . . No, I'm sure you'd put the high technology and weapons systems to good use . . . No, I don't care about the export textiles being made in your country's prisons. Why would I care? . . . Well, right, exactly . . . I mean, they wouldn't be in a Chinese prison in the first place if they hadn't done something very, very bad . . . Right, and why would you treat a valuable and productive worker inhumanely? . . . Exactly, yes, that's what you should say if *The Weekly Standard* calls . . . No, don't say you got it from me . . . say it was your idea . . . No, my pleasure, a gift from me to you, Tom . . . because we're friends . . . Okay, but getting back to coffee . . .

"Will you be videotaped while you're here? Hell, I don't know, Tommy. Do you want to be videotaped? . . . Uh-huh, you don't. Okay. 'Cause problems with your boss.' 'Don't want to see yourself on *Nightline.*' Wait, don't talk so fast, I'm just jotting down notes here . . . As I've tried to explain to you before, the coffees are private . . . No, the Secret Service isn't going to tell anyone that you were there . . . They're the *Secret* Service, they're supposed to keep things secret . . . Tom, what's really going on here? Why are you getting cold feet? . . . You *what*? You're not sure Clinton's gonna be around much longer? . . . Where did you get that? . . . Have you been talking to members of the vast right-wing conspiracy? Tom, an investment in this President is an investment in the future. Ken Starr, Paula Jones, Monica Lewinsky—that's going nowhere. Didn't Mao have girlfriends? . . . Right, he had lots of them. Tom, it boils down to: 'What did the President ask Monica Lewinsky to blow and when did he ask her to blow it?' . . . No, that's a joke. But it's the President's word against Monica Lewinsky's . . . Exactly. Monica Lewinsky is a girl. If she were born in China she would have been thrown down a well before her first birthday . . . No, that's a joke, too. The point is, there's no hard evidence, Tom . . . Right. *Hard* evidence. Right. It's a joke. You're catching on!

"No, look, Tom, I can't make any promises about the restrictions. I don't control trade policy. Not yet. Here's the . . . How can I put this the best way? . . . The guests at the White House coffees are all favored people . . . Right, you got it . . . Favored, exactly . . . And the most favored of the guests are the ones who make generous donations within two weeks of the coffee in question . . . Oh, come on, you wild man! I know it's not your money, anyway! So, what do you care? Right, exactly . . . all right then, Tom, shall we say the fourteenth? . . . Works for you? . . . Great . . . See you then . . . Oh, and Tommy . . . Tom, you still there? . . . Don't forget to bring your checkbook . . . Okay, bye, now . . ."

Outside, the shadows were shortening as noon approached. A lawn mower coughed to life in the distance. Across the lawn, Sam Donaldson stood immobile with his back toward me while Wolf Blitzer and the lovely Claire Shipman waited in line to do stand-up reports with the White House in the background for that night's news. Claire looked like she was cribbing over Wolf's shoulder.

And next door, Harold Ickes began another call.

15
Going Both Ways: The Bipartisan Brunch

☆ ☆ ☆

I'm not sure when the invitation was slipped under my door. I only know that there it was, lying on the carpet. The paper was rich and creamy, and the invitation itself was as stiff as a board and formally engraved.

> THE PLEASURE OF YOUR COMPANY
> IS REQUESTED AT
> A BIPARTISAN BRUNCH
>
> ———
>
> SATURDAY, 12:30 P.M.
> THE BLUISH DINING ROOM
> THE WHITE HOUSE

I looked at my watch. It was just before noon. I would have to hurry. Socks was stretched out languorously in front of my closet.

"Listen, Socks, I'm off to a Bipartisan Brunch. Want to come along? I'll slip you some scraps."

Socks scowled and batted at a fly-shaped aerial listening device that was buzzing around. "No chance," he hissed.

By now I was used to Socks's speech, but I still found his nearly human facial expressions disconcerting. Still, he was pretty cute and I couldn't resist reaching out to pet him.

He froze. "I hope you realize your petting of me does not constitute a sexual relationship or emotional bond of any kind."

"Oh, please. Of course not," I responded, beginning to rub his stomach.

He relaxed. "Really? Then how about a blow job?"

"Oh, God." I pulled my hand away.

"Come on, baby. I have a friend who could get you a job at Purina."

"Shut up and tell me about this brunch."

"Well, I wouldn't touch the pap bipartisans eat. The food is awful and the portions are chintzy."

"You're a cat of firm convictions, Socks. I know it's bad manners to discuss politics in a social setting, but I have to ask you—do you have a party affiliation?"

"I used to be a yellow-dog Democrat. But now I'm just a frustrated populist."

A few minutes later I was lost once again in the halls of the White House. I asked directions to the "Bluish Dining Room" without initial success. People seemed to remember blue rooms, pink rooms, red rooms, and vermeil rooms, but no one was able to recall any place with such an equivocal color scheme.

Left to my own devices, I tried to think logically. A "Bipartisan Brunch" would not be on the left or right side of the White House, or particularly north or south. Sure enough, by positioning myself in the middle of the White House, facing a spot in between the DNC and the RNC headquarters, I found myself outside a nondescript doorway. I opened it and went inside.

The walls were indeed an indefinable, vaguely bluish tint, and a long table was set for brunch. Walter stood silently and impassively behind a buffet.

"Good day, Mrs. Huffington. I trust everything has been in order so far."

"Actually, Walter, nothing has. Where have you been? I've had to make do with Kent."

"Well, Mrs. Huffington. I've been pretty busy. The Thomasons are in town, and Harry's going off half-cocked about firing all the Swedish massage girls. Plus Mrs. Clinton wants to cut back the number of interns again, so we're a bit short-handed."

"Say no more."

I looked around. The rest of the room was empty. I checked my watch. Twelve-thirty on the nose. Where were the bipartisan brunchers?

"Hello! Greetings!"

The voice came from the head of the table. I walked toward it. A seated figure rose to greet me. The person was of medium build and height. But he was dressed outlandishly in overalls on one side and a business suit on the other. His collar was blue on the left and white on the right. From one angle I could have sworn he looked like Bill Clinton, but when I tilted my head, I saw Newt Gingrich.

"Where is everyone?" I asked, concealing my amazement as best I could.

"I am everyone. Everyone is here."

"Right here." A voice came from my left, but I could see nothing.

"No . . . wait . . . over here," I heard the voice from behind now.

"Arianna, are you blind? I'm right in front of you!"

I seized at the air, only to find nothing.

"HA! HA! HA!" The Bipartisan enjoyed a hearty laugh. "Don't worry, Arianna, that's just my friend the Vital Center, having a little fun. You see, no one can ever quite manage to get his hands around him, though everyone thinks he knows where he is. Much sought, never caught."

"Who, or what, are you?" I asked.

"Well, Arianna," the voice said, swirling around me, "when Arthur Schlesinger coined me forty-nine years ago, I was the common ground between fascism and communism. But now I'm just the mushy middle."

"Kind of a living metaphor?" I ventured. "Like Henry Kissinger."

"Most politicians use me like that," he replied. "They just like to invoke my name."

"That's enough, Vital Center!" said the Bipartisan. "It's a shame you have to go, but I know you've got a bill-signing to attend. Good-bye!"

With a rush of air, the elusive Vital Center departed, giggling maniacally.

Forcing a wide grin on one side of his mouth, the Bipartisan turned to me. "I've ordered a wonderful brunch, Arianna. It's the perfect meal, both breakfast and lunch—and neither. Something for everyone . . ."

"And nothing substantial for anyone," I said.

As I looked closer, I noticed more extraordinary details about my host—on one side it appeared to be female; on the other, it looked all male. On one side of its face, the skin was brown with almond-shaped eyes; on the other, white with oval eyes. The upper part of the face was wrinkled with age; the lower had the smooth skin of a child.

So this was the Bipartisan. Not a group, but a single being. I sat down next to him.

"Well, it's certainly nice to finally meet you, Mr.—or, uh, Mrs.—"

"Just Bipartisan will do fine."

How did one talk to a Bipartisan? Familiarly or formally? In slangy vernacular or in perfect newscaster's English? Of high culture or low? I decided to break the ice with something noncontroversial. "Tell me, are you reading anything these days?"

"Just the newspapers. I love the Paula Jones and Monica Lewinsky stories."

"Really! That seems oddly partisan."

"Well, I love politics, but I prefer surface to substance, so political scandal suits me fine. Today it's a Democrat; tomorrow it will be a Republican. Scandal is bipartisan, just like me."

"And what's your take on Clinton's peccadilloes?"

"His alleged behavior, if proven to have occurred, is reprehensible. And yet I deplore the snoops and busybodies of the press who invade private lives, while not forgetting that a free press in turn helps guarantee our freedoms, which include the freedom to snoop and busybody as we please. Now if the President did something wrong, he should be punished. However, we don't have all the facts, and if we dig too hard we risk a witch hunt. I'm in favor of fidelity in marriage, but the First Amendment says we have the right to lie to anyone, even our spouses, except under oath, but what is truth anyway?"

I was in danger of losing my appetite. Fortunately, at that moment Walter entered, bearing a steaming tureen which emitted a mouthwatering scent. My mounting queasiness died away.

"We're going to start with sweet-and-sour soup," said the Bipartisan. "It's one of my favorites."

Walter served. Despite the clash of flavors, the soup was good: Bipartisanship at its best.

"Bipartisan, do you think Bipartisanship is the wave of the future?"

"Well, yes and no. On the one hand, it's not possible to get anything done in government these days without support from both sides of the aisle. Partisans say that the middle of the road is for yellow lines and dead armadillos, but trust me, the *hard-line* radical middle of the road—*that's* where the action is."

The Bipartisan took a slow, thoughtful sip of his bourbon and milk, and continued.

"On the other hand, I must admit, the intellectual vigor in our political culture is concentrated on the fringes. And some people find compromise unsatisfying. In short, when it's win-win, then everyone loves me; when it's lose-lose, I'm as popular as a tax hike."

"Win-win, lose-lose, lose-win, win-lose," I laughed. "I lose track!"

The Bipartisan smiled and frowned at the same time.

"But nobody really loses over the long run," I went on. "Except the American people."

He shrugged a shoulder. The Bipartisan didn't seem to care what I thought. After all, he had been on a winning streak lately.

He gestured to Walter, standing a few discreet yards away. Compared with his polite friendliness during our earlier encounters, Walter seemed unusually grim as he whisked away our empty soup bowls and presented us with a Hobson's choice of entrées. Before I could speak, the Bipartisan ordered both.

Walter returned with a tureen of mushy stew that smelled rank.

I peered into it. It contained what looked like pieces of hot dog, chicken bits, egg yolk, asparagus, parsley, sage, rosemary, thyme, and cornflakes.

"It has something for everybody," the Bipartisan chirped proudly, "just like the budget deal. Tax cuts for families and investors, new entitlements, new spending on education for the middle classes. And a balanced budget! A Bipartisan triumph!"

"A Bipartisan fraud is more like it."

"Eat," he said firmly. "That should lift your spirits."

I stirred the slush in my bowl and tinkered with my fork to simulate the sounds of busy eating.

The Bipartisan continued. "Besides, the public is on our side. We don't do anything without the right poll numbers behind us. People may say we're out of touch here in the Beltway, but we're always working to find out what people want."

"But isn't that the problem?" I asked. "It seems like Washington is way too *in* touch. That's all politicians do—spend time and money on endless polling and focus groups figuring out what people want and then feeding it back to them."

"Finally we agree on something," the Bipartisan said eagerly.

"Not quite. Maybe what people really want is someone who doesn't care what they want day to day. Maybe people really want leadership—someone who will take an unpopular position and then, with force and conviction, explain it to the public and bring them along. Can you imagine a politician today signing something that was as controversial as the Emancipation Proclamation?"

"That way is so hard," said the Bipartisan. "This way is so much easier. You know, early on, Ross Perot proposed an 'electronic democracy' where everybody would vote on everything with little computers. But we don't need that. Through the miracle of polling, we've already got it. It's democracy perfected. It's automatic Bipartisanship."

Then I saw something odd. His hand, resting on the table, was a lot hairier than previously. His eyebrows were also darker and bushier, even on his female side. And now I found myself looking up at him, whereas earlier in the brunch he was at eye level.

Was he growing larger? Or was it just my imagination?

Walter arrived with a huge silver tray and pulled off the shiny top. Beneath it was our second choice entrée: a mighty chunk of dark brown meat. It was covered with a thick yellowish ingredient that smelled oddly familiar.

"Peanut butter and lamb chops! One of my favorites!" The Bipartisan licked one side of its lips. "Medium-rare, just the way I like them."

"I'd have thought you'd prefer just medium," I said.

I cut a small piece, trying to be polite. The mixture of flavors made me queasy. It was revolting.

"So," I asked, trying to avoid eating, "do you spend a lot of time here in the White House?"

"Oh yes!" the Bipartisan responded enthusiastically. "Bill Clinton really listens to everything I say. And he runs all of his ideas by me in order to get my opinion. I always give him both sides of any argument, you know, sort of like David Gergen. And the President strongly agrees with everything I say—although he's really only interested in the upside. And we've achieved Bipartisan consensus on so many important issues during his presidency: like agreeing to do nothing about campaign finance reform and agreeing that oral sex does not constitute adultery."

I had been getting rather apprehensive about dessert, but it turned out that I need not have worried. Walter delivered a baked Alaska, a perfect Bipartisan dessert: flaming on the outside, ice cold on the inside.

I took a taste, then another, and another. It was delicious. I guess even with Bipartisanship, every now and again you get something decent—like killing the tax write-off for big tobacco.

"Mmmmm," I said with a smile. "Win-win."

The Bipartisan beamed. To top it off, Walter brought out some Dom Pérignon.

"Bipartisans celebrate their converts with a toast," the Bipartisan said. We clicked glasses like old friends. "And a tattoo," he added.

I froze.

"I'm just kidding," he said. "That's only for jailhouse converts."

"How do you get along with the true partisans?" I asked.

"Oh, there aren't many of them anymore," he responded. "They hate me, of course. But these days it's the partisans who have the image problem. Remember when Hillary talked about a vast right-wing conspiracy to ruin her husband? And the right wing responded by complaining about a vast left-wing conspiracy? That kind of stuff is like mother's milk to me. The true partisans know that, in the end, I can't lose—even if I lose."

That sounded logical; but then again, everything seems logical after a few glasses of champagne. "I don't hold it against them," the Bipartisan said, adding, "After all, my parents were partisans."

"Why don't you join us, Arianna?" he went on, looking at me salaciously from both of the wildly different sides of his face. "It's so peaceful in here. None of that ideological bickering; no battles won or lost. You're everything—and nothing—all at the same time."

I had to admit it did sound relaxing. Bipartisanship was so reasonable, so comfortable, so . . . In fact, I was getting drowsy just thinking about immersing myself into the great river of humankind. Individualism was such a chore . . . It was so easy to go along with the crowd, to support that important Mother's Day resolution, a Congressional Siblings Day, that wonderful budget that helps everybody and harms no one, that forty-eight-hour maternity bill to be followed by the thirty-six-hour appendectomy bill, the twenty-four-hour kidney stone bill, and the eight-hour sprained-ankle bill. . . .

I was awakened by Walter shaking me frantically. "Mrs. Huffington! You've got to get out of here right away!"

The Bipartisan's head reared up behind me. Its face had grown monstrous; the maw gaped and drooled. It was preparing to consume me.

Walter pulled me out of my chair and dragged me out of the room, just a few steps ahead of the hideous beast, now no longer recognizably human but part donkey, part elephant, part dinosaur, part Packwood, and part political hire in Revlon's smudged lipstick department. How could I have ever believed that I had anything in common with this creature?

Walter slammed the door in the Bipartisan's face and then leaned against it. I could hear the Bipartisan howling in rage.

"You don't want nothing to do with them Bipartisans, Mrs. Huffington. They're the worst bunch here. I've never trusted them. Almost nobody gets out of a Bipartisan Brunch alive—or at least with their integrity intact."

"I do have to say that was the scariest brunch I've ever had," I said, still a little shaky. "It really transcended the form."

"You'd do well to avoid them in the future," Walter said sternly.

"Brunches or Bipartisans?"

"Both."

16
Boy Wonder in the Umbrella Stand

☆ ☆ ☆

With my pulse still racing from my disastrous flirtation with Bipartisanship, I returned to the Lincoln Bedroom and collapsed on Mrs. Lincoln's exquisitely carved bed, grateful to have made a narrow escape from the horror of Death by Equivocation.

The Television sprang to life—well, not life as we know it, exactly, but a reasonably accurate simulacrum thereof—with a buzz and a crackle. "Are you all right, Mrs. Huffington?" it asked solicitously.

"I think so, thank you, Television," I replied. "But I've just had a near-death brunch and I'd like to relax for a while."

I lay back and found myself hearing a rather cheery tune. "What is that tune you're humming, Television? I won't be able to get it out of my head now."

"Oh, that's not me humming, Mrs. Huffington. That's *him.*"

"*Him* who? Where?"

"Over there, in the umbrella stand. He's always looking at the bright side. I don't know what his secret is, but he's one happy, happy guy."

"Who is?"

"George Stephanopoulos! Who else? Listen to him! Shoved down into the bottom of a damp umbrella stand and he's *still* humming away. I wish I knew his secret!"

"What is he doing in the umbrella stand?"

"You'll have to ask him that, Mrs. H. I don't like to be talking out of school."

I threw Television a skeptical look. For as long as I had known it, it had done nothing but talk out of school—just like its civilian cohorts. It cleared its electronic throat.

"Ahem, that is to say, that is . . . I don't like to talk about people if I'm not behind their backs. Not that Mr. Stephanopoulos would hold it against me or anything. He's really a sweet guy."

I sensed that George Stephanopoulos was the one person in the Clinton White House that my hypercritical Television actually approved of. It was too bad he no longer worked here.

I went over and peered into the umbrella stand. Down there in the bottom I could just make out an enormous mop of hair. Sort of a tousle-headed Mediterranean Ken doll.

"Hello, George. Is that you?" The humming stopped.

"Oh, hey, Arianna!" George Stephanopoulos's boyish voice was unmistakable.

"George, I'm very surprised to find you here. I thought they'd never let you back in."

"Why? What are you talking about?"

"Well, you were one of the first to bring up the Big *I* word after the Monica Lewinsky story broke."

"The Big *I*? You mean impeachment? I was just establishing my independence from the White House and my bona fides as a legitimate commentator."

"Well, you were wrong, at least so far."

"Yeah, thank God."

"But wasn't the President mad at you?"

"Aw, he was sore for a bit. He called and threatened to, you know, pull out my tongue and shove it down my throat and stuff, but he's forgiven me. It's not like I said Hillary might be gay, like Dick Morris did. Anyway, enough about me. How are you, Arianna? Are you having fun?"

"Well, George, since you ask, staying at the White House has been a bit of a trial."

"Really? When is your trial date?"

"No, I was speaking metaphorically," I said.

"Hey, well, around here you never know," he said. "But I'm sorry about your stay, just look on the bright side and it all rolls off your back."

"George, that's the attitude that almost got me killed at brunch."

"That's odd. Brunch is usually so casual. You know, it's not really breakfast, and it's not really—"

"I know it seems innocuous, but a lot of the most dangerous things seem harmless—like Barney."

"Oh, hey now, Arianna. Don't say that! Above all, we Greeks can't afford to get cynical. There's always a bright side. When life gives you lemons, make lemonade! Let me give you an example: Whenever Bill Clinton used to lose his temper and yell at me and swear and call me things and threaten to kill me and stuff, why, I'd just count to ten and think about the Chemical Weapons Convention. Imagine 130 nations, some with powerful military-industrial complexes, coming together to forswear chemical weapons. Forever! Now that's one for the ages. When the President would blow his stack, I'd just close my eyes and think of chemical arms control. And I'd feel better right away."

"But, George, you sound just like Neville Chamberlain! It's a really neat idea, but here's the not-so-bright side of that: The treaty's unenforceable. And a lot of those regimes won't be in power in a year's time. And what about terrorist groups? I bet none of them signed. See? Sometimes the glass really is half-empty."

The humming had begun again.

"What's that, Arianna? I can't hear you."

"George. George!" I would have been tempted to poke him with an umbrella if I had had one.

"Arianna, life is all about choices. And you can choose to be happy. Every morning when I wake up, I say to myself, 'George,' I say, and I really say it out loud, 'you have two choices today. You can choose to be in a good mood or you can choose to be in a bad mood.' Each time something bad happens, I can choose to be a victim or I can choose to learn from it. I choose to learn from it. Every time someone comes to me complaining, I can choose to accept their complaining or I can point out the positive side of life. I choose the positive side of life. And then when I'm finished, I look in the mirror and I say, 'Somebody needs a hug.' And then I say, 'I do!' And then I give myself a big hug."

"And ABC is paying you how much?"

"Here's another example of what I'm talking about," he said, ignoring me. "Sometimes all the spin control would get me down a bit, you know, dealing with bimbo eruptions or corrupt cabinet members, all that stuff. Anyway, whenever I would say to myself, 'I just can't go on, I just can't do this anymore, I can't deal with the hypocrisy and self-loathing,' I'd pause, look in the mirror and say, 'Remember the blue signs.'"

"I'm sorry, I don't remember the blue signs."

"In '92! In New York! At the convention! Dee Dee wanted a mix of different-colored handwritten Clinton signs on the floor; Ickes wanted red; Carville was on the fence; and Thomason had some wacky idea about glow-in-the-dark Bill and Hillary masks. Boy, what a disaster that would have been! Anyway, I thought all-blue signs would look great and I went with it. And five months later we won the election!"

"But do you really think it was the signs that put you over the top?"

"Well, who knows? Anyway, they didn't hurt, did they? Boy, you sure are a Gloomy Gus, aren't you?"

"No, but it's just that you don't really know for sure, do you? I mean maybe you'd have carried all fifty states if you'd used Dee Dee's idea or the thing with the masks. The electoral college can be very quirky."

George started humming the names of various (I assumed) treaty signatories: Bangladesh, Belarus, Belgium, Brazil, Bulgaria . . . He got to Burkina Faso, then stopped.

"Attitude is everything, Arianna. Let me tell you about one time when Bill and Hillary started fighting and . . . man, I just hate it when they fight. It's like watching your parents argue or something. Anyway, he was shouting at her about, you know, how it wasn't his fault, how he couldn't control himself and all, and she, she finally threw a lamp at him. I mean it wasn't a real valuable lamp or anything, but it made a big noise and . . . and I just put my fingers in my ears and I started humming and I thought about the line-item veto. And I just felt better right away. That was a real accomplishment!"

"I know, George. I supported it, too, and so did every President since Nixon, but lining out a $15,000 police training center or a $900,000 veterans' cemetery hardly constitutes a serious inroad into congressional pork."

George was humming up a storm. I tried to shout over him.

". . . IT'S JUST WINDOW DRESSING! HE'S TRYING TO LOOK TOUGH ON SPECIAL INTERESTS WITHOUT TAKING ANY REAL RISKS!!"

I waited for the humming to stop. After a minute, it did.

"George?"

"God grant me the serenity to accept—"

"Oh, dear God, no, not the serenity prayer."

"—the things I cannot change, the courage to—"

"George, wait! I'm not going to argue anymore! Please stop, I want to look on the bright side, really I do."

"I'm glad to hear it, Arianna. You'll find it really makes a big difference. We Greeks are happy people! *Opa!*" He seemed momentarily doubtful. "Aren't we?"

"George, I just have to know one thing. What are you doing in the umbrella stand?"

"Oh, I just come here to relax, Arianna. To keep my head down. I used to do it all the time when I worked here. It's become my special place. And it's juuuuuuust the right size."

"But you're at ABC News now. Why come back here?"

"Have you ever been to ABC News, Arianna? Man, I mean, I thought I was shell-shocked working in the White House! But now I've got to cross swords with Sam Donaldson and Cokie Roberts, and Bill Kristol. But I wouldn't mind, I wouldn't mind any of it, if George Will didn't treat me like a precocious sixth-grader. Carville called the other week after the show and, well, let's put it this way, he was laughing so hard that his nose started to bleed. I felt like a fool! And what do I have to look forward to? Forty years from now I can retire like David Brinkley, try to make a few bucks off Archer-Daniels-Midland, and watch all my old friends turn their backs on me."

"Poor George! I had no idea. No wonder you like to come back to where you feel at home. Please stay as long as you like."

"Thanks, Arianna. Thanks for being so understanding. You know, I liked it here and all, but by '96 I started to feel like I was just marking time, just going through the motions. So when the opportunity came to get out, to go over to ABC, I took it. Now, I'm not so sure. Do you think . . . do you think I made the right decision?"

"Well, George, in my opinion you barely made it out in time. And since you always like to look on the bright side, I'll just add this: Wherever you go—there you are."

"Hey, thanks, Arianna, thanks a lot. Can I use that one?"

"It's all yours."

The humming resumed.

17
The Red Queen's Tea Party

☆ ☆ ☆

An unladylike grumble from the vicinity of my stomach was a reminder that my brunch (or lack thereof) with the Bipartisan had left me peckish. George seemed happy in the umbrella stand, so I left him to his humming and stepped out for a bite to eat.

It was a relief to know where I was going for a change. I made a beeline for the Presidential Snack Room.

Kent saw me coming as I cruised down the hall.

"Hi there, Mrs. Huffington! What can I do for you? Should I get my camera?"

"Out of my way, Kent." I was in no mood for Kent's unhelpful brand of personal service.

Kent continued to grin at me.

"More ice, perhaps?"

"Kent, I know where your boss keeps his snacks. And I'm on my way to get some. I've had it with this place. I practically got eaten myself earlier today, by a Bipartisan, no less!"

Just as I said it, I realized that that hadn't come out in quite the right way.

"Boy, it sure didn't take you long to get into the spirit of the place, Mrs. Huffington!"

I resisted the powerful urge to slap Kent. Instead, I marched purposefully to Bill Clinton's walk-in snack closet.

"I don't think you'll have much luck there," he said, sounding positively gleeful.

Ignoring the KEEP OUT, THIS MEANS YOU! sign, I yanked on the doorknob. Locked. I should have known.

"Mrs. Huffington, if you'll listen to me for a minute, I was just coming to tell you that Mrs. Clinton has invited you for tea. In the Old Family Dining Room. It's just ladies, so you can do your ladies' talk or whatever. Plus there's heaps of food. Oh, and don't mention Monica Lewinsky to the First Lady. She's liable to scratch your eyes out."

I resisted the powerful urge to kiss Kent.

Upon entering the Old Family Dining Room—the White House's most intimate dining experience short of breakfast in bed—I found a raucous tea party in full swing. Hillary sat at the head of the table, and as Kent had said, the other guests were all women. I grabbed a crustless sandwich and gobbled it quickly to restore my blood sugar level. That done, I took a closer look at my fellow tea partiers.

Hillary gave me a friendly wave.

"Ah, Arianna. There you are. You know everyone, don't you?"

Without waiting for an answer, she proceeded to introduce me all around.

"Arianna, I'd like you to meet Tipper Gore . . ."

The blond, smiling Mrs. Gore shook my hand.

". . . Madonna and her baby, Lourdes . . ."

I was relieved. I had initially mistaken the woman across the table for Evita Peron.

". . . Dr. Maya Angelou . . ."

Ah, yes, the Clintons' poet laureate. She was wearing a large hat.

". . . Attorney General Janet Reno . . ." The legal giantess took my hand in a crushing grip. I hoped that she didn't associate me with the delay at the front gate. If she did, I was toast.

". . . Gloria Allred, the well-known attorney from Los Angeles, a courageous advocate for those in justifiable pursuit of publicity." The stern, cranky-looking lawyer with a sculptured swoop of black hair thanked me for interrupting my shopping to attend the tea.

". . . Secretary of State Madeleine Albright . . ." A comfortably upholstered older woman said hello. She was wearing an aggressive brooch that looked as if it should be hanging on the wall of a castle armory somewhere, along with all the rest of the medieval weapons, instead of on the ample bosom of the nation's chief diplomat.

". . . Lynn, Jennifer, and Laura and their babies . . ."

She indicated three breast-feeding women, who nodded at me. As I nodded back to them, Madonna unbuttoned her shirt, exposing a globe-like breast, and joined the celebration of lactation.

". . . and our guest of honor, former welfare recipient Wanda Muldaur, now enjoying her third straight week as a cleaning woman at Milwaukee General Medical Center, courtesy of the Welfare Reform Bill."

A thin, slightly frightened-looking young woman stood up nervously and looked at me. I smiled at her.

I sat down in an empty chair. Walter poured me some tea.

"Am I safe here, Walter?" I whispered.

"Safe as houses, ma'am. Safe as houses. This crowd is so wrapped up in themselves, you'll be lucky if they pay any attention to you at all. It's only men who have to watch out. Speaking of which"—he looked up at Mrs. Clinton—"now that everyone has gotten their tea, I'll be moving along."

As Walter left, a tittering intern with a beret—could it really be Monica?—glided in, grabbed half a dozen linzer tarts and glided out. Gloria Allred gave her the hairy eyeball as she departed. The remarkably composed Mrs. Clinton rose from her chair.

"Now that we've all assembled, I'd like to go over the ground rules briefly and then we can get back to Gloria's interesting anecdote.

"First of all, there is to be no mention of . . . um, you know . . ."

Some of the ladies seemed to know what she was referring to. Others didn't. Madonna was in the latter category.

"What? What's she talking about?" she asked Dr. Angelou. Tipper elbowed her. Hillary continued.

"Second, there's to be absolutely no discussion of . . . of . . . I think you all know what I mean . . ."

"I don't know," Madonna whispered. "What does she mean?"

"And finally," Hillary went on, "under no circumstances is anyone to allude to the topic of . . . of . . . the topic that everyone's been talking about lately or to refer in any manner to any of the people, places, or things associated with the . . . you know . . . stuff."

"What?!" Madonna was getting riled. Maya Angelou whispered urgently in her ear. A smile of comprehension spread across Madonna's face. "Ohhh . . . that . . . the thing about her husband and the blow jobs. So what doesn't she want us to say? Blow job? Sperm? Penis? Monica? White House movie theater? Or is it just blow job? Is that what she has a problem with? Blow job?"

Everyone was staring at Madonna. "What? What is it? Blow job?"

Hillary looked to be in momentary danger of losing her remarkable composure. She cleared her throat and nodded toward Gloria Allred.

"Arianna, Gloria was just telling us about her latest fascinating lawsuit. She's asserting the right of girls to be boys."

"Boy *Scouts,* Hillary. Boy *Scouts.* You see, my client, a thirteen-year-old girl in northern California, is being shamefully deprived of her constitutional right to go hiking and camping with what I like to call the 'young boys' club.'"

"Oh yes, I saw something about that," I interjected. "Aren't there only twelve different Girl Scout troops in her area that do precisely the same thing?"

"Without the opportunity to earn merit badges in direct competition with the opposite sex, she could suffer second-class status and have to endure lower pay for the rest of her life."

"Yes, her future ball-busting skills would definitely suffer," I agreed.

Something furry rubbed my leg. I looked at Janet Reno sitting on my left. It didn't seem to be her. It brushed me again, and I heard a gentle purr.

"Socks! This tea is for ladies only!" I whispered.

"There are virtually no benefits to being neutered," said the cat, "except being able to attend these teas. Actually, scratch that. There are *absolutely* no benefits to being neutered. But I do get a kick out of Gloria. Ask her who's paying her fees."

"Who's paying your fees, Gloria?" I asked innocently.

"That is privileged information," she said stiffly.

"Privileged, my foot," Socks snorted. "She's paying herself in media money. It's all self-promotion. Next thing you know, she'll be trying to make cats hang out with dogs. And we all know where that will lead."

Hillary had risen again from her chair. She clinked the edge of her glass with a knife.

"I would now like to invite Dr. Maya Angelou to inspire us all with a poem. Maya?"

Maya Angelou fished around in her purse for some bifocals, affixed them to her nose, and stood up. She opened up a folded sheet of paper and began to read.

"The History of Time," she announced. "A stone, a bush, a mountain, another stone, some more bushes, a mastodon, wait! A third stone."

Hillary had her schoolteacher-listening-to-an-assembly-presentation-by-a-very-special-guest expression on her face. Madonna was bobbing her head like a beatnik at a be-in. Gloria Allred smiled as if each word really struck home for her personally. Janet Reno looked stern. The Secretary of State looked genuinely concerned about the mastodon, the rock, and so forth. And Wanda Muldaur, the former welfare recipient, looked as if she'd walked in on a surprise party at a mental institution. Dr. Angelou continued.

"The dry tokens of the dinosaurs cry out to us across the gloom of ages, 'Remember us! Even the crumbling excreta of the thunder lizard will not turn to dust and blow away until we have delivered our message in petrified waste products. For it is this: the bush and the stone—not the first stone, but the second one, the one in the middle—do not turn your face away from us, the bush and the stone. Okay, maybe the tree, you can ignore it—not all natural phenomena are equally eloquent—but don't ignore us. We've got a lot to say. The Creator gave to us a beautiful song. Do you not hear? It is the song of the river, of the shiny pebble, of the seashell, of the dinosaur dump, of all these and a million more silent speakers trod upon by bloody feet in the mad quest for silver and gold . . .'"

Maya was starting to lose the crowd. The breast-feeders were still blissed out, but everyone else was getting restless. Gloria Allred broke the ice by turning to Madonna and saying, "Who's doing your hair these days, girlfriend?"

"I've found somebody new, a Rastafarian surfer who mixes his own hair-care products in a big backyard vat in Trancas."

"It looks stunning. And who does your legal work?"

The conversation became general. Maya Angelou appeared not to notice. She droned on.

". . . Plant yourself here and listen to the songs of the Gay Pawnee Rabbi, the Chinese happy-sad, rich-poor person, and the Handicapped Yoruba Home Depot Sales Associate . . ."

Wanda, the welfare-reform success story, could not contain her bad case of the fidgets any longer. She lit up a cigarette. Hillary glared. Even Dr. Angelou paused for a moment. Hillary appeared to wrestle with herself, and then, her voice tightened by her strenuous effort at retaining her remarkable composure, said, "Wanda, dear, we don't smoke here in the White House."

Wanda sullenly stubbed out her cigarette.

"Sorry, Mrs. Clinton, sorry," Wanda said, looking down at her place mat. "Cigarettes just help me relax, you know? Deal with my stress. As soon as I can afford some of that Prozac everyone at the hospital takes, I'm gonna give it a try. But for now, you know, I just love my smokes."

"Wanda, if those of us who support universal health care have our way," Hillary said, "everyone in the United States will get all the medical care they need, whenever they need it. You'll have all the antidepressants you'd ever want, and you won't need those nasty, unhealthy cigarettes anymore."

"Wanda, the Jewish people have an old and wise saying," Mrs. Albright interjected. "Early to bed, early to rise."

A couple of the other women stared hungrily at Wanda's stubbed-out cigarette. Madonna and Gloria Allred, in particular, looked as if they would kill for an American Spirit Light just then.

"Besides," added Hillary, "it's not good for the babies." She indicated the suckling infants. "Maya, go on, please."

". . . the rock and the plant and the shrimp and the Traveler. They hear the Speaking of the Acorn, which says . . ."

I leaned over to Janet Reno. "What are those babies doing here? I mean, I'm all in favor of public breast-feeding, but who are they?" I asked.

"ENORMOUS DONORS." Janet Reno's stentorian voice boomed out across the room.

Dr. Angelou smiled as if to thank Reno for her helpful contribution to the aimless poem. I couldn't suppress my curiosity.

"How much did those women donate?"

"Not the women," said Reno, only slightly less loudly, "the babies."

I was baffled, but I didn't want to risk causing any more loud outbursts from the Attorney General. I bent over discreetly, and Socks helpfully filled in the blanks. "The parents give the money in the name of the children. The Boss got $217,450 from the little tykes. It's all quite legal if you can convince the judge that the money's independently controlled by the kids and that it's their decision to contribute it.'

Madonna was hazarding some conversation with Wanda, no doubt hoping to forge a bond so that she could bum a cigarette as soon as tea was over.

"It must be so satisfying to work in a hospital, Wanda."

Wanda looked utterly baffled.

"You know, helping people and all," Madonna added.

"Health care is such an enormous growth industry, Wanda," Janet Reno added. "You're a very lucky young lady to be getting in on the ground floor."

"Are there good prospects for advancement in your current position, Wanda?" Gloria Allred asked, picking up the thread. "Because if there aren't, I'd be happy to sue someone, anyone, on your behalf."

The women looked expectantly at Wanda, waiting for her answer. But there was none.

Hillary rushed in with more questions: "Is Milwaukee General a good hospital? Is it part of an HMO or a for-profit chain? Is it a teaching hospital? Does it provide an adequate package of Medicaid benefits to children and the indigent? How is it rated on consumer rights issues? Do patients have an ombudsman? Are doctors given a financial incentive to withhold treatment? Do they operate under a gag rule?"

Madonna's ears pricked up. "*Gag rule?* What?! I thought she didn't want anyone talking about blow jobs."

Madeleine Albright, ever the diplomat, tried a new line of questioning: "You know, Wanda, I've always been intrigued by cleaning ladies, indeed by janitorial personnel of all sorts. Tell me, those big carts that you push around . . . how do you decide which cleaning products to put on the top shelf and which on the lower shelves? And how often do you go through vacuum bags?"

Wanda sat there, staring wildly at her inquisitors. Her right hand, as if it had a mind of its own, began crawling across the table toward the carcass of her stubbed-out cigarette.

Dr. Angelou and the slurping babies were the only ones not watching in horror.

". . . the bright morning carnival cannot go on without the shade of the tree where the dwarf can sleep . . ."

Secretary Albright cleared her throat and said, evidently referring to the poem, "That reminds me of the old story about the two rabbis and the priest on the golf course . . ."

"You know, Wanda," Hillary interrupted, "there's a little place just outside the West Portico where the staff goes to smoke. I think there's a bench and some ashtrays. You can take your tea if you like."

Wanda got up so hurriedly she almost forgot her pack of cigarettes on the table. But, at the last minute, she grabbed them—one step ahead of Gloria and Madonna, who were waiting to pounce—and walked out the door.

Hillary shook her head sadly. The tea continued. Gloria and Hillary began a lively discussion about the so-called nuts and sluts defense used by victims of sexual harassment suits. Hillary pressed Gloria for detailed examples of what all agreed was an exceptionally pernicious methodology. Janet Reno offered to show me a few wrestling holds (I declined). Madeleine Albright offered up a smorgasbord of Jewish wisdom, parables, jokes, and quotes from the Talmud. And Maya Angelou's poem went on . . . and on . . . and on . . .

Tipper and Madonna started talking about warning labels on record albums.

"Would you want Lourdes—" Tipper said.

"It's Lourd-ess," Madonna interrupted, correcting Tipper's pronunciation.

"I'm sorry, Lourd-ess. Would you want her to listen to your records, Madonna? When she is at an impressionable age?" the Second Lady asked.

"Oh yeah, sure," Madonna answered, looking down affectionately at the suckling infant. "But I'm sure she won't want to. She'll probably rebel and listen only to classical flute recordings or something. No, I'll have to make her listen to my records, really force them down her throat."

Realizing that the last comment might have brought her close to forbidden territory, Madonna shot a quick glance at Hillary.

"What about you, Tipper? You let your kids listen to my music, don't you?"

Tipper patted Madonna reassuringly on the hand.

"In the Gore household, we always viewed you as the lesser evil, Madonna. In any event, my kids are growing up and I'm not so concerned about suggestive lyrics anymore. I've gotten more involved in the issue of mental health."

"Oh, really? And what are some of the things you're doing?"

"Well, I'm launching a campaign to have warning labels put on records to indicate whether any of the performers involved suffer from mental illness of any sort. If only we'd caught Kurt Cobain's records in time . . ."

Madonna seemed to approve. "Well, I could tell you a lot about who's nuts in the music business. For starters, there's . . ."

She leaned over and began whispering to Tipper, whose eyes grew wider and wider. I thought I heard the Second Lady say, "No, not Paul Anka!" but I can't be sure.

The tea was winding down and Maya Angelou was winding up. The chitchat died away as the tea guests paid her respectful attention for the slam-bang conclusion.

". . . men, children, women. Shake off your chains of brutishness. You deserve a break. Maybe not today, maybe not tomorrow, but soon and for the rest of your life. And listen to the tree—sorry, not the tree—I meant the rock. Forget you ever met the tree. Good morning!"

The women took Maya's cue and began to disperse, wishing each other a cheery good morning, even though it was now late afternoon.

"Good morning, Tipper!"

"Good morning, Janet!"

"Good morning, Madonna!"

Hillary gave Maya a remarkably composed hug. "Thank you, Maya, for that beautiful poem and for not including any references to . . . you know, the thing I don't want anyone to talk about."

"Yeah, Maya," said Madonna, "thanks for not including anything about blow jobs in your poem. There's a time and a place for talking about blow jobs, of course, but this isn't it. Right, Hillary?"

The First Lady remained remarkably composed.

I joined in the general farewells, happy to have eaten something and to have spent time with such a representative slice of American womanhood.

Socks ogled the breast-feeder moms and Madonna as they put their breasts back into their blouses.

"Yum-yum, I'll take some of that!" the cat leered.

"Socks, please! Breast-feeding is not a sexual act. It's a way of nourishing your child."

"Aw, I can look, can't I?" said the cat, chagrined. "Jesus, that's about all I can do."

I felt guilty for lecturing him.

"Poor Socks, I keep forgetting that you're neutered."

"That's the whole idea," said the cat. "That's why you never notice me looking up your skirt."

18
State Dinner at Eight

☆ ☆ ☆

A **state** dinner at the White House is a majestic event in democratic America—no less glittering when the honoree, in this case President Jiang Zemin of China, has given democratic principles a pass. But after all the Chinese money that has blown through the White House and into the coffers of the DNC, I suppose the least Clinton could do was give Jiang a nice meal.

Tiananmen Square? Labor camps? Forced abortions? None seemed to ring any ethical bells these days. In a worldview consisting purely of debits and credits, China's special brand of totalitarianism was particularly popular with foreign investors, of whom an honor roll was at the dinner.

In the magnificent hallway outside the East Room, I wondered what I was doing there. On the one hand, by being at the dinner, I was sanctioning the moral rehabilitation of a gang of thugs the likes of which the world has not seen since Alaric the Visigoth roamed the Steppes (my apologies to Alaric and the Visigoth family). On the other hand, I was staying at the White House as an invited guest of the President and not to attend would have been a serious breach of protocol. I was walking an ethical tightrope.

"Good evening, Mrs. Huffington," Social Secretary Capricia Marshall said in a first class stewardess voice. "Welcome to the White House. I trust the staff has taken care of all of your needs."

"Staff" seemed like too grand a word to include someone like Kent, but this was neither the time nor the place, so I just said, "The staff has been very conscientious, thank you."

Inside the East Room I saw nothing unusual, except one thing: all the guests were wearing name tags that glimmered in the soft lighting of the chandeliers. At least they looked like name tags—name tags on steroids.

The first one I got a close look at was pinned to the grosgrained lapel of Michael Bowman, the chairman of Atlantic Richfield. It was an elegant gold-plated picture frame, inside which his name was beautifully rendered in calligraphy. Beneath that was the amount he apparently had donated: $486,372. The frame was encrusted with several rows of tiny lights, all flickering at once. The effect was almost blinding.

Robert Allen, the outgoing chairman of AT&T, and C. Michael Armstrong, his successor, were both wearing more tasteful matching name tags, slightly smaller than Mr. Bowman's and with fewer lights. Accompanying them, however, was a small child walking before them tossing rose petals in their path. Both name tags read $422,184, the amount AT&T had donated.

There were scores of others, sporting sums that started at about $50,000 and averaged around $200,000. But the undisputed heavyweight champion contributor was the Lion King himself, Disney Chairman Michael Eisner, who clocked in at a hefty $1,036,050. His was a normal-size tag, but upon closer examination one could plainly see that a series of small diamonds had been carefully arranged to spell out both his name and the amount he had donated. Classy.

I watched as the cavalcade of CEOs made its way through the receiving line.

Michael Bowman enveloped the Chinese President's hand in both of his own, dreaming, doubtless, of a Beijing dotted with ARCO gas stations.

Jack Welch, chairman of General Electric, paid his respects. As he shook the most favored dictator's hand, he leaned in very close. I thought I heard him ask Jiang how to say "We bring good things to life" in Chinese.

Looking around, I realized the room was crowded not only with executives with fancy pins. There were a large number of young women wearing, I thought, surprisingly revealing clothing for such a formal occasion. Curious, I sidled close to two of them. I could see now that they wore plain sticky HELLO MY NAME IS tags; one young lady was "White

House Intern Janet Muldoon" and the other was "White House Intern Bree McNair."

"But, I mean, I'm saving myself for marriage." Bree was saying. She tugged nervously at her black cocktail dress, trying unsuccessfully to get the hem to cover her slip.

"Don't worry," Janet responded confidently. She quickly checked her makeup with a small compact. "He's only into oral stuff."

"Oh, well then," said Bree, obviously relieved. "That's not the same thing at all."

"That's what he says. Apparently it's in the Bible or the Kabbalah or something. Anyway, it's totally worth it. Check this out."

Janet removed a laminated card from her clutch and showed it to Bree. It was an ID badge that read "PENTAGON—TOP SECRET CLEARANCE—J. MULDOON."

"Not too shabby, huh?"

"I guess. I was hoping for Commerce or HUD, though."

Janet rolled her eyes. "You'll learn."

Just then a commotion at the door interrupted the hum of conversation. A round-faced woman with straight dark hair was trying to crash, it seemed. "Don't you know who I am?" she screamed, as two Secret Service men dragged her away.

"Who's that?" Bree looked scared.

"Monica," Janet sighed. "She gets so worked up sometimes—all jealous and everything. You've got to understand, you won't be the only one."

Bree nodded, but it didn't seem as though she really did understand.

"Look, I've got to talk to the Revlon guy about a job. One more thing—it helps if you say you like Whitman. He's got a closet full of the books, makes his gift-giving easier. Good luck."

As Janet swept away, leaving Bree in uncertain thought, I saw the eyes of several other young women follow her—eyes that were filled with envy, and, I thought, rancor.

The guests began taking their seats for dinner. The State Dining Room shares the neoclassical architecture of the rest of the White House. There is a cornice of white plaster, and the delicately carved frieze is offset by a painted paneling with Corinthian pilasters.

My eye was immediately drawn to one thing that seemed out of place: a large number of trophies, set on a special table, each with two hands clasped in a handshake with a one-hundred-dollar bill peeping out.

I didn't know what they were for, but they stood out like a mustache on the Mona Lisa.

A waiter came by with a platter of appetizers and promotional brochures. I took a crab cake and a pamphlet and discovered a menu of items that were available. What you got apparently depended on how much you were willing to contribute to the Democratic National Committee. But, as in the most exclusive restaurants, there were no prices listed on the menus given to the ladies—that would be tacky. The line items included the following:

1. **Two seats on Air Force One**
2. **Six seats at all White House private dinners**
3. **Six to eight spots at all White House events**
4. **Invitations to participate in official delegation tours overseas**
5. **Better coordination on appointments on boards and commissions**
6. **White House Mess privileges**
7. **White House residence visits and overnight stays**
8. **Guaranteed Kennedy Center tickets (at least one month in advance)**
9. **Six spots to sit with the President as he gives his weekly radio address**
10. **Photo opportunities with the President and Vice-President**
11. **Two places per week at the presidential CEO lunches**
12. **Phone time from the Vice-President**
13. **Ten places per month at White House film screenings**
14. **One lunch with Mack McLarty**
15. **One lunch with Rahm Emanuel**
16. **One lunch with the First Lady**
17. **Use of the President's Box at the Warner Theater and at Wolf Trap**
18. **Ability to reserve time on the White House tennis court**
19. **Meeting time with Vice-President Gore**
20. **Jogging and/or golf with the President**

I folded the pamphlet and stuck it in my purse.

At the most successful state dinners, guests are seated with a delightful marketplace-of-ideas concept at work. A fashion designer next to a linguistics professor, next to a Buddhist nun, next to a Texas wildcatter, next to a supermodel or a superathlete. This night, however, seemed to have a different theme. It was more like a plain old marketplace. Big-time contributors mixed with smaller-time contributors, with a generous sprinkling of young female interns. Take the guests at my table: Jack Welch of General Electric, better known to the DNC as $325,092; Frank Biondi, President of Viacom (i.e., Mr. $226,400); David Geffen of DreamWorks (aka $425,127); Steven Spielberg of DreamWorks (aka $436,023); Gerald Levin, CEO of Time Warner ($401,250); George David, chairman of United Technologies ($231,400); Steven Jobs, formerly of NeXT, now of Apple ($150,000); Raymond Smith, chairman of Bell Atlantic ($159,600); and finally, Martin Greenberg, CEO of American International Group ($198,492).

A hush fell over the table when I mentioned that I was spending the weekend in the Lincoln Bedroom. I could just hear the question going through their minds: I wonder how much she contributed? Was it so much that she doesn't even need a tag like the rest of the *hoi polloi*? Should we be feeling envy or awe?

We started in on the sumptuous feast, chilled lobster, followed by pepper-crusted Oregon beef (from Asian cattle crossbred with American Angus, no less) with Yukon Gold whipped potatoes and spring vegetables, and then—the *coup de grâce*—a dessert of marzipan pandas arranged neatly around orange sherbet.

Conversation at my table focused on the usual stuff multimillionaires talk about when they gather—you know, whether the transpacific capability and stand-up cabin of the Gulfstream G-5 is really worth the extra twelve million, that sort of thing. (My table was of the opinion that it is.) After a decent interval, the President rose to begin the evening's toasts.

"Good evening, ladies and gentlemen, and welcome," he began. "All of you are here for a reason. The reason is that you all are basically the reason why I'm here. Now before we let the press in and launch into the usual state dinner rigmarole, where I toast the Chinese President and he toasts me, yadda, yadda, yadda, I'd like to introduce a new annual feature of my administration, the bestowal of a very special new award."

There was a noticeable rise in the excitement level in the room.

Clinton paused for a moment and proudly displayed one of the trophies on the table beside him for all to see.

"Ladies and gentlemen, it's my pleasure to introduce (drumroll, please) . . . the first annual Fundie Awards! And the first Fundie goes to my good friend Johnny Chung, who brought new people into the White House and into the political process—making the immigrant dream come true. Some members of the press have claimed that these people weren't really immigrants, that they were Chinese citizens, agents of the Chinese government. Well, to those ugly nativists I would like to say my vision of America includes everybody in the world. Just because someone is, say, a foreigner or a Communist agent, does that mean he can't participate in our political process? And I would also say that Johnny Chung showed me 366,000 good reasons why a narrow view of who should—and who shouldn't—participate in the political process is just plain un-American."

The Chinese were applauding wildly. I felt something brush up against my leg. I glared at Jack Welch, but he looked innocent. I peered under the table, and there was Socks. He asked me to hand him some of the leftover lobster.

Clinton continued, "I couldn't let this moment pass without also thanking my good friend Charlie Trie. Charlie, we're delighted that the terms of your fifteen-count indictment allow you to be here tonight. Folks, Charlie recently went to China to seek traditional remedies for severe back pain. I don't think many of you realize how heavy a manila envelope stuffed with $460,000 can be. But let me tell you what kind of man Charlie is. The instant he heard about Ken Starr's investigation he took a long, painful flight back to the States. This remarkable man risked personal injury just to help the authorities find the truth. Charlie, refresh my memory. You never funneled any illegal foreign donations to the DNC, right? You never gave the money to straw donors who then gave the money to the DNC, correct? And we've never been alone together, right? Don't worry, my secretary can vouch for anything."

Charlie nodded vigorously with each assertion. Clinton went on. "John Huang. I want to thank you, my good friend, for being so darned effective. Many of you may already be aware of what I consider John's most touching achievement—bringing in thousands of dollars from some penniless Buddhist nuns—Buddhist nuns who really got behind this administration and what we're trying to accomplish. All thanks to John. They gave their all so we could give our all. And, you know, this is really a touching story. A Good Samaritan in Taiwan sent those nuns $5,000 apiece so they could eat instead of fasting or chanting or whatever penniless Buddhist nuns do when they're $5,000 in debt. Somebody up there was looking after those nuns. And that was just a small part of what John accomplished—I won't even go into the way he used his CIA security clearance to build better relations with the Chinese government."

A knowing chuckle swept through the crowd.

"Creative thinking was a big part of our success. I give Harold Ickes a lot of credit for that. That is why I will never forget his unstinting devotion, that is why I fired him, and that is why I called on him to help fight the vast right-wing conspiracy. We wish Harold well in his new life as a full-time lobbyist and part-time defendant. It seems like just yesterday when a fellow named Warren Medoff handed me a business card saying 'My associate has $5 million he is prepared to donate to the DNC,' and I said to myself, 'Ickes will know what to do.' And he did. Thought up a way to make it all tax-deductible by funneling the money through nonprofit organizations. Even gave Medoff the bank account numbers. Sadly, we never actually got the money. But with a little fine-tuning, the 'Ickes shuffle' will be a big help in the future.

"Of course Don Fowler, the Chairman of the DNC, was central to our fund-raising campaign. His tireless efforts to make sure big Democratic donors had the chance to share their ideas with government officials are legendary. And you know something? He proved that the bigger the donor, the better the ideas. And he kept on despite the objections of some unenlightened members of this administration. I won't name them, but they include Laura Tyson and the National Security Council among others. Eventually, of course, most of the skeptics came around. Money has some marvelous persuasive powers, eh?

"Don Fowler is just a great human being and a terrific example for our nation's young people. Aspiring fund-raisers would do well to sit in on Don's lectures at the University of South Carolina. Speaking of education, that reminds me that sometime next month, after years of quiet reflection late at night and weighing the pros and cons, I will issue an executive order restoring discipline to our schools by mandating that *all* high school students embrace my favorite aspect of the Catholic school system, namely, the wearing of uniforms, particularly the girls—with white cotton blouses . . . and those socks . . . not to mention the pleated skirts—"

At this point the two interns seated at the table next to me, Sue

Harte and Alison Kellner, gave each other knowing looks. Hillary coughed violently, startling her husband.

The President continued, his voice slightly subdued after his wife's upbraiding. "Don's special genius was in persuading donors to give even when they weren't members of our party and didn't support our goals. Don was able to remind those people just how much they love democracy. Carl Linder and Dwayne Andreas, both of them here tonight, are great examples of this bipartisan giving. It takes an inspired fund-raiser like Don to persuade some of the big guns that usually play for the other team to hedge their bets. Hey, there's no point in backing a loser! I call Don the world's greatest insurance salesman, and those of you who bet your money on *both* sides last time know that that's no insult.

"'No controlling legal authority.' Those words were spoken by one of the brightest minds ever to pass through the doors of the Vice-President's residence since Dan Quayle. Al, I'm kiddin' you. Al is a great, great Vice-President. The exuberance with which he tackled those fund-raising calls would surprise anybody who still thinks he's just a stiff.

"Hell, Al didn't just make one call or two calls. He made at least eighty-six, bringing in over three point seven million dollars for the cause—that is, me. I mean us. Not only that, he made our administration proud as he was named MCI's 'Friends and Family Man of the Year.' And as far as I'm concerned, every dollar was perfectly legal, because everyone knows that the same laws that apply to every other federal employee don't apply to me and my buddy Al."

The entire audience turned upon hearing a sharp crack, as Al Gore, positioned to the right of the President, attempted a modest smile.

"And only a mind with as good a grasp of advanced telecommunications as Al Gore's would have realized that, hey, when you make a fund-raising call from federal property, you're not really breaking the law. That is, of course, if the law even applied to you in the first place. 'Cause the fund-raising really takes place in cyberspace. I think. Al tried to explain it to me, but I was pretty busy keeping those cold-hearted Republicans in line. I swear, I never worked harder in my life trying to save Medicare and keep the radical right wing from endangering our senior citizens.

"Anyway, thank you and God bless everyone who helped."

Clinton stepped away from the podium to a standing ovation. Hillary stepped forward and grabbed the microphone, sending feedback echoing throughout the White House:

"Surprisingly, my husband is being too modest." Laughter rippled through the hall at this. Bill forced a smile. "So I just want to be the one to toot his horn for a change."

She smiled, waiting for the laughter, but the audience was puzzled by Hillary's attempt at a smutty joke. The two interns I could see seemed positively alarmed. Hillary continued, a little flustered.

"Other Presidents have rewarded campaign contributors with stays in the Lincoln Bedroom, and bad coffee and crullers, but they lacked the true grit and determination of my husband. He was the first to have the courage to put the policy in writing. And he is the first President in history to throw the doors of the White House wide open to his wealthy supporters so they can share their concerns with him on a wide range of issues.

"The Riady family, old friends of ours—well, they were just overjoyed when we resumed relations with Vietnam and continued normal trade with China. The Riadys' businesses there are booming. Carl Lindner—he's a new friend—the administration helped him win a trade war over banana exports. In this day and age, that's probably as significant as the Gulf War. And FedEx—gosh, their chairman, Fred Smith, didn't even vote for us, I mean Bill. But his company gave $275,000. And now we're talking to Japan about the trade restrictions FedEx is facing over there.

"By the way, none of the policies I've referred to were instituted just because someone gave us money. I believe that people are smart enough to realize that our actions are going to help everybody, and they give money in advance because, like us, they want to help everybody and they're so grateful. And to those who point out that some of the people we met with are convicted criminals, arms smugglers, tax evaders, nuclear black marketeers, I would say, since when do convicted criminals, arms smugglers, tax evaders, and nuclear black marketeers have no rights? They are citizens of this great republic, too. For the most part. And therefore the policy of this administration on these supposed fund-raising scandals, including the Congressional hearings, will continue to be— everybody join me—'Don't ask . . .'"

The audience roared it with her: "DON'T TELL!"

A thunderous ovation followed. I scanned the crowd, picking out the tear-streaked faces of Clinton donors: convicted drug smuggler Jorge Cabreras, out on a weekend pass; Wang Jun, not yet convicted of smuggling AK-47s into the United States; convicted tax evader Eric Wynn;

convicted tax evader Chong Lo; convicted tax evader Russ Barakat; suspected Russian plutonium smuggler Grigori Loutchinsky; Yogesh Gandhi, destitute President of the Gandhi Memorial International Foundation; and a large, unidentified contingent of middle-aged Asian men wearing boxy, ill-fitting Communist formal wear.

I could feel Socks brushing up against my leg again, so I dropped my napkin on the floor so that I would not be seen talking to myself.

"Makes you proud to be an American, doesn't it?" said Socks. "I only wish I could cry."

"Why do you even stick around for these things?" I asked.

"Affirms my self-esteem as a nonhuman."

I couldn't argue with that.

As the evening went on, my table walked away with several Fundies. In fact, by the time the champagne was being served, I was the only guest at my table without one of the small statues. Some of my tablemates were upset because time didn't permit them to give acceptance speeches. Frank Biondi made a point of reading his out loud to those of us who would listen. Right after that, discussion turned to where the best after-parties would be.

When all the Fundies had been passed out, then and only then was the press allowed into the room. They crashed through the door like the bulls of Pamplona. The President welcomed them and the dinner instantly became very formal and very scripted. Clinton took the lead in the toast *pas de deux* with Jiang Zemin. Through a translator, the Chinese President returned the favor. Flashbulbs flashed and tape recorders whirred. "What exactly did President Jiang mean when he said that China has much to learn from the U.S.?" I heard a reporter call.

"He wants to know more about the White House intern program," Clinton joshed. The babble of questions continued as the illusion of democracy was maintained. The guests were all invited to move to the East Room for the evening's entertainment.

Just before walking out, I looked up at the ceiling and beheld an amazing spectacle: dozens of people sitting in what seemed like sky boxes at a ball game. They were separated from us by a clear plastic shield, which muffled the noise of the gawkers and sightseers.

"What on earth?" I asked Socks. "Is this another fund-raising device?"

"Five hundred bucks a head," he said. "They all get commemorative baseball caps."

As we made our way to the East Room, we were checked in our progress by the enormous crush of people at the door. All of the White House interns were clustered around the President, and he was tossing gifts into the throng. I saw Bree McNair looking adoringly at Clinton as she clutched one of those cheap Guatemalan cotton dresses you see at crafts fairs. Her friend Janet Muldoon looked distinctly nonplussed by her haul—a T-shirt from that store on Martha's Vineyard, the Black Cat or something.

While I waited for the crowd to disperse, I fell into conversation with a building contractor from St. Louis who was waiting for his wife to return from the ladies' room. His name tag read "Stan Lundegaard—$312,000." He was one of those men who had never accepted his expanding waistline—but he had, clearly, expanded. So, as the years wore on and the pounds piled on, he had, through considerable force of will, kept his belt constant, forcing the pounds to settle in just above the belt line. I wondered how long it would be before he just became so top-heavy he fell over. Or maybe some sort of training wheel would be in his future. Nevertheless, I found him quite pleasant.

"You must be a very enthusiastic Democrat," I said, looking at his name tag.

"Oh, heck, Mrs. Huffington, it's just the price of doing business," he said cheerfully. "I'm more of a Republican myself—I've got another tag with the same amount for Republican Senatorial Trust get-togethers. It's really my wife who's interested in the Democrats." He slipped his arm around a young and attractive woman, who introduced herself as Sandy Lundegaard.

"That's right," Sandy continued. "But, you know, Stan supports the President just as much as I do. It's still hush-hush"—her voice dropped to a whisper, but a loud whisper, the kind everyone around us could hear—"but we may be named ambassador to Grenada soon."

"We?"

"Well, Stan, most likely. But that makes me ambassadress, right?"

I was a little surprised. "Now, Stan, Sandy, stop me if I'm wrong, but neither of you know anything about the Caribbean, right?"

Stan shrugged and smiled. "We took a long weekend in Bermuda once."

"But that's not . . . never mind. I hate to presume on our short acquaintance, but I have to be blunt. Do you think your contributions had anything to do with this?"

"Oh, no," said Stan, visibly shocked. "Not at all. I only gave money because of the construction tax break—"

"You run along and mingle, honey," Sandy interrupted. "Maybe you can sneak out back and have a cigar with the President."

"Oh, boy," he burbled, and we were left alone.

"Now, Arianna, you must know that money isn't the only thing that buys a favor." Her lips puckered in a little moue as her pale blue eyes fixed me with a knowing stare. "Do you follow me?"

"I'm not sure," I said faintly, but I was afraid I did.

"Let me put it to you this way. See that couple over there? Do you think they're contributors?"

I followed the tilt of her head. In the crush of people I spied—but surely my eyes deceived me . . . No, they didn't. Amid the blue suits and evening gowns were the leather-clad forms of Pamela Anderson Lee and her husband, Tommy Lee. And unless I was very much mistaken, that was a video camera clutched in Mr. Lee's hand . . .

"They didn't give a cent, Arianna. And yet he's about to become . . ."

"Ambassador Lee? Where?"

Sandy laughed, not a pleasant laugh. "I hear he wants 'someplace sexy,' like France. Or Italy. Or maybe, what was it . . ."

"No—"

"Greece."

I fled to the East Room, Sandy's laughter ringing in my ears.

19
Ladies and Gentlemen, Mr. Mark Russell

☆ ☆ ☆

My guess is that a big name must have canceled as the evening's entertainment and some calls were made at the last minute. I don't know this for sure, but I'm assuming that Mark Russell is an all-purpose pinch-hitter for White House social events. They probably keep him on retainer with his own special pager. Or maybe there's a special signal, like the one Commissioner Gordon uses to summon Batman. Come to think of it, I've often wondered about the giant bow tie I'd seen projected on the low clouds above the capital.

I gazed at the full-length portrait of George Washington on the wall of the East Room. Abraham Lincoln had sheltered Union troops in this room. Harry Truman had played a bit of Paderewski's Minuet for President Kennedy and his guests. Now 232 dinner guests—most of them big donors—awaited the iron man of Washington postprandial entertainment, Mark Russell.

Socks, of course, couldn't let a star turn go unstoned: "For what these people are paying, they should get Enrico Caruso resurrected from the dead and singing the entire Verdi catalog with the Vienna Philharmonic."

"I didn't know you were an opera fan."

"High-pitched screeching? I'm a cat. I love it. I'm in heaven when Hillary pitches a hissy."

I must have looked unconvinced, because Socks went on indignantly, "Do you think it makes me gay that I like opera? You haven't been talking to Dick Morris, have you? Did you hear what he said about me on the radio? 'Let's assume that some of the allegations that Socks is not into regular sex are true. You would then expect a variety of things of a quasihomosexual nature, like a love of opera.' Where does that guy get off?"

"I just wouldn't have pegged you for an opera fan, that's all," I said, not really sure if he was joking.

"You know, plenty of straight cats like opera," he said.

Was I really having this conversation? "Socks," I said, "I'm in favor of cats of all sexual orientations liking opera. I'm sorry if I implied other-wise."

Mark Russell bounded onstage with an energy that belied the amount of food and drink I'd seen him put away at dinner. "Good evening, ladies and gentlemen. Mr. President. Mrs. President." This line got some nervous chuckles and a few tentative groans. The few guests who'd dared to laugh quickly swiveled their heads to make sure the First Couple wasn't disapproving. "It's sure great to be here," Russell went on. "I got the call just a short time ago. Apparently Weird Al Yankovic wasn't available."

As the crowd chortled, Socks whispered, "How did he know?"

"I love performing at the White House," Russell continued. "It's the only place where the green room is the Green Room." Scattered guffaws.

"But, you know, one great thing about this country is that we can poke fun at our leaders and not end up like Susan McDougal. Because you have to be a *very* close friend of the President to land in jail. Anyway, if a couple of Arkansas state troopers show up at the end of the show, you'll know I crossed the line. By the way, I'm not suicidal, so if I turn up dead anytime soon, don't believe the official story!" The President frowned. Russell hurried on.

"My first little recitation is for a member of the audience, the most important and powerful man in the world right now. Of course, I'm talk-ing about Alan Greenspan. Am I right? Is this on? Hello?"

Most of the audience laughed. One noble exception was Janet Reno, who didn't seem to get the joke. "Yes, of course it's on. We hear you just fine," she said loudly, then, under her breath, "Idiot."

Russell continued his patter. "This guy hiccups and the stock mar-ket jumps a hundred points. He institutes Casual Friday at the Federal Reserve, up two hundred points. He gets married and the business cycle is tamed forever."

"But it's a tough job, being chairman of the Federal Reserve Board. I know I couldn't do it, because . . ."

And with that introduction out of the way, he launched into "It's Not Easy Being Greenspan," a parody of the classic Ray Charles/Kermit the Frog duet. The point seemed to be to mention politely the names of as many people in the audience as possible in order to elicit an appreciative laugh of recognition. That, and to conduct in one short song the most cursory examination of economics since the Indians of Manhattan said, "No, the beads and mirrors will be fine."

"Wow, this sounds strangely similar to the song he did at the fundraiser for Ruth Messinger last year in New York," said Socks cynically.

"How do cats of various sexual orientations feel about Mark Russell?" I asked him.

Socks chose to register his feelings by pretending to cough up a fur ball. At least I think he was pretending. Anyway, I laughed, so the little troublemaker did it several more times during Russell's performance. He was very funny. The cat, that is.

The first song shuddered to its pun-laden conclusion. Applause, applause, applause.

"Thank you, ladies and gentlemen, you're too kind." Russell was on a roll. He turned to Greenspan and said, "Mr. Greenspan, I just hope to God that you're amused."

"Just avoid irrational exuberance, Russell," Greenspan joked. His wife, the lovely and powerful journalist Andrea Mitchell, beamed at her husband's little sally.

"I have a personal theory about Andrea Mitchell," Socks hissed. "If you were lost in the Arctic with her, just the two of you, and you were running out of food, and you had to catch some fish to survive, you could pick her up by the ankles and use her to chop through the ice."

"That's terrible!"

"Hey, Alan told me that one," Socks said.

"You're kidding!"

"Yeah, I am, but that would be something if he had, wouldn't it?"

"Are you drunk, Socks, or am I?"

He just smiled.

We turned our attention back to Russell, who was rattling on. "You know, there's a lot in the news these days about whether the President did or didn't accept illegal campaign contributions, but ultimately doesn't it just come down to the fact that people are people? Huh? Isn't that right?"

"What the hell does that mean?" asked Socks.

Mark Russell plowed on inexorably, like a force of nature. Like a hurricane, or a mysterious rain of fish out of a clear blue sky.

"But, you know, when push comes to shove Bill will have to go on record again, saying:

"I get no kickback from campaign
The Chinese with their money, will happily explain

It was part of their game
To see me remain—

'Cause I get a kick out of moo-goo-gai-pan
All the food from that land

Ask me no questions, I'll tell you no lies
It goes right to my thighs

'Cause I get a kick out of that kind of stew
Especially in lieu

Of getting no kickback from you . . ."

The audience went nuts, whooping and hollering for his rambling version of the Cole Porter classic, probably because it seemed to justify the presence of a lot of the guests. But if it's true that the dead really do turn in their graves, Porter must have been rotating like Nora Charles on the revolving dance floor of the Rainbow Room after half a dozen stiff martinis.

"Give me shelter," Socks cried. "He's not even trying anymore. I mean, we're not even getting top-quality Russell here."

"It's frightening that you even know the difference," I said.

The song ended and Russell went back into interstitial patter.

"Speaking of illegal contributions," he said, "who among us here tonight can honestly say that, from time to time, they haven't accepted big wads of cash in sealed manila envelopes—huh? I know I'm looking forward to one at the end of tonight. I'm donating it to my favorite charity, which some of you might recognize by its initials, T.M.R.F.F.M.R., The Mark Russell Fund for Mark Russell. It's a worthy, worthy charity with a very simple, clear-sighted goal: Make Mark Russell a wealthy, wealthy man. The direct mail goes like this. 'Please, folks, please, for just $7,500 a day you can help Mark Russell maintain a lifestyle far more opulent than the one he's currently grown accustomed to.' My motto? Same as the DNC: 'If it doesn't fold, I'm not interested.'

"But Washington isn't only about money and power—it's about love." The guests stirred uneasily, not sure where this was going. "Yes, love. Love of country, certainly, but if you're in the armed services, Washington can be about the love of men for other men." At this, William Cohen looked like he'd swallowed even more than his usual daily dose of alum. "Gosh, D.C.'s even about the love of dog for cat—Socks? Buddy? Are you with us? Just kidding, fellas." Socks began to arch his back and bristle.

"Peace, Socks," I said, hoping to avert calamity. "Revenge is a dish best served cold. Pee on his coat or something."

"You're right. Thanks."

"But most of all, Washington is about the love of man for woman—or should I say women." Russell began to tickle out the familiar samba strains of "The Girl from Ipanema," and after an instrumental moment he burst into inglorious song:

"Short and dark and young and chubby,
Another intern eyes the First Hubby,
And when she passes, the First Lady's glasses get fogged

Tall and gray and fat and reddish,
The Big Guy sure has quite a fetish,
Oral only, 'cause that's not a-dul-te-ry.

Ohhh, and he loves them so madly
How can he tell them he loves them
With a dress brought back from the Andes
Or a book of Whitman's po-e-try, oh . . .

It's hard to stop at just one cutie,
The President needs a lot of bootie
Especially if he gets none from Hillary.

Linda Tripp's tapes and Paula's trial,
Monica's face around the dial,
And then there's coping with groping Kathleen Wiley

Ohh, and he handles it badly
W-i-i-ith unconvincing denials,

His wife blames a con-spi-ra-cy
While Ken Starr searches out per-ju-ry-eee.

But Clinton's head is not uneasy,
He just needs something new on TV,
Attacking Iraq will just about do him nicely . . ."

There was dead silence in the room. After a moment Jiang's aides, who didn't seem to have caught the drift of the song, applauded softly, then stopped in confusion. Russell seemed to realize that possibly he'd taken the court-jester role too far; he stood there, flop sweat standing out on his face, no doubt recalling tales of Bill Clinton's near-murderous temper. For myself, I kept thinking back to the throngs of interns at the state dinner.

One of Hillary's aides—an ex–Children's Defense Fund type who looked as if she took the "Defense" part very literally—leaned forward and whispered something in Hillary's ear. Hillary nodded and said something to her husband. He began to chuckle awkwardly, and Hillary joined in. Then they began to laugh loudly. "That Russell, he's a card!" the President hooted. "If only, Mark, if only!"

"It almost seemed like he was going to kill Mark Russell there," I said to Socks. "I mean, *really* kill him."

"It was close," Socks said. "Put it this way, what have you heard from Lanny Davis lately? 'Nuff said."

The rest of the audience burst out in great animal roars of laughter. They too were relieved that the threat of Bill Clinton barehandedly tearing Russell's limbs off had been averted.

Russell seemed puzzled. He paused for a moment and scanned the room, as if searching for a face in the crowd. "Is the Press Secretary, the venerable Mike McCurry, around? What? Not invited? Well, he's probably out at a pay phone begging David Gergen for help.

"It's a tough job, though, bending the truth into pretzels all day. And some days are worse than others. Some days the truth is a balloon animal in the shape of a *T. rex* . . . to scale! It's a job that requires a lot of creativity. Mike's gotta have all the euphemisms, excuse me, all the *facts,* at his fingertips, all those qualifying adjectives that convince the press things aren't that bad. Sometimes he even slips into understatement . . ."

And to the tune of "That's Entertainment," Mark Russell again launched into song:

"John Huang didn't do any wrong
Paula Jones—just a right-wing crone
No news here—this came out last year

That's understatement!

Says Bill may bomb Paris
Claims the tail will not wag the dog
Kenneth Starr, he's gone way too far

That's understatement!

McCurry, in a hurry, tries to quell all our fears
Says "the truth will prevail" over Monica's smears
Leaves Donaldson and Blitzer in a pool of their tears

Of journalists' frustration
They can't get information

About all these things that we doubt
Like a bash for some Chinese with clout
Broken laws become "social calls"

That's understatement!

The press is amazed by the show
Forget the scandals! How 'bout that Super Bowl?
That Mike McCurry, he's one slippery troll

The world is a stage
The stage is outraged
By understa-a-a-a-te-ment!"

"Encore, encore," the crowd shouted.

"Oh, I couldn't possibly," Russell demurred. Without pausing, he continued, "Well, sure, if you insist."

Suddenly, the tune of "Officer Krupke" from *West Side Story* filled the East Room.

"Dear kindly Mr. Clinton,
Why won't you take my calls?
You just ignore my hintin',
You snub me in the halls.
You never say the sweet things

You used to say to me
Like 'Oral sex is not adultery!'

Young Miss Lewinsky,
It's really a sin
That now-a-days I don't have time to pencil you in.
So go and deny what you gotta deny
And thanks for the sex tapes and the tie!

Love the tie!
Yes the tie! What a tie!
Nearly made me cry!
Yes, you've made the Prez a happy guy!

Dear kindly Bill's friend Vernon,
The Pentagon I hate.
I much preferred internin'
Close to the Head of State.
And though I've met a colonel,
I doubt he ever will
Stand up and salute as well as Bill!

Now, Miss Lewinsky,
We'll find you a place,
A private sector job where you can hide your disgrace—
At Revlon or even Amer'can Express
But first burn the semen-covered dress!

Yes, the dress!
Burn the dress, with the mess,
I'll accept no less,
And make sure to keep it from the press!

Dear kindly Mrs. Linda,
I fell for ev'ry trick.
He knew it was a sin ta,
But, boy, is Willie slick!
He told me to deny it
But lying makes it worse,
What's that humming coming from your purse?

There, Miss Lewinsky,
It's time you should learn,

He plays the same lip service game with each gal in-tern.
I know a guy who's much nicer by far—
Come say hello to Kenneth Starr!

Kenneth Starr!
Here we are, Kenneth Starr, we're at Larry's Bar!
Since you're listening, come and bring the car!

Dear kindly-ish Grand Jury,
My guts I'm gonna spill.
I know you're in a hurry
To unemploy my Bill.
But, still, I'll always love him
In ways you'll never guess;
My eyes said 'No,' but my lips said 'Yes!'

Whoa, Miss Lewinsky,
Now don't bet the ranch,
Although you've put the squeeze on his Executive Branch,
You've made us all envy our poor President,
We, too, love oral argument!

So, young Miss Lewinsky,
We're setting him free,
We like the way you pled his case while down on one knee.
Bravo, Miss Lewinsky,
You're loyal and true!
We want a Lewinsky . . .
Like you!"

And then it was over. Mr. Russell took a bow and the audience applauded and rose to its feet in a standing ovation. Over the clapping, Bill Clinton quipped, "I'd just like to thank Mark Russell personally and say that, Mark, you can perform at the White House anytime—you'll just have to give all your material to Ken Starr afterward. He's in charge of my presidential library now."

"Too bad we can't get Mark Russell to take the fifth like everybody else around here," said a surly Socks.

"Look, he's no Mort Sahl, but he wasn't that bad," I said.

"It's not really Mark Russell. Well, it's partly Mark Russell—I mean, where's a little 'prior restraint' when you need it? But mostly it's Clinton."

"I thought he was pretty good-natured about the whole thing," I said. "The point of political humor is to make a tough point by making people laugh."

"Thanks, Harold Bloom. But taking a joke is one thing. And pretending there is no problem is another. Especially when the butt of the joke uses the joke as the ultimate cover—it softens the true nature of a scandal."

Conversation had resumed. Russell was pretending that his wallet had disappeared and trying to search the President's pockets, to the amusement of all.

"You know, they have Prozac for animals now, Socks."

"Hey, you can laugh as hard as you want," Socks shot back, "but sometimes people need to see things clearly for what they are. See, when Clinton laughs at a joke about fund-raising, he's being magnanimous. But when he tells a joke about fund-raising, he's trying to tell people, 'Hey, obviously there's nothing sleazy here—I can joke about it!' And then everybody laughs and it's all a big joke."

"Like for instance . . ."

"Like at the White House Correspondents' Dinner, when Clinton made fun of his own meaningless rhetoric. He got up there and said, 'We are going to build that bridge to the twenty-first century—yadda, yadda, yadda.' I mean, what's everybody laughing about? He got elected on that little joke.

"What he's really doing is sending a signal: He doesn't believe in anything he says or does. Except maybe for trade. Trade with China. Trade _über alles_. The rest is all provisional. If a policy or an idea doesn't work out, then, hey, he was just kidding. Only a jackass would have taken it seriously!"

"So what does that leave Clinton?"

"Almost nothing. He can't win over the public with bold new initiatives, or decisive leadership, or moral rectitude. The only thing left is to make them laugh."

"Socks, you're actually starting to make sense."

"There's nothing like a guy in a bow tie to put everything in perspective."

20

Closed-Captioned for the Ethically Impaired

☆ ☆ ☆

With Mark Russell tunes dancing in my head, I returned to the Lincoln Bedroom ready to kick back and relax. But the White House is not a good place to kick back and relax, unless you're just phoning in a lackluster second term or hiding out from a media feeding frenzy or two. Perhaps this is why all Presidents at least since the invention of the camera have succumbed to that form of media leprosy otherwise known as "visible aging while in office." Of course, some of it could just be the fact that they have to work and sleep in the same place.

My own remedy for White House anxiety was to follow the example of millions of Americans and turn to a trusted and reliable friend: television.

The nocturnal infomercials were already out in force and on the prowl—men in loud sweaters being goaded on by paid television audiences to pour lighter fluid onto Jaguars or make beef jerky. And of course, there was singer/astrologer Dionne Warwick. Do you know the way to San Jose? Or Mars? Or Jupiter?

Then the parade of channels I'd never heard of, which these days seem to pop up like endless new breeds of dogs or plants: the Hitler Channel, the Libertarian Cooking Channel, the Amish Weather Channel, the Gay Sports Channel. I was about to check out what was on the

Emergency Room Aerobicize Channel when I saw the familiar, gloriously plain logo of C-SPAN.

I feared that it might have mutated since my stay had begun, that I'd see Brian Lamb making real-life rescues, or Steven Scully judging a freestyle snowboard competition. But, no, it was simple, unalloyed C-SPAN—the boring friend that outlasts all the others.

I was greeted with something you don't hear much on C-SPAN—thunderous applause. The President was about to begin the State of the Union speech. Not many people can—in the middle of a scandal, no less—walk into a room where half of the people present hate them and still get ninety or a hundred standing ovations. When I'd watched the address in years past, I'd never known which was the worse lie, the sure-to-vanish promise or the standing ovation it received from the political enemy.

It looked like Bill was just starting.

Mr. Speaker, Mr. Vice President, members of the 105th Congress, distinguished guests, my fellow Americans.

Suddenly, at the bottom of the screen, appeared the words: *(Except the vast right-wing conspiracy arrayed against me and my wife. If you're out there Monica, stand firm! Don't let them crack you.)*

What was going on? Had the Americans with Disabilities Act included some sort of Truth in Closed-Captioning clause for the ethically impaired?

"Do you like this feature?" asked Television.

"You can show people's thoughts?"

"Or something," answered Television. "It's still in the experimental phase. I call it BS Filter '98. The BS chip for short."

"This is incredible. Can you do this for the whole thing?" I asked.

"To the last standing ovation," it answered.

And with that, the sound and the special clarifying captioning came back on.

These are good times for America. We have more than fourteen million new jobs. *(Unfortunately, ten million of those jobs are as bouncers on the* Jerry Springer Show, *two million are as beauty consultants to Paula Jones, and the rest are on my legal defense team.)*

Crime has dropped for a record five years in a row. *(Although, according to the latest FBI statistics, the number of incidents of fondling, groping, leering, brushing up against, and copping a feel of White House interns has risen dramatically during my tenure in office.)*

Our leadership in the world is unrivaled. The state of our union is strong. *(And by "our" I mean the whole country, not Hillary and me.)*

It is time to build the America within our reach. *(Stop giggling over there in the Supreme Court Justice row.)*

Where every citizen can live in a safe community. Where families are strong, schools are good, and all young people can go to college. *(And then all of them, literally all of them, can come to the White House. Or at least, be reachable by phone. Betty, set that up, ASAP.)*

But, with barely seven hundred days left in the twentieth century, this is not a time to rest. *(And rest I have not. If you know what I mean. I've been eagerly tending to the nation's business: talking to Vernon Jordan, meeting with my attorneys, denying allegations that I had "improper relations" with Monica Lewinsky . . . See, busy. Not resting.)*

For five years now, we have met the challenge of these changes as Americans have at every turning point—by renewing the very idea of America: widening the circle of opportunity, deepening the meaning of our freedom, forging a more perfect union. *(And if you're like me, taking off your pants when they feel too, you know, confining.)*

We have shaped a new kind of government for the Information Age. A government that gives the American people the tools they need to make the most of their own lives. *("Tool." That's pretty funny. I see you laughing, Clarence. Okay, really, stop laughing, or you're going to crack me up, too.)*

We have the smallest government in thirty-five years, but a more progressive one. We have a smaller government but a stronger nation. *(And that's my legacy: that size doesn't matter. It's what you do with the government that counts.)*

Tonight I come before you to announce that the federal deficit—once so incomprehensibly large that it had eleven zeroes—will be, simply, zero. *(That's ten zeroes less, but still one too many. That's why I've asked NASA to spend ten billion to find a way to get rid of that last zero. That's right—I intend to submit a budget with zero zeroes.)*

Last year, we enacted targeted tax cuts, so that typical middle class families will now have the lowest tax rate in twenty years. *(Or, to put it another way, since my last girlfriend was only four years old! That's a long time!)*

If we balance the budget for next year, it is projected that we'll then have a sizable surplus in the years that immediately follow. What should we do with this projected surplus? I have four words. Save Social Security first. *(Kill Kenneth Starr second. Or here are four more words. Pay off my lawyers. Or Big Macs for everyone. Or dry-clean Monica's dress. Or kegger in my office. Or more oral sex. OK, that's only three words. But that's what I want to do with the money. And I'm the President!)*

In an economy that honors opportunity, all Americans must be able to reap the rewards of prosperity. We should raise the minimum wage. *(And lower the age of consent.)*

And because of these actions, I have something to say to every family listening tonight. Your children can go on to college. If you know a child from a poor family, tell her not to give up. *(If she has big breasts, supple lips, and the ability to keep her fat yap shut, she can always get work as a White House intern.)*

I ask Congress to support our efforts . . . to reach out to disadvantaged children . . . so they too will be able to go on to college. *(The girls particularly, to go on to become cheerleaders or sorority sisters.)*

We have more than doubled funding for training dislocated workers since 1993, and if my new budget is adopted, we will triple funding. *(Most of which goes directly to Vernon Jordan, for his tireless efforts to find jobs for so many dislocated, beautiful young women.)*

Millions of Americans between fifty-five and sixty-five have lost their health insurance. Some retired. Some were laid off. *(And some were squeezed out in order to make room for younger, prettier, bustier employees.)*

Next, we must help parents protect their children from the gravest health threat they face: *(Being alone in a room with the President and a certain Supreme Court Justice, am I right, C.T.?)* An epidemic of teen smoking, spread by multi-million-dollar market campaigns. *(Here's my slogan: "If you've been smoking, I won't let you kiss it.")*

Tomorrow, like every day, 3000 children will start smoking; 1000 of them will die early as a result. *(721 will enter into a close "emotional relationship" with me, 467 will be subpoenaed by Ken Starr, and 346 of them will be granted immunity to testify against me. All because you wanted to save Social Security before killing Ken Starr.)*

The Family Medical Leave Act was the very first bill I was privileged to sign into law as President. I ask you to extend the law to cover ten million more workers, and to give parents time off when they have to see their children's teachers, or take them to the doctor. *(Or accompany them to a sexual harassment deposition.)*

We have formed a crime fighting partnership with local law enforcement and citizen groups. Violent crime is down, robbery is down, assault is down, burglary is down. *(Suborning of perjury is slightly up, but, hey, can't win 'em all—I'm not Superman here.)*

We must exercise responsibility not just at home, but around the world. *(Of course, I'm talking about you. Not me!)*

To meet these challenges, we are helping to write international rules of the road for the twenty-first century, protecting those who join the family of nations, isolating those who do not. *(And in that family of nations, I think it's important that the older nations take the younger and less experienced nations under their wing and help them out and buy them a dress and stuff.)*

Like every taxpayer, I'm outraged by the reports of abuses by the IRS. We need some changes there. New citizen advocacy panels, phone lines that are open twenty-four hours a day. *(And you can talk dirty to the operators. It's a lot cheaper than those calls to the 900 numbers.)*

We must also ban the cloning of human beings. *(Unless, of course, it's the Dallas Cowboys cheerleaders.)*

This year, Hillary and I launched the White House Millennium Program to promote America's creativity and innovation. *(Like not being so uptight about open marriage and oral sex. I mean, that whole adultery thing is, like, so twentieth century.)*

In schools, homes, and libraries, millions and millions of Americans surf the net every day. We must give parents the tools they need to help protect their children from inappropriate material on the net. *(Scandalous rags filled with lies like* Time, Newsweek, *the AP wire.)*

Throughout history, humankind has had only one place to call home—the planet Earth. Beginning this year, 1998, men and women from sixteen countries will build a permanent foothold in the heavens—the international space station. *(Note to self: add to trip one more young woman. I mean, they can't go into outer space without an intern. Bill, my friend, you are a genius. Problemo solved.)*

With its vast expanses, scientists and engineers will set sail on this uncharted sea of limitless mystery and unlimited potential. *(And they will never, ever come back, and there will be no phone contact whatsoever.)*

"I can't take it anymore," said Television.

"Okay. I've had enough too," I said.

"I've actually blown out two BS chips on the campaign finance hearings alone."

"Do you use it on any other stations?"

"Occasionally," said Television. "It's actually fun to watch *60 Minutes.*"

"Why's that?" I asked.

"Turns out whatever Morley Safer says, he's actually thinking about Hugh Downs."

"I wouldn't have figured it."

"That's the paradox of BS Filter '98," said Television. "There are some things you just don't want to know."

21
The Two Mr. Clintons

☆ ☆ ☆

Instead of relaxing me, the television had left me wired. I read once that when you're experiencing insomnia, reading is okay, but you're not supposed to read in bed. The bed should only be identified with sleep—or whatever one does as a preamble. But the Lincoln Bedroom was already associated with so many unrestful things for me, I figured reading was comfortably at the soporific end of the scale. So I curled up with a Russian novel—Mikhail Bulgakov's *The Master and Margarita*. Socks was sprawled at the foot of the bed, his tail occasionally twitching, no doubt dreaming of a better and better mousetrap—and the world beating a path to his door.

Suddenly the quiet was shattered by a knock on my door. Who could it be? At this late hour? If it was more ice, the world was going to have to get by with one fewer Kent. As I gathered my robe around my shoulders and made my way to the door, I imagined the emergency radio call that would go out: "We've got a bellboy down! Repeat, bellboy down!"

Gingerly I cracked the door. "Yes?"

The door opened. Standing there were Bill Clinton and . . Bill Clinton. Both had slick graying hair, and wore blue suits with red ties. Socks had awakened and was standing with his back arched and fur bristling.

"Hey, Arianna, sorry to bug you so late, but . . . can we come in?"

I motioned for them to enter. Socks hissed and took off through the

open door. I felt uneasy. Two Bill Clintons were at least one and a half Bill Clintons too many. I wished Socks had stayed.

Clinton laughed. "Crazy cat. Sometimes I swear he enjoys the fact that I'm allergic to him. Arianna, I don't know if you've met the other Bill Clinton yet. Bill Clinton, Arianna. Arianna, Bill Clinton."

"Hello," said the second Bill Clinton. "It's nice to know you."

"I'm sorry," I said, "but which of you is the real Bill Clinton?"

"Oh, we both are!" said the first Bill Clinton, laughing. "But I'm default Bill Clinton, and Bill Clinton here"—he motioned toward the other Bill Clinton—"is mostly used for all that ceremonial stuff, so I can have more time for serious fund-raising. Which, of course, only allows us to implement our party's policies, which benefit all Americans. Plus, I'm the one who gets all the White House groupie sex," he said. "I'm kidding, Arianna. That's a joke." I wasn't so sure.

The second Bill Clinton elaborated. "While Bill Clinton here is meeting with Secretary Cohen or Prime Minister Blair or a donor who wants to generously participate in our political system, I'm down in the Oval Office having my picture taken with Boy Scout troops, small-town mayors, and, of course, lower-level donors, those who are also participating in our political process, but less wholeheartedly."

"But I thought you were opposed to human cloning."

"Oh, we are opposed to human cloning, Arianna, we are," said one Clinton.

"Despite the fact that if we were to clone ourselves we could be even more efficient," said the other.

"Yeah, we could attend maybe thirty, forty, hell, a hundred fundraisers a night."

"Right, and we could have hundreds of alibis every time Ken Starr accused us of anything."

"You're right," said a Clinton. "Perhaps we should rethink our cloning position—but, no, we're not clones. Think of us as dual manifestations of a complex, multifaceted personality."

"So are you two alike in every distinguishing characteristic?"

They looked at each other sheepishly.

"I don't think so," said one Clinton.

"If Bill Clinton has done one thing for this country, it's create jobs," said Bill Clinton Number Two. "And you can see that right here tonight. He created my job. Before I—I mean, Bill Clinton—was elected President, I was just another low-level, disbarred lawyer, running around Arkansas, shootin' guys and roughing up prostitutes. I was a nobody, a zero. You think Vince Foster was depressed? But now that's all changed. I owe everything I am today to one man: Bill Clinton."

The two Bill Clintons sat down on the edge of my, er, Mrs. Lincoln's bed. They both looked at me appraisingly.

One smiled, looked at the other. He smiled. Both looked at me. I didn't smile.

After a pause, Bill spoke.

"Arianna, can I ask for your opinion on something? I mean, you're a woman and all, and I thought, well, maybe you'd have some insight . . ."

The President got up and started to pace. His doppelgänger stayed seated on the bed.

"It's this whole Sexgate mess. Paula, Monica, Gennifer Flowers, Kathleen Willey, Janet Reno . . ."

"Oh, no, Mr. President, you didn't . . . not Janet Reno, too. Where did you grope her?" I asked.

"No, it's not what you think with Janet, Arianna. She's not one of the forty-three distinct types that scientists now recognize as 'my' type.

No, it's just that she knows about a lot of the others. Look, everyone's always known that I have . . . a large appetite. I never tried to hide that. Hillary and I have acknowledged some tough times in our marriage, and on *60 Minutes,* I all but came out and admitted that I have strayed from the marital bed from time to time. But, dammit, if a President wants to get a little head from one of his interns in his hideaway office in, say, the White House movie theater and then ejaculate all over her navy blue dress, well, I think those sort of clinical details, they ought to be private. Even for a President."

His double picked up the thread. "Now, sometimes the whole testosterone thing has worked for us. We get the female vote every time, and things like the Kathleen Willey business. That could have worked for us."

He glared at Bill Clinton Number One: "But every woman in the country just about melted when they heard that the President of the United States had fondled an older woman, leaving her, as Linda Tripp put it, 'flushed and joyful.' I mean, aren't those words in the Bible? Wasn't that how Mary was described after giving birth to baby Jesus? Hey, you gotta love the Good Book, right? I mean, just about everything is in there—if you know where to look. For example, there's a whole long bit about how phone sex isn't adultery. I'll show it to you sometime."

The President sat down, and the other Bill Clinton got up and went over to the window. I was beginning to get extremely confused. Who was who?

The seated Clinton continued, "It's true that sometimes I feel like the luckiest man in America. Except for maybe Steve Guttenberg—man, that guy's career, I mean, he *must* have naked photos of somebody. Anyway, the womanizing, my bad temper, the whole Whitewater thing, all that nonpolitical *character* stuff that Bob Dole used to go on about so much, that's always been deflected by my Teflon coating. It just doesn't seem to stick."

The other Clinton bit a nail. His lower lip trembled. "But I'm worried about Paula. And Monica. Can you imagine? The President in court talking about the distinguishing characteristics of his penis? Or trying to convince the jury that oral sex is not adultery?"

The other Bill Clinton stifled a giggle.

"It will irreparably damage the institution of the presidency!" one Bill Clinton said.

"Oh, shut up!" said the other. "It'll irreparably damage my prospects of getting laid for the rest of the century! Back in Jack

Kennedy's day, a guy could get away with just about anything. If he was President now, he'd be waving his pecker around in courtrooms from here to Hyannisport every day of the week. He was my idol. All I did was follow his example."

"But I made one big mistake," said a Bill Clinton ruefully, "I hit on women who didn't have the good taste to keep their mouths shut. Of course, Paula *did* keep her mouth shut in that hotel room. That was the whole problem. But Monica? Mouth never shut. Never."

Both Clintons kept silent for a time, lost in a swirling gas of regret and recrimination.

"It's a strange thing to want something and then, when you get it, realize it's not what it's cracked up to be," said one of the Bill Clintons.

"You thought that Monica was the silent, stiff-upper-lip type?" I asked.

"I'm talking about the presidency," Bill Clinton replied. "I mean, I'm not the first to say so either. Just look at Nixon. You must've heard those stories about him walking around late at night, bourbon in hand, talking to all the portraits in the hallway. Well, now I understand what he was going through. I really identify with him."

I flashed back to Nixon's funeral. I'd been amazed by Clinton's plea during his syrupy eulogy that we stop judging the Watergate President on anything less than his entire life and career. Then I thought of that photograph—of Nixon and Elvis shaking hands in the Oval Office. And then it hit me. It was as if at that moment in the Oval Office a peculiar process had been initiated. The two men, one insistent that whatever he did was okay because he was the President, and the other insatiably obsessed with food, women, and himself, had somehow fused into an entirely new person: William Jefferson Clinton.

I looked at Bill Clinton and the other Bill Clinton. So in a sense, there had always been two Clintons. Or, rather, Clinton had always been two people—not just any two, but two very specific people: Nixon and Elvis.

Suddenly, one Bill Clinton broke down and began to weep.

"Mr. President," I said awkwardly, "you've still got a couple of years left to work on your presidency."

"Maybe, maybe not, Arianna. But well . . ." Another wave of emotion rolled over him, and he blurted out, "Why couldn't things have worked out between Paula and me? We were such a great couple!"

"Weren't you together for about ten minutes?" I asked.

"I mean, *right at that time* we were a great couple. We could have spent a delightful few hours . . ."

The other Clinton tilted his head and looked mockingly at the speaker.

"All right, all right, maybe just a few *minutes,* but she would have remembered those few minutes for the rest of her life."

"The distinguishing characteristics of my penis could have been part of a happy memory for Paula instead of a piece of evidence in a civil suit."

"I feel so *dirty.* Paula Jones—she broke my heart."

The Clintons put their heads in their hands. I mean, each one in his own hands. Then, one looked up.

"Say, Arianna, you don't think it's too late for flowers, do you?"

"Gennifer Flowers?" I asked.

"No, no, no. Flowers with a note."

"You mean one of those 'Sorry I dropped my pants in your job interview' bouquets?" I said.

"They have those? This is a great, great country, Arianna!"

"I was kidding, Mr. President."

"How about the government job she wanted?" the other asked excitedly. "Any job she wants, it's hers."

"Her whole family can have jobs!"

"How does this sound? 'Paula Jones, Secretary of Energy'?"

"Oh, sir, she could never fill Secretary O'Leary's shoes," I said.

"You're kidding again, right?"

"Right."

"See, we catch on pretty quick," said the other Bill Clinton.

The Clintons high-fived each other. But their ebullience was short-lived. The mood changed—again.

The Clintons' Inner Nixon seemed to be gaining the upper hand over their Inner Elvis.

"You see, if Paula hadn't gotten so mad, she'd never have subpoenaed Monica or Kathleen, and Bob Bennett would never have gotten Linda Tripp so upset—talk about Mad Cow Disease—and then she would never have blabbed to Lucianne Goldberg. See! It's all Paula's fault. Am I right? When I'm right, I'm right."

The Presidents' Inner Elvis struggled with their Inner Nixon and came out victorious. The Clintons' voice got a little husky.

"Arianna, you must be tired . . ." a Clinton said.

"Well, actually, I am a bit," I said, and then stretched and yawned to reinforce the point.

"You know, Arianna, I'm pretty upset about all of this, as you can see. I'm not sure that I should be alone tonight."

"Well then, it's a good thing your other self is here," I said reassuringly, moving them toward the door.

"Have you ever before been with two men at the same time?"

"Two virtually identical men, both of whom are one of the most famous lovers in the world?"

A sparkle bloomed in the eyes of both Clintons. The situation called for drastic measures.

"You know, Mr. President, er, Mr. Presidents . . ."

"We prefer 'Misters President,'" said a Bill Clinton, "like 'attorneys general.'"

"Okay, Misters President, when I was talking to Paula Jones the other day, she told me all about your, uh, *technique,* and you know something? So far she's right on the money."

The two Clintons went pale.

"You . . . you talked to Paula?"

"Susan Carpenter McMillan called me when she heard I was coming to the White House. She is one determined lady. She told me what to expect, and then she put me on with Paula. She asked me to call her on Monday just to help her make sure she got your whole standard approach right. Said something about 'establishing a pattern of behavior' or something like that."

The Bill Clintons backed off. One laughed. Then the other laughed, as if it had all been a joke. In a few seconds they were hooting and slapping their knees with laughter. For a brief moment I had a glimpse of what it must be like to walk through life as Mark Russell.

"I feel like a movie. I'm gonna watch *The Mirror Has Two Faces* on tape. I just love that picture," one Clinton said. Then he asked the other one, "You want to join me?"

"I think I'll stay here awhile," the other Bill Clinton said casually.

"Join him," I said sternly.

"Okay, what the hell. Good night, Arianna."

"Good night, Arianna, and you tell Paula Jones and her lawyers one thing for me. You tell them that they'll never make it stick. Because if things get really rough, I've got an emergency plan. It's a beauty. Can't lose."

"Well, what is it?" I asked.

The first Bill Clinton didn't say anything, but just looked at the other Bill Clinton, who stared blankly for a second.

"Oh no. You are not pinning it on me," he said. The two Clintons hastily backed out the door as they argued, nearly wedging themselves in the frame in the process. They extricated themselves, and as the door to the Lincoln Bedroom slammed shut, a small black-and-white streak entered the room. Socks had barely missed catching his tail in the door.

"Sorry, Arianna, but those guys give me the creeps. Who did you think was phonier, the first Clinton or the second one?" He offered his head for a scratch.

"That's a tough call, Socks. And it may be like counting angels on the head of a pin. Frankly, it's hard to see the appeal of *either* of them."

"Put it this way. If Bush was like every woman's first husband, Clinton is like every woman's first affair. He sweeps into your life, charms you, understands you—deeply, intimately—treasures you. He makes a lot of beautiful promises. Of course, it never works out—it turns out he was married or, in Clinton's case, has seen the tops of more women's heads than most hairdressers."

"Are you describing the political Bill Clinton or the priapic Bill Clinton?"

"You can separate them? The thing is, women know he's a cad. But they are trapped in this dysfunctional relationship, this cycle of seductive lies and broken promises, rationalizations, blame-shifting, and assurances that all will be better."

"How does all this explain Paula Jones or Monica Lewinsky?"

"No idea. But that's for a jury to decide, isn't it? To me, though, the Paula Jones thing doesn't seem like his MO. The Bill Clinton I know would have compromised. He would have settled for a hand job."

"Perhaps. Anyway, I don't think we'll learn the truth at the trial."

"Arianna, you mean you don't have faith in the American system of jurisprudence?" Socks asked mockingly. "How can you say that after the Juice?"

"Paula's case had its ups and downs. I meant now that the judge has decreed the distinguishing characteristics off limits, all we are left with is crooked penis jokes. Socks, you've been with the Clintons a long time. Surely you must have caught a glimpse . . ."

Socks rolled his eyes. "Think about it. Bill is always on both sides of every issue. Remember what he said about the congressional vote authorizing Desert Storm? First he agreed with the vote against it, then after victory had been declared, he said Bush was right to kick Saddam Hussein out of Kuwait. Or the IRS. First he was defending it, then after he saw the poll numbers, he decided that it was in dire need of reform after all and went along with the Republicans. We haven't seen a big tub of vice like this since Warren Harding. He's a Democratic President, completely at home with a Republican Congress. Isn't it obvious?"

"Oh no, Socks . . ."

"Oh yes. Bill Clinton is a hermaphrodite."

INTERLUDE IN MOSCOW

The news was already two days old by the time the Russian President awoke from his most recent vodka-induced blackout.

"Aiiee! Some idiot vomited on me!"

First Deputy Prime Minister Anatoly Chubais grimaced. "Mister President, that is your own vomit."

Yeltsin took a closer look. "Ahh. So it is."

Chubais signaled to a pair of apparatchiks to pick the President up from the floor and commence cleaning him. As they did so, Chubais held up a dossier of news clippings.

"Mr. President, there is very important news from America."

Yeltsin nodded impatiently. "I know. They canceled *Seinfeld*. That's why I went on a bender. I mean . . . on vacation in the Crimea."

"No, there is other news. President Clinton has been accused of having an affair with a twenty-one-year-old White House intern."

"What the hell is an intern?"

"I don't know, either. But here is her picture."

Chubais handed Yeltsin a photo. The Russian President's eyes bugged out.

"Tell me about her, Anatoly. Does she have big tits?"

"That's not clear from the photo, Mr. President."

"But she is a Russian girl. I can tell."

"Her name is Monica Lewinsky, sir."

"Lewinsky! I knew it! Nice Russian peasant girl with big, big tits! We must discuss."

He began looking excitedly around the room.

"Where is the red phone?!"

"Don't you remember? You threw it out the window. We had to replace it." Chubais gestured toward a green phone.

Yeltsin looked at him sternly. Chubais shrugged.

"They were out of red ones."

Yeltsin picked up his direct line to the President of the United States.

"Hello, Bill . . . ? Bill, I have only just heard the news. Bill, this is very important. I must know immediately! You like it with Russian girl, huh? Russian girl is good, yes?"

A grin spread across Yeltsin's face as he listened. He began to nod excitedly.

"Oh boy, oh boy, Bill!" Yeltsin looked at the photo in his hand. "She looks like she has big tits. Am I right?"

Chubais waved his hands in a desperate effort to get Yeltsin's attention. "While you've got him on the phone, ask about the loan guarantees!"

Yeltsin waved off his closest adviser. This was no time for matters of State.

"Bill, Bill! Next time I come to Washington, you find me intern, yes?"

At the White House
Sunday

22

Newt Crawls Out from Under His Rock

★ ★ ★

I awoke on Sunday morning to find bright sunlight streaming through the windows. A brisk wind rocked the branches of the trees on the South Lawn. The Sturm und Drang of the past two days was a distant memory, rapidly fading. Besides the relentless subversion of democracy, all was right with the world.

Someone knocked on the door. Walter with my breakfast, no doubt. I opened it and there, to my horror, stood Newt Gingrich. No, I told myself, it can't be. I rubbed my eyes. I must be dreaming. I would wake up in a moment. It must be every woman's nightmare (except Marianne's, I guess), having Newt Gingrich's face be the first one you see in the morning. Wake up, wake up, wake up!

I closed my eyes tightly and then opened them again. My door and my eyes were still filled with Newt.

"Hi, Arianna! Rise and shine!" said my nightmare.

"Newt, it's a little early . . ."

"No rest for the wicked! Listen, we need to talk."

Newt brushed past me and into the room, revealing in the process another equally bloated gentleman standing behind him. The cheery, chubby man emerging from Newt's eclipse shook my hand.

"Arianna, you know Haley Barbour, of course?"

Looking at Newt and Haley together, I saw that Newt was actually shaped almost exactly like Haley, but about twenty-five percent less bloated—Haley in Canadian currency. Haley clasped my hand in both of his and looked me in the eye with the sort of awesome mock sincerity that makes an honest man's blood run cold.

"Wow, get a load of this place!" the speaker said. He proceeded to do a 360-degree, wide-eyed, mouth-hanging-open, near-pirouette. "No wonder everybody and their brother wants to stay here."

"Don't tell me you've never seen the Lincoln Bedroom before," I said.

"All right, I won't. But I haven't. There are some places that are off limits to me. At least for the time being."

"I'm sure it's just an oversight."

"No, it's because no one likes me. Well, a few people like me, but I don't like them—"

"Arianna," Haley interrupted in a deep Southern drawl, "you look too young to be staying here in the Lincoln Bedroom all by yourself. Where's your mom and dad?" He let out a big laugh, which tapered off when no one joined him. "Aw, now, don't blush!"

I wasn't.

"When Newt told me that we were going to pay a call on a very important donor to the Democratic Party, I was expecting someone old and wrinkly and ugly—"

"Cut the crap, Haley," Newt said abruptly.

The Speaker settled into a deeply upholstered chair: an overstuffed man in an overstuffed chair. I slipped on my robe.

"Arianna, I need to know. Just whose team are you playing for here?"

"I . . . I'm sorry?"

"Listen, I can play the bipartisan game as well as the next fellow, and I'm chummy enough with Clinton and his boys when it suits my purpose"—I recalled the grisly scene in the second-floor kitchen on Friday night—"but I always . . . keep . . . my . . . eye . . . on . . . the . . ."

He punctuated this last statement with sharp jabs of his right forefinger.

I waited. "The prize?" I ventured.

"No, the ball, the ball, we keep our eyes on the ball," Newt said, looking to Haley for affirmation.

Haley nodded. "The ball. Absolutely, Newt, I always, uh, try to keep my eye on the ball."

I still had no idea what either of them was talking about. "So let's all keep our eyes on the ball," I said, motioning to the door. "Thanks for stopping by."

"Arianna, do you mind if I ask you what the hell you're doing here?" Newt asked, finally getting to the point. "Are you some kind of spy or are you undercover trying to dig up dirt on Bill? Are you wearing a wire, Arianna? 'Cause if you aren't, we can get you wired up in no time. Just takes a single phone call to Ken Starr."

"I lost a bet with Al Franken, Newt. That's really where it all started. It's a long story. But anyway, now that I'm here, I'm trying to use the opportunity to understand the mechanics of the Clinton White House."

"Um-hmm, um-hmm." Newt didn't seem to be buying it.

"I'm not buying it, Arianna." I was right. He wasn't buying it.

Haley Barbour dove in: "Arianna, the recent fund-raising and sex scandals have been pretty good for us, for our side. Not that they couldn't have been a real gold mine if some people hadn't had ethics problems of their own . . ." He cast a glance at Newt, who started looking curiously at his nails.

"But be that as it may—the point is, and please turn your wire off now, if you are wearing one, that we could spend enough money to burn a wet mule in 2000—all money raised legally, I might add—and run against that fallen Dudley Do-Right Al Gore and we *still* might not win the White House. These Democrats, they're agile, nimble, slippery . . . and some of 'em got political skills out the yin-yang. We need an issue. A clear statement of purpose. Something to really catch the public's attention. You know, grab 'em by the balls."

"Sounds like you've got the gender gap all taken care of, at least. Grabbing 'em by the balls, huh? Well, that sure would be a change from *this* administration," I said.

Haley paid no attention. "To explain simply and clearly what our party stands for. What we're all about."

Newt followed up, on a slightly different tack.

"Arianna, we've had our differences over the last two years and, frankly, I've never really felt that you liked me."

"I did like you, Newt, when you said things like 'balancing the budget doesn't have the moral urgency of coming to grips with what's happening to the poorest Americans.' And then I realized you didn't mean a word of it."

"So you don't like me now."

"Oh, that's not true!" I lied.

"Really? You like me?"

"No."

"Okay, Arianna, look—Haley and I have been up all night working on something, something that's really gonna win back the momentum for our side. It's big. It's real big. Let me refresh your memory: How did we take over Congress in '94?"

Before I could say anything, he answered his own question.

"We won it by running on a clear, straightforward platform that captured America's imagination: the Contract with America. But lately we've been drifting, Arianna. Like Haley says, we need something new that will really get people fired up about the Republican Party, something that will really show America where we stand."

"I agree, Newt. So what is it? The charitable tax credit? Or school choice for inner-city kids?"

"No, no, no. Boy, you just don't get it, do you? Here's what we've come up with—and I'd like to get a quick read on it from you—the Contract with Corporate America. It's real compassion for American corporations, and we'd like you so-called Compassion Conservatives to get on the ground floor with us."

He handed me a document.

THE CONTRACT WITH CORPORATE AMERICA

THE CONTRACT'S CORE PRINCIPLES. The Contract with Corporate America is rooted in three core principles, which we refer to by their first three letters, CEO:

COMPETITIVENESS. In today's tough global marketplace, our corporations need all the help they can get to stay competitive. But staying competitive can take a lot of time and a lot of money. Often, corporations would prefer to keep that money and not put forth the effort. But how can they still stay competitive? With a compassionate "leg up" from the U.S. government. The GOP's Contract with Corporate America opens doors for American companies overseas and helps keep the fortunate in the forefront of the dynamic worldwide business environment.

EFFICIENCY. When corporations spend a lot of money, they have to raise the prices of goods and services. And, more alarmingly, greater expenditures can lead to lower profits and a depressed stock price—which can be devastating for senior management. But if government helps our corporations, they won't have to use so much of their own money and will be able to lower prices while raising profits, the stock price—and their level of security. The GOP's Contract with Corporate America helps corporations become more efficient, and as a result helps the American family.

OPTIMISM. Martin Luther King once said that a society is only as good as it treats its corporations and multinationals. And as we look across America, we are proud to say that many corporations seem to be doing very, very well. But sometimes prosperous companies want to become more prosperous. Often they could do it themselves—but it would be hard. Can we, as a party, turn our backs on them? We want a staggeringly profitable corporate tide that lifts *all* corporate boats and yachts. We must safeguard one of America's greatest natural resources: its corporations. A party must have certain core values, and within "corporate," you find that core. A party must also serve its constituency, and that constituency will reward the party—sometimes with votes, sometimes with hundreds of millions of dollars. Listen to the words of Dr. King, my friends. Who will help the more fortunate who don't want to help themselves? We will. That's our pledge to Corporate America.

1. The Global Village Marketing Saturation Act—It's a Big World After All!

All good Americans know what it means to "Just Do It" or have a glass of "The Real Thing" or "Reach Out and Touch Someone," but what about the poor French people who "just" want to "do it"? Or the Malays, or the Azerbaijanis? Worse, what about Nike and Coke and AT&T, who want so badly for those people to do it? It's easy for those companies to advertise in America—we all speak English. But in other countries it's very hard—those people have so many languages and folkways that, to stay competitive, our multinationals need a "leg up." Each of these countries is different, and it would take a lot of time and effort to get it right. Even with really good lip-synching, few Russians will understand the subtleties of an Obsession ad. But with a little help, in the form of a lot of rubles or yen or zlotys or drachmas, it would be much easier. So this act will be a great improvement on the Market Access Program, which is how we now subsidize our multinationals' overseas advertising.

2. The Greenhouse Gas Reduction/Greenback Increase Act—Agribusiness Is Hard Business.

Three important words with regard to the future: Eth, An, Ol! And three important words with regard to ethanol: Archer-Daniels-Midland. No, it's not a law firm, it's a ten-billion-dollar agribusiness giant. Unsubsidized ethanol costs three times more than gasoline and is far less efficient, but ADM chairman and agrivisionary Dwayne Andreas has assured us since the seventies that ethanol is the wave of the future, and apparently now the future is getting really close. To help Mr. Andreas keep ethanol cheap, he's going to need a lot of money—more than the $75-million-a-year subsidy he already gets for producing ethanol. Mr. Andreas even gave $750,000 back to both parties in last year's election. But let's show him that we're the party that feels his pain. It's an investment in the future. And if you have any doubts that Mr. Andreas is not operating in America's best interest, just ask David Brinkley. He'll vouch for Dwayne 100 percent!

3. The Expatriate Patriot Act—Gone But Not Forgotten.

If it takes a village to raise a child, then sometimes it can take an offshore village to raise an adult. Being a captain of industry can be very lucrative, but it can also be very costly. Do you know that when you're extremely wealthy, you have to pay a lot of money in taxes? Well, it's no surprise that many distinguished moguls prefer not to pay so much. So is it fair that they have to renounce their citizenship and move away just to get out of paying taxes? Just because a corporate overlord has moved to Bermuda to be closer to his offshore account(s), does that mean the public should be deprived of the fruits of his talent and expertise? Shouldn't those expatriates, on whom the sun never sets, be able to stay in the good ol U.S. of A., keep their citizenship, and pay no taxes? This act will improve an existing loophole in the tax code and will provide a touching reunion with our overseas bigwigs. Won't it feel good, at long last, to say, "Welcome home, Billionaire!"?

4. The How-Sweet-It-Is Act—It Makes You Go Fast.

"Sugar and spice and everything nice." Delightful childhood rhyme, or corporate cry for help? Just look at the place that sugar holds in our American lives: longtime childhood friend, proud occupant of most of the finer American kitchen tables, and the only chemical substance the brain can actually use. With all that, shouldn't we thank the corporate humanitarians who provide it to us? Of course! And chief among them is agribenefactor Dwayne Andreas. Yes, you have read about him before, but that's because of his overwhelming significance. And yet he's so modest that, instead of flowers or "National Dwayne Day," Mr.

Andreas requested that we not "make a big deal" and just give a quiet $200 million subsidy to ADM's corn sweetener, a staple of American "junk food" companies. Isn't Dwayne sweet? We only wish we could do more—and, with your help, maybe we can.

5. The Turning-a-New-Leaf Assistance Act—Follow the Yellow Tobacco Road.

If there's one thing we can all agree on, it's that smoking is bad. But that doesn't necessarily mean tobacco is bad. Reflect a moment on what America really is, and you'll see that tobacco is a huge part of our great heritage. The peace pipe, the Virginia plantation, the jazz musician—where would any of these fine American institutions be without golden brown, home-grown tobacco? Now tobacco needs us. And we'll be there. Our tobacco giants were gracious enough to settle that big lawsuit brought by the states for $368 billion (not that the settlement means they're in any way culpable). That kind of noblesse deserves our support—and we tried to give it to them in the form of a $50 billion tax write-off that we attached to the budget. Unfortunately, some spoilsports in Congress told the American people about it and we had to kill it—this year. But if at first we don't succeed, we'll try and try again. After all, like a fine sonnet or a beautiful haiku, the sublime heights of linguistic artistry reached by the tobacco lawyers who wrote the provision have practically created a new American art form. God Bless Tobacco.

6. The High-Definition High Entitlement Act—Must-See TV.

Isn't *Seinfeld* funny? With Jerry and Elaine and that crazy Kramer? And what about those lovable roomies—and friends—on *Friends*? Wouldn't it be great if there could be more Jerrys and Kramers and Rosses and Rachels? Of course—because it's TV, and TV is fun. And what's the only thing better than TV? That's right—more TV. Recently, scientists created something wonderful called HDTV. It will allow you to see Jerry and Kramer and Morley in brilliant high definition—it will be as if Larry King and George Clooney and Jimmy Smits's ass are right there in your living room! But first the networks need certain parts of the digital spectrum. How can they get them? That's the beauty part—they're owned by the American public. Certainly the networks would be willing to pay what the spectrum is worth—about $70 billion, according to an FCC estimate—but they'd prefer to get them for free. And why shouldn't they? They've given us a lot of laughs, a lot of tears, and hundreds of thousands of campaign dollars. The networks need us. Let's help them. TV is good.

7. The Superfund Forest Cleanup Act—A Tree-Free Bridge to the 21st Century.

What would have happened if, when Paul Revere rode into town to sound the alert that the British were coming, there had been trees all over the place? He would have been much slower, for one thing. If his way hadn't been cleared of trees, America might never have been founded. Well, now you know how timber companies feel. How are they expected to drive their trucks into a government-owned forest and bring the trees out when there are trees all over the place? Environmentalists want the forests left alone so they can have more places to hold nude love-ins and gay séances. But America's not about that; it's about not having trees in your way. And since it's a government forest, it only seems sporting that the government should provide the roads for the timber companies. "Log it, don't hog it" is our motto. At a cost of only $50 million, we can help provide a nicely paved safety net for these American heroes. Next time you see an ambulance speeding by on a tree-free road to save somebody, say a silent prayer for American timber conglomerates.

8. The Racial Reconciliation Act—Sometimes You Feel Like a Nut.

It's not just our beloved Speaker's Georgia constituents who "sometimes feel like a nut." All of America often feels like a nut, and when they do, whose nuts do they reach for? That's right, those of the American nut growers, known affectionately as agribusiness giants. Yes, it's true that foreign growers have nuts, and that they could be sold cheaper here. But doesn't it feel good to know that your nuts are American? And, yes, American nut growers could be competitive, but when they came to us and said, "We'd rather sell our nuts for $610 a ton than something less than that," our only question was "How fast can we do this for you?" And peanut butter—the humble peanut's most celebrated offspring—was created by a black American, George Washington Carver. So when we prop up the nuts of American growers, we're also fostering racial and ethnic diversity. Isn't that a "win-win" situation?

9. The American Transportation Infrastructure Improvement Act—Highways to Heaven, Paved with Green.

America, God bless it, has a lot of roads. And for that we can thank America's Big Contractors for all their hard work. But now that many parts of the United States have all the roads they need, what are these contractors to do? After all that hot, stinky paving, can we really ask them now to go do something for which there's a real market? What about the ones that don't want to do that? That's why we pledge to provide funds for roads that, while technically "unnecessary," are very necessary if huge contracting companies are going to keep a healthy cash flow. And these "demonstration" highways, as we like to call them, are downright essential for individual members of Congress seeking reelection. They put $800 million into the pockets of big contractors who know how to return a favor. Keep on truckin'!

10. The Aid to Financially Dependent Corporations (AFDC) Act—Every Penny Helps.

Just because a country's in the Third World doesn't mean there's not a lot of money to be made there. And it turns out that many Fortune 500 companies, like Citicorp, Amoco, Coca-Cola, and General Electric, would like to do this. But, off the top of your head, would you know how to start a business in Addis Ababa? How about São Paulo, or Karachi? Well then,

> how should these companies know how—they're only
> human. Apparently it's much easier and less expensive
> for them to make all this money in the Third World
> if we provide them with low-interest loans and loan
> guarantees. The best part is, it's free—other than
> $100 million a year on overhead that the Overseas
> Private Investment Corporation spends. These coun-
> tries may be poor, but a few baht here and a few yuan
> there, and pretty soon you're talking millions of
> dollars. Let's help corporate America bring it home.

They looked at me with their pudgy, expectant smiles the entire time I read, little by little moving in closer to me until by the time I finished and looked up, we all reacted with a start.

"Well," I said, "this is some document you've got here."

"Don't forget, Arianna," Newt said, "it's a *contract!*"

"Yeah, a *contract!*" Haley added helpfully.

"Okay, a 'contract,'" I said. "Good luck in the midterms. I'll be waiting with champagne."

"We were thinking of having it done up like a real contract," said Newt, "all official-like, signed at the bottom by me and Haley . . . and Dwayne Andreas and David Brinkley!"

Newt and Haley rose in unison, looking like one of those improbable Guinness record breakers: the world's fattest Siamese twins.

"Thanks for giving it the once-over, Arianna. We're counting on you to spread the word," said Newt as he started to leave. "I guess all we have to do now is spell-check this thing and hit the fax machines. There's not a moment to waste."

As they left the room, arguing about which parts were their favorites, I, like thousands before me I'm sure, made the observation that the sight of Newt leaving is only slightly less horrifying than the sight of Newt approaching. A small distinction but an important one.

23
Lame Duck of the Millennium

☆ ☆ ☆

A sudden knock on the door caused Socks to puff up his fur, hop onto Lincoln's rocker, and arch his back. After a discreet pause, Walter entered, bearing a heavy silver tray with what seemed like effortless ease.

"Good morning, Mrs. Huffington. Here's your breakfast."

Socks hissed. Walter noticed the cat for the first time. The ancient butler rolled up the copy of *Roll Call* that I had requested with my breakfast and waved it in Socks's general direction. The cat jumped off the chair and ran out the door.

"Go on, shoo!" Walter called after it. He closed the door, shaking his head.

"That cat sure does get into plenty of mischief, especially since Buddy arrived," Walter lamented.

"He must be a little resentful," I said.

"We've tried telling him it wasn't personal," Walter replied. "It's just that the polls came in saying more Americans like dogs, so the President did what he had to do."

"Very touching."

Walter seemed not to hear. "I don't know where people get the idea they can bring some tomcat into the White House and let it scratch and climb all over everything. But that's the problem with holding a general election, if you don't mind my saying so. It sure does give some people ideas above their station."

Walter began laying out the breakfast.

"Here's your coffee, ma'am, and your juice, toast, eggs. And here are those FBI files you asked for under 'special requests,' along with the Greek baklava . . ."

Walter was interrupted by an uproar just outside my door. Someone was howling, "You can't do this to me! Do you know who I am?"

I sure didn't. Who was it?

"I'm Buzzy the Giant Ostrich!" the voice replied as if in answer to my unspoken question. Then it began to whoop and bark.

"That's Mr. Emanuel, Mrs. Huffington," Walter explained. "I'm afraid all that coffee he was having finally put him right over the top. You see, once he found out that people would pay twenty or thirty thousand dollars just to have coffee at the White House, well, he began having coffee all the time, twenty-four hours a day. Last night he finally snapped. Right in front of a very nice couple from Thailand. He put on her hat and marched around the room and made everybody say he was 'the prettiest one of all.' I guess Mr. Begala, he must have seen it coming, because he had a straitjacket waiting. And this morning they're taking Mr. Emanuel over to the Bethesda Naval Medical Center, to the Hamilton Jordan Wing. I'm sure he'll be very comfortable there."

Walter picked up his tray. At the door he paused. "Oh, and by the way, Mrs. Huffington, the President asked if you would stop by the Yellow Parlor. He'd like to have a word with you."

"What? Right now? I need time to get ready, have my breakfast, call my lawyers, put a new tape in my recorder . . ."

"The President said whenever you're ready, Mrs. Huffington. There's no rush."

Half an hour later, I was wandering the halls once more, looking for the Yellow Parlor.

It was Mrs. Clinton's raised voice, hard Midwestern—like a Chicago winter—that led me to it. She was yelling something, and I heard the sound of china breaking. As I approached the end of a hallway, Kent came running toward me from the other direction. He ducked and a coffee cup skimmed past his head, breaking against the wall. He ran off down the hall. I was about to follow his example when the President caught sight of me.

"Hey, everyone Here's Arianna! Arianna, come on in here, we're having a little debate and we need you to break a tie."

I had a bad feeling that this was going to be like intervening in the former Yugoslavia.

The White House Breakfast Menu

FEBRUARY 8

"The most important contribution of the day!"

A lurid White House breakfast morsel: When Democratic presidential nominee Grover Cleveland fathered an illegitimate child, Cleveland's opponents came up with the slogan, "Ma, ma, where's my pa?" Cleveland handled this controversy, dubbed the "Buffalo scandal," by taking responsibility for the child's paternity. Cleveland's candor under duress is credited as a factor in his victory over Republican candidate James G. Blaine. Cleveland's victorious supporters thus responded to the anti-Cleveland sloganeering with their own word play: "Gone to the White House, ha, ha, ha."

PLEASE NOTE: Portions come in three sizes: "Chelsea," "Hillary," and "Bill."

PRESIDENTIAL WAFFLES
Is it a pancake? Is it French toast? Who knows? But we do know this: Just think of what you want it to be, and that's the thing it will be. Served with strawberries.

POACHED EGGS À LA BUSH
They seem like a reasonable choice now,
but later you'll wonder what you were thinking.

THE MAYA ANGELOU PLATE
An egg. A grapefruit. A sausage link.

THE FIRST LADY
Muesli, carob, dried fruit, tofu, kale, wheat gluten, and soy bacon.
It may not taste great, but it's good for you, so eat it anyway and be thankful for it.
If the President has to, so do you.

THE ROSS PEROT OMELETTE
A hearty western omelette with tomatoes, peppers, onions, and cheese.
If you don't want it, it won't be served to you. It's not our choice—it's up to you.
If you want it, it will be served, but it's entirely up to you.

THE AL D'AMATO
Bacon, sausage, and ham. Just like you'd suspect, lots and lots and lots of pork.

SILVER DOLLAR HOT CAKES
Note—size of hot cakes is tied to the dollar, so servings may vary
depending on how the Asian markets closed.

THE AL GORE
No ordinary bagel and lox, but one that's been reinvented by the Vice-President himself. This newer version is much more efficient, with the lox served on top of the bagel and the cream cheese baked right in. Over the course of the next millennium, that will save 24 minutes. And, of course, they're all baked right here on the premises.

THE JANET RENO
Simple, plain omelette, served with home fries and toast. Note—takes 16 hours to prepare.

THE MONICA LEWINSKY
These scrambled eggs are hot and loose. Comes with hot sticky buns.

THE AMERICAN PEOPLE
Made up of whatever breakfast meal the American people say they want most in the latest tracking poll, plus or minus four percent. Served with whatever sides the American people say they want it served with.

THE MARIAN WRIGHT EDELMAN KIDDIE PLATE
Prepared fresh each day and made up of whatever the child wants, because we really, really, really love children. (Most popular ingredient requested: candy.)

• •

Except where otherwise noted, our breakfast specials come with your choice of bacon, sausages, or ham. The following side orders are also available for a nominal extra charge:

Hash browns	$75,000	**BEVERAGES**	
One egg	$90,000		
Cereals	$65,000	Orange juice	$65,000
Oatmeal	$70,000	Tea	$70,000
Canadian bacon	$95,000	Coffee	$20,000
Smoked ham	$80,000	Starbucks coffee	$300,000
Fruit plate	$65,000		

THE WHITE HOUSE ACCEPTS ALL MAJOR CREDIT CARDS, TRAVELER'S CHECKS, AND LARGE BAGS OF CASH. YOU MAY ALSO CHARGE YOUR BILL TO ONE OF SEVERAL SUGGESTED DEMOCRAT-LEANING ORGANIZATIONS AND THEN MAKE A DONATION IN THE SAME AMOUNT AT A LATER (BUT NOT THAT MUCH LATER) DATE.

"Uh, you know something, Mr. President, I'm not sure it's really appropriate for me to be getting involved in your personal affairs. As far as I'm concerned, that stuff is between you and your wife."

"I didn't ask you here to talk about *that*," the President responded, ushering me into the room. "We've hashed all that out. You heard my wife on the *Today Show*, we know everything about each other. Except," he added under his breath, "about my visit to your room last night. But, speaking of my wife, you know Hillary."

Hillary, in a gray sweatsuit, tennis shoes with no socks, hair pulled back in a tight ponytail, and absolutely no makeup, managed a smile. "And you know the Thomasons, of course." Linda was sitting next to Hillary. Harry was in charge of a large dry-erase board. A very tall, gangly man was next to him. "And this is our friend and adviser Mr. Tony Robbins. Perhaps you've seen his infomercials—uh, sorry, Tony, 'motivationals.'"

Tony favored me with a dazzling smile composed of the most thoroughly capped teeth I'd ever seen in my life.

"And these are . . . uh . . ." The President indicated two new Chinese men sitting off to one side. "Oh, hell, I can never remember. Introduce yourselves, guys." One said he was Danny Chen. The other was Billy Lim. "And here are Paul Begala and Sidney Blumenthal. Watch out around these two. They're nuts!" Clinton added jocularly.

Clinton waved at the board next to Harry. The word "Millennium" was written at the top. "What we're trying to do here, Arianna, is come up with some really kick-ass plans for the Millennium. We want people to remember the start of the third millennium every bit as fondly as they remember the start of the second one. Anyway, I've appointed my wife to be in charge of the whole thing and we're just trying to help her out with some suggestions that are, you know, *practical*."

Hillary gave me an exasperated look. She was obviously very upset. "It's the same old gender-bias thing, Arianna. They want to put me in the traditional sex role of a hostess throwing a big party for the whole country. They want Tammy Wynette. Well, if that's what they want, fine. But I'm going to do it my way. I'll give 'em a millennium they won't soon forget."

Clinton laughed. "And you see, Arianna, that's where we disagree. That's why I asked Tony here to join us. We want to do something that really drives home the terrific theme that Harry came up with: 'Honor the past, imagine the future.'"

I might have known that was one of Harry's.

Harry picked up the ball. He began to draw on the board. "We've decided to focus on three broad goals: preserving American culture and history, encouraging creativity and exploration, and extending the bonds of international understanding." A small murmur of applause from Harry's ubiquitous soundtrack accompanied the enumeration of each goal.

"Right? You with me so far?" Clinton looked at his wife. "Now, my wife here, she wants to—"

Hillary interrupted. "All I said was that it might be a good idea to focus on some important issues like health care. I suggested different ways to spotlight the epidemic of sexually transmitted diseases as a result of promiscuous and indiscriminate sexual behavior." She glared at her husband. "Or maybe a parade of breast cancer victims to highlight breast cancer awareness."

"But you see, darling, that would be a downer. We're trying to make this a celebration."

"You haven't even seen the Breast Cancer Dancers perform yet," she said. "They're hardly downers."

"Hillary," Sidney Blumenthal piped in, "all of our recent polls indicate that Americans like good things and dislike bad things. In fact, the disapproval rating of unpleasantness is just, well, it's off the charts. We just can't see any good reason to focus on anything negative."

"But, Sidney, you know as well as I that the first two millennia had plenty of unpleasant aspects: war, famine, pestilence, genocide, and inhumanity and depravity of the most appalling variety. And, although our own history is only a very small span in the years since Christ's birth, it too is full of as many instructive examples of what *not* to do as it is of examples of behavior we ought to emulate." Hillary looked patient—and stubborn.

"Have you been reading *Tikkun* again?" asked the President.

The men glanced around the room at one another. Clinton looked pleadingly at Linda. She chimed in, "Hillary, honey, I'm with you on this, believe me. *(Applause.)* No one has a stronger record on tackling difficult issues than I do. *(Cheers.)* In *Designing Women* for example, we put out a very strong message that women ought to have the right to work and also to associate with gay people. *(Loud applause.)* We took a lot of flack for that. We were ahead of our time, and maybe we made a few enemies among the fanatic Christian Right crowd and their cronies in the vast right-wing conspiracy. *(Loud boos.)* Fine, so be it. But I've got to say there's a time and a place for everything, and I don't think a concert played by rock stars with sexually transmitted diseases is a particularly wholesome way to ring in the new millennium. We think it might be a little, well, risqué." *(Sober, approving applause with an occasional "hear, hear.")*

"The point, Linda," Hillary said through gritted teeth, "is for the rock stars to acknowledge their sexually transmitted diseases and get treated right there onstage, between sets. It will encourage kids to get tested and treated. There's nothing risqué about a catheter and a shot of penicillin. It's all there in my book, Linda. I don't support sexual licentiousness any more than the next fellow."

The next fellow, as it turned out, was her husband. Everyone looked at him. He looked down.

"Poor choice of words," Hillary said. I thought I heard Bill mumble something under his breath, in a kind of singsong: "Oral's okay, this I know, for the Bible tells me so."

Hillary went on. "But the point is, Linda, that people who know me well actually say I'm a bit of a prude. And I don't mind being called that. Actually, I'm proud to be a prude. But you know that already, from reading my book."

There was an awkward pause.

"You *did* read my book, didn't you?"

Linda looked very guilty.

"Oh, Linda," said Hillary, disappointment dripping in her voice.

"I'm planning on reading it, Hillary, really I am, and—don't get me wrong about your millennium ideas. I mean I *love* the idea of some kind of concert. I just think the sexually transmitted disease thing is a bit, well, over the top. I mean, sexually transmitted diseases, after all, how long have they been around?" *(Applause, shouts of "Right on," etc.)*

Clinton turned to Tony Robbins. "Tony has some ideas I know you're going to love, sweetheart. Powerful stuff, very motivational, with a great positive message."

Hillary folded her arms over her chest and looked skeptical.

"Mrs. Clinton, what I have in mind is the world's largest firewalk. We're going to fill the entire Mall with hot coals and get hundreds of thousands of people to walk the whole length. We think we can really awaken this country's giant within." Tony talked with his hands.

Paul Begala interrupted. "Tony, Mr. President, just so you know, we've had Bob Bennett's firm do a once-over on the liability aspects of a mass national firewalk and, well, he's got some serious concerns. Plus, McCurry thinks there is always the possibility of, say, a small child stumbling and being roasted alive on national TV—and that would really send the wrong message. And I made some calls, and it turns out a colossal national walk on hot coals is very difficult to get insurance for. Although we did manage to insure this last State of the Union address."

Tony was unfazed. "Paul, you're not listening to your giant, your giant in here," he said, pointing to his chest.

"Tony," Paul said, "if your giant within can get a reasonable policy from Allstate on this, you've got my blessing."

"That's the spirit," boomed Tony, slapping him on the shoulder. Then he turned to Clinton. "Mr. President, I've got an idea for the climax, for New Year's Eve to usher in the Year 2000, that I think you'll agree will be remembered until the year 3000. And it'll jump-start the country into the next millennium by using a technique that I've made work for business leaders, celebrities, and top athletes all over the world. Here's the idea. At the stroke of midnight you jump off the Washington Monument, making the world's highest 'trust fall.' You'll be relying on nothing other than the goodwill and affection of the ordinary citizens gathered at the base of the monument to save you. Imagine how great the country's going to feel when some lucky person who happens to be walking by the Washington Monument actually catches the President of the United States! I tell you, it'll be pandemonium!"

There was a long silence. Clinton made a small gesture to Paul Begala, who reached over and pulled a bell rope. Two Secret Service agents entered, grabbed Tony Robbins, dragged him out of his chair, and began beating him.

"Boys, boys, go on, take it outside," Clinton said. We heard Robbins being removed. Without missing a beat, Clinton continued. "No, but I like what Harry was saying about the 'Millennium Minutes' for TV. I didn't understand it—but I liked it. Sounds cute."

Hillary rolled her eyes. "So you're just going to blow a chance to really do something meaningful, something powerfully symbolic, in favor of doing some lame public-service announcements about Ben Franklin and Harriet Tubman?"

Blumenthal jumped in, "Not Tubman. Too controversial. Jesse Helms will never stand for it."

Hillary was exasperated. "So you're saying that my idea of the fireworks display set off by victims of sexual harassment is out, right?"

Begala fielded this one. "Frankly, Mrs. Clinton, it just doesn't seem like a good idea to have Paula Jones involved *at all,* much less setting off any kind of explosives."

At that point a previously unheard voice chimed in from the corner. "Excuse me. Excuse me."

I turned and saw the statue of Al Gore, which had been standing unnoticed in the corner. "My goodness, Mr. Vice-President, I didn't see you standing there. Did they bring you up just for this?"

"This, and some routine maintenance." He tried to look around the room, but his neck did not afford sufficient mobility. He managed to scan the group with his eyes. "Look, *I'm* the one who is going to be elected President in the year 2000. Doesn't anyone want to know what I think we ought to do to mark this historic occasion?"

There was a pause while everyone mulled it over for a moment. Then all responded in unison.

"No!"

24
Eat the Press
☆ ☆ ☆

Mike McCurry was once the darling of the Washington press corps—trustworthy, good-natured, witty. At the State Department he starred as the aging surfer dude, with his dusty blond locks and impish charm. He always knew what his bosses were thinking, or at least what they wanted him to think they were thinking.

But at the White House, McCurry shorted out. His deftness with words started crumbling when he had to deal with words like *Huang, Trie,* and *Riady,* or *Lewinsky, Willey,* and *Jones.* He was forced to spin the unspinnable. Cozy big-donor meetings with the President became "social calls." Buddhist fund-raisers were "voter outreach," unsavory characters were always "Who?" until they had safely left the country or pled the Fifth. And he added his own layer of obfuscation to the President's semantic defense of his personal behavior, trying the patience of even such calm and reasonable reporters as Sam Donaldson.

Nevertheless, I had never been as glad to see him as when he burst into the room and rescued us all from the millennial discussion of the millennium.

"You're late, Mr. President," he said.

"Mike, you're here, great!" Clinton said enthusiastically, wrapping his press secretary in a bear hug. "We're just spitballing on this millennium thing. How about this for a hook: 'If you liked the American Century, then you'll love the American Millennium.'"

McCurry seemed noncommittal. Apparently he had only so much spin left, and had to save it for the press. I took a good look at him. He looked nothing like the old Mike McCurry. He was shrunken, cramped, and slightly viperous, his comb-over refusing to stay combed over, as if he had finally learned that trying to tell the truth in the Clinton White House was like trying to dam a river without getting wet.

"Just an idea . . . just an idea," said Clinton, looking a bit hurt.

McCurry glanced meaningfully at his watch.

"Your press conference, sir. On educational initiatives. It was supposed to begin ten minutes ago."

"Okay, okay. Is this tie gonna be good for television?" the Commander-in-Chief asked.

"Anything but bright red or busy patterns, sir. Now, sir, if you please." He gestured toward the door. Clinton waved to me.

"Hey, Arianna! We're on our way to a press conference on education. You've got kids in school, why don't you tag along?"

"Uh, Mr. President," McCurry grumbled, "you know we've talked about how the First Lady is the only woman who should accompany you in front of the cameras. Don't forget the ape-tay of you ugging-hay Ewinsky-lay," he said significantly. Clinton dismissed this gibberish with a wave of his hand.

As we walked downstairs and into the "official" White House, where the President's offices and public rooms are, Clinton rehearsed his speech with me.

"What we're hoping to do here is seize the moral high ground on the issue of education. We think that our party can 'own' education, so to speak. See, we really, really care about kids, and we've got to get the message out about that."

I hazarded a little feedback.

"But, Mr. President, no one doubts that both sides care about children. I mean, forgive the allusion, but the Nazis loved their kids too."

Something clicked in Clinton's brain.

"Right, but Hitler was childless, right? Mike, can we use that?"

"Uh, Hitler's always risky, sir," McCurry answered, "what with the whole World War Two thing and the Holocaust . . ."

"Okay, maybe you're right. Stalin had kids, right?"

I persisted.

"Mr. President, my point is that politics and educational policy don't mix well. The problem is too much politics. Our kids pay the price.

Every day, 160,000 students miss class just because they're afraid to go to school. Twenty-two percent of college freshmen need remedial courses in writing and math, another twenty-seven percent simply drop out, and an astonishing sixty-eight percent of sorority girls have *you* on their speed dial."

"Yes," Clinton broke in. "And I'm told—anecdotally, mind you, but I'm having a study done—I understand that there's a real problem out there with drama teachers seducing former students. Simply ruining their lives. Denying them a wholesome educational experience. Something's got to be done." He stuck out his lower lip in a fair approximation of concerned sympathy.

"Well, yes, that too. But my point, sir, is that politicians want easy solutions, but there aren't any."

And right there I could see that I had lost him.

"Well, thanks, Arianna. I always enjoy a chin-wag with a fellow parent. But I think you're wrong about the no-easy-solutions thing. We've got some easy solutions worked out that everyone's gonna love. When you really, really love children, it's just not that difficult. Boy, old Newt's gonna sweat off another thirty pounds when he hears about this!"

We had reached the entrance to the White House Press Briefing Room. McCurry and the Secret Service men held back and I did the same. The President entered and the press corps stood. McCurry, the Secret Service, and I followed and stood by the doorway.

The President began to read from his prepared text.

"Ladies and gentlemen, I'm very pleased to announce to you today a sweeping educational policy initiative which we call Operation Band-Aid. We truly believe that this unique partnership of federal, state, and local government resources will better the lot of every child in this country by making our schools more responsive to our culture as it exists today. In short, Operation Band-Aid will make school more fun, more entertaining, and more exciting than it's ever been before for our children, whom we really, really love."

I took a moment to scan the assembled press corps. It was a mixed crowd. The print people looked like the people you see at the grocery store who know the price of everything without having to check. The TV people were another story—especially the women, in their brightly colored, mostly pundit-red business suits, topped off by their short aspiring-anchorwoman hairdos.

Clinton continued.

"Now, I know that a lot of you in the media made sport of us for having so many Hollywood people over to spend the night at the White House, friends of ours like Steven Spielberg and Ron Howard. Well, even though we had a lot of laughs, saw a lot of movies, and ate a lot of popcorn, these overnight encounters with some of the most imaginative members of our creative community served a more serious purpose. Our Hollywood friends formed a sort of ad hoc task force on the subject of how to get our kids to pay attention in school and get more out of their classes.

"And that's how we came up with Operation Band-Aid."

I could see several reporters shifting restlessly in their seats, already bored out of their skulls. One man was vigorously writing on a pad. Perhaps he was new on the job.

"In a nutshell, our idea is to use the information delivery systems that school-age children are already familiar with—some might say addicted to—to teach them the essentials of a nationally uniform curriculum. Imagine, if you will, in place of classrooms full of bored kids listening to an overworked, underpaid, and, frankly, boring teacher repeating the same irrelevant lessons that we all grew up with—imagine, instead of that, space-age learning labs with each kid learning whatever they want, whenever they want, by watching their own personal 'information appliance.' This interactive 'information appliance' will be every student's personal instructor, and in place of rote memorization, pop quizzes, and analytical book reports, it will use the tools every kid loves: television shows and computer games.

"What's more, we'll be lining up commitments from major entertainment superstars to actually appear in the instructional television programs. Kids will learn an important lesson from their real-life idols: They'll get the message that education is 'cool.' Just think of it: Your child, whether he or she lives in Anchorage or Baton Rouge, can learn biology from Michael Jackson or civics from Macaulay Culkin, or anatomy from Sharon Stone."

He paused for a moment and laughed. "I'll tell you, I think she's terrific. Real terrific."

Mike McCurry leaned over and whispered urgently in the President's ear, "Sir, it's better if you don't improvise. Just stick with the prepared text."

Clinton cleared his throat.

"I'd like to stress again that our goal is relevance. That's what Operation Band-Aid is all about: relevant education. And here I owe a nod of thanks to Scott Martin, the math department head at L. C. Roberts High School just outside of Dallas, who's done some very innovative work to make that school's math program one of the most relevant in the country. What they've done is to replace dry hypothetical questions with contemporary math problems that apply to real life.

The press corps collectively stifled a collective yawn.

"For instance, they challenge their students with problems like these:

" 'Hector has knocked up six girls in his gang. There are twenty-seven girls in the gang. What percentage of girls in the gang has Hector knocked up?'

"and

" 'Jerome wants to cut his half-pound of heroin to make 20 percent more profit. How many ounces of cut will he need?'

"or

" 'Rufus is pimping for three girls. If the price is $65 for each trick, how many tricks will each girl have to turn so Rufus can pay for his $800-per-day crack habit?'

"Do you see what we're getting at here? This is as relevant as it gets. And our Operation Band-Aid math programs will be just as hip and happenin' in the comfortable upper-middle-class suburbs and the intellectual precincts of our college towns as they will in the drug- and violence-ridden barrios and ghettos.

"For instance, in Greenwich, Connecticut, the problem might be:

" 'Howard's Beemer gets 34 miles to the gallon. His father's gas credit card can only be used once every 24 hours. Assuming that the card cannot be used until midnight, that Howard has 4.5 gallons of gas, that it is now 9:20, and that it is 80 miles to the keg party at Hotchkiss, will Howard get there before the keg runs out at 1:00 A.M.?'

"For kids growing up on Manhattan's Upper East Side, we'd ask:

" 'Leonard has been insider trading for the last 3 years and 8 months. The federal statute of limitations on securities fraud is 7 years. The Dow is now at 8100 and going up by, say, 100 points per month. If Leonard stops his insider trading now and waits until he's immune from prosecution for his past crimes before he resumes, how much of a rise in the Dow will he have sat out?'

"Whereas in Beverly Hills, the question would be more along these lines:

" 'Miranda is a student at Beverly Hills High. Miranda's father has promised her a new Range Rover if she raises her grade-point average to 3.0 or above; if she fails to do so, he will only buy her a Jeep Cherokee. Miranda is taking five classes and has two Bs, one C, one D, and an F. She can raise the grade of any class one full level by having intimate relations with the teacher. However, Miranda can only risk having intimate relations with any one teacher twice and can have no more than five total sexual encounters; otherwise people will talk and she will have to transfer. Can Miranda get the Range Rover while remaining at Beverly Hills High?' "

Changing gears, Clinton went on.

"Now, contrary to what you may have heard, my administration does not support either the West Coast or the East Coast faction in the current dispute among rap artists. Nor have we taken sides in the ongoing disagreement between the Crips and the Bloods. We think all sides have valid points of view that deserve respect and esteem. We have learned something from all elements of the rap community as well as from our friends in Hollywood. The lessons we teach our children should not only be life-affirming and imbued with positive value; they should also be entertaining and, above all, relevant."

Then, as an afterthought, he added: "And of course, the 'Internet Superhighway' will also be integrally involved. I don't really have time to look into it, but the Vice-President assures me it's all very exciting. And I urge kids out there surfing the web to tap into our home page at http://www

.president/~whitehouse.usa.government/clinton.operationbandaid/gore2000.gov.html.

"I will now take your questions."

The press corps, which had, in the previous fifteen minutes, resembled more of a press corpse, came instantly to life. They shouted, together, "Mr. President! Mr. President!"

Clinton pointed a finger in the general direction of the throng. They all sat down except for one indistinguishable clone, who asked, "Mr. President, for years now, people have been proposing so-called innovations of the sort you describe, and they never lead to improved test scores or lower dropout rates. So my question, sir, is, could you summarize your plan in one sentence for us? Could you give us a catchy, pithy sound bite? And as far as we're concerned, it doesn't have to be about education."

McCurry, who had become increasingly agitated during the last part of the President's speech, suddenly stepped forward and shouted, "Our standards for accuracy are one thousand. We are at one thousand percent!"

The President seemed a bit stunned, but, being one of the most publicly unflappable men ever to reside in the White House, quickly laughed off the outburst and said, "Thanks, Mike . . . and you know, he's right, our standards are one thousand percent."

McCurry stepped back against the wall, and put his head down a bit. His eyes darted all over the room, and he looked as though he might hyperventilate.

"I'm sorry, what was your question again?" asked the President.

"Your policy in one sentence, sir," replied one of the clones.

"Oh yes," said the President, "how about this: 'Hey, you dudes, listen up, school is cool.'" Then he made a hip-hop hand signal by pointing the index finger and pinky of both hands at the crowd and folding his arms. The press corps ate it up, and I could see them all writing it down.

McCurry then stepped forward again, prompting a nervous look from his boss. "The President considered these people personal guests," McCurry blurted, "and he appreciated their interest and support!"

Everyone looked at him in silence. It seemed that McCurry's spin cycle was being disrupted by an unbalanced load. The President stepped off the platform and gently guided McCurry back against the wall. "Thanks, Mike, I'll take it from here," said the President, and he went back to the microphone. "Next question."

An identical man rose—or was it the same one?

"Mr. President, would you mind giving us another one of those more 'accessible' explanations?"

The President thought and, after a moment, leaned forward and said, "We're gonna create schools where even Beavis and Butthead could graduate Phi Beta Kappa."

The press corps murmured and nodded their approval. As they were eagerly writing the sentence down, they didn't see McCurry stepping forward again.

"The full nature and seriousness of the allegations against Mr. Hubbell were not fully known to anyone at the White House until he pled guilty!"

McCurry's anger was now uncontainable. "And if you came all the way to Brazil and all you care about is the story of the President's phone calls, the timing is such that you can contact the Travel Office and drop off the trip and get to Washington in time to cover it, probably."

President Clinton looked questioningly at the row of aides clogging the entrance, all of whom looked as stunned as the President. He then motioned at a few in the front, who came forward and tried to lead McCurry away.

"Dan Burton!" cried McCurry, tossing a quarter to a reporter. "Go call him. Tell him to come on down here, and he can look in any document he wants to!"

The President managed a nervous laugh. "Please excuse my press secretary, he's been rehearsing a bit too hard for the White House Correspondents' Dinner."

The press corps nodded and murmured, and I could see the few nearest me writing, "McCurry rehearsing a bit too hard for the White House Correspondents' Dinner."

McCurry, led away by the aides, had just disappeared from view. But I could still hear him in the hall. "Anytime the general perception is that I've not been completely accurate, I'd leave. I'd leave!"

As his voice grew fainter, I could just barely make out, "One thousand percent! Ten thousand percent! A million percent! . . ."

The President took a deep breath: "Next question?" He pointed to a female reporter in the middle of the pack.

She rose. "Mr. President, the timeless canon of Western literature, the writings of Plato, Aristotle, Thomas Aquinas, Shakespeare, and Milton, has been destroyed by the fashion-conscious tinkerings of pressure groups and self-appointed experts, with the result that today's schoolchildren learn less about the shared values of our Judeo-Christian tradition than they do about voguish situational ethics and dubious revisionist history informed more by wishful thinking than historical fact. With that in mind, my question to you, sir, is, have you ever used the seduction techniques you tried on Paula Jones and Monica Lewinsky on your wife? And, if so, did they work?"

"Thomas Aquinas is one of my favorites. I was rereading the *Summa Theologica* just last week, and I told Hillary, 'Wouldn't it be wonderful if all our children could read Aquinas by the third grade?' A wonderful goal to add to Operation Band-Aid in the future." Clinton turned to leave.

"Hold on, Mr. President," Sam Donaldson shouted.

Clinton paused. "Yes, Sam?"

Sam was perplexed. "I don't . . . I don't really have a question, Mr. President. I just always say, 'Hold on, Mr. President.' It's sort of a reflex. No President ever held on before, sir. I'm sorry. I'll go now."

The President thanked the assembled company and stepped down. Another press aide took his place.

"We'll have copies of those two sentences at the door for you," he said.

I looked down and saw one of the crack reporters writing "copies at the door."

As the members of the press corps rose and walked out single file, I could hear them earnestly debating whether to use the "dude" sound bite or the "Beavis and Butthead" sound bite.

25
A Bizarre Bazaar
☆ ☆ ☆

Making my way back from the press conference, I passed an open door. In the room beyond, I could see rows of people, all with their backs turned. Unlike the press corps, they were paying rapt attention to whatever was going on inside. I decided to stick my head in.

The room had a little bit of everything—and a lot of gold Rolexes. There were American business types with thick waists and thin hair. A half-dozen trim, dark-suited Asians. Several people of vaguely Latin American and Middle Eastern background. I saw fedoras, fezzes, and burnooses. I was disappointed not to see any Greeks. Maybe they were still tapped out after Dukakis did his Icarus thing.

The center of attention was James Carville, standing at the podium. Those eyes! Two black bullets buried under a large and shiny forehead. Mary Matalin, his Republican-pundit wife, fondly called him "serpent head." In the Garden of Eden, Eve got in big trouble with something that probably looked a lot like Carville.

"Sold!" Carville barked in his Southern twang, just as I walked in. "To yet another friend and associate of John Huang." The audience laughed and winked at each other. A bespectacled Chinese man made his way to the front.

"Howdy, Jimmy-Bob Ling." Carville grinned. He gave the lucky winner a small velvet box. The Chinese man handed over a check and proudly waved the box in the air as his friends clapped and cheered.

Carville looked at the check with an expression that could have curdled milk. "Jimmy! We can't take this." He looked around the room pleadingly.

"I'm gonna remind you guys one more time that all checks must be made out to the Democratic National Committee, not to the President personally. And if you wanna help the President battle the sleazy sex smears of the far right, send your money directly to Bob Bennett. We do not want to do anything that would appear unethical in the slightest."

Murmurs of agreement.

"So let's do it right. We don't want Ken Starr all over our ass, now do we?" Nobody wanted Ken Starr all over his ass. "Don't forget, we take Visa, MasterCard, American Express, Diner's Club, Carte Blanche, checks, cash, change. We'll also barter. But we won't take those goddam Asian currencies. No tellin' what they're worth these days."

I assumed that was good news to a man who had come in a few minutes before with several live chickens.

"And we also don't want the Republicans to get elected, do we? They'll cut Medicare for our senior citizens and cut education for our kids!" Carville shrieked.

Nobody wanted that either.

Carville's mastery of the political craft was clearly apparent. He had only gotten better since his timeless "It's the economy, stupid" slogan. After watching him work, you had to wonder what was next for this excitable eccentric—a cabinet position or a rubber room. Probably the one that wouldn't require Senate confirmation.

I was surprised to see him here, actually, because I knew that, to date, Carville had conspicuously spurned any official public duties in the Clinton administration. I remember him joking once that, à la Groucho Marx, he didn't want to work for any country that would hire somebody like him. Or maybe it was just the fact that part of the benefits package of a White House staff job was the opportunity to have a legal bill of a few hundred thousand dollars. So he hit the speechmaking trail, addressing just about any group that would drag a $20,000 bill through his exclusive neighborhood. But he also stayed close to Bill and Hill and never failed to come to their defense against vast right-wing conspiracies—real or imagined. They owed him a lot.

Carville waved another box in the air. "Now, I've got cuff links here. And this ain't no ordinary set of cuff links. This ain't some souvenir crap we'd give to a White House intern—not that they'd get cuff links anyway. Usually it's just a beret or some book of smutty poetry."

The audience nodded sympathetically.

"No sirree, Bob. These came straight from the President of France himself. President She-rack personally handed 'em to President Clinton at an economic summit."

The crowd oohed.

"Fourteen-carat gold. With itty-bitty little diamonds in 'em!"

He opened the box and looked at them admiringly. "This stuff's the shit!"

He peered closer at the rare specimen.

"And if you look real close, you can see the President's initials. *WJC.* William Jefferson Clinton."

He looked up at the crowd. "Ordinarily I'd pass 'em around so that everybody could have a look-see. But too many guys in this audience are on parole or otherwise under the supervision of the justice system." He cackled wickedly. A couple of shifty-eyed men shifted uneasily in their chairs.

"Lemme tell ya." Carville returned his attention to the magic little box. "This ain't no garbage that the President just tossed in the corner and forgot all about. These were worn by the President himself," he said, "while being deposed in the Paula Jones case."

The crowd oohed and ahhed.

"In fact, they still have some drops of cold sweat on them," Carville joked. "That is their distinguishing characteristic." The crowd laughed.

"So do I hear twenty thousand? Twenty-five? Thirty? Sold!" Carville said. A beaming man stood up, and bowed repeatedly to Carville and the audience.

"Ah yes," Carville said. "Pauley, my good buddy from Indonesia!"

"The Republic of Korea, sir," the man corrected him.

"Exactly!" Carville said. "Any shady business associate of John Huang's is a shady business associate of mine, no matter where you come from—so long as you pay in hard currency, hard *western* currency."

Carville gave him the cuff links, and the business associates shook hands.

An aide wheeled up a waiter's tray filled with dinner plates. Carville held up one of them.

"I have in my hand some of the finest china in the world. Rare porcelain. Lenox. I'm told that it's 'translucent.'"

He held it up to the light. "That means you can see through it, right?" he joked. A staffer nodded as the audience giggled.

"Okay, okay, just a po' boy from the bayou," he said, raising his hands in mock protest.

"I am also told that this china has been used at state dinners since 1982. Why, these plates have been eaten off of by kings! princes! Presidents! movie stars! starry-eyed delusional interns! motivational speakers! self-esteem counselors! recovered-memory channelers! licensed astrologers! And now you too, in the privacy of your very own home, can share in this unique dining experience!"

Hands were raised eagerly.

"First Lady Nancy Reagan, a woman of great taste, though hardly my cup of tea politically, personally selected this fine porcelain. And would personally shoot all of us if she knew what we were up to. So let's just keep this between us, shall we?" Carville intoned, sotto voce.

Next he waved a plate in the air. "The President ate a Big Mac on this one! Thirty thousand? Forty? Gone! For fifty thousand dollars!"

Carville looked at his watch as the burger plate made its way to the back. "C'mon, we need to hurry! We need this cash now! Folks, the mid-term elections are just around the corner. We've got to take Congress back! We need to get the word out, and we need to get it out now. Preemptive early spending—that's the name of the campaign game. Starting tomorrow morning, the Republicans are running a nasty attack ad in every major media market in the country! Each and every dollar you spend here goes to combat that vast right-wing conspiracy! Minus a small commission for the auctioneer, naturally."

He held up another rare plate. "George Bush! From the Halcion days—you can still see a forehead print if you hold it up to the light right! Ten thousand dollars? Twenty? Sold! For twenty-seven thousand dollars!"

A man stood up in the back.

"Here, catch!" Carville tossed the plate like a Frisbee across the room. The man barely caught it. Soon plates were flying across the room right and left. But it was fine with me. It was like the end of a good dinner at a Greek *taverna*. There's nothing like a Democratic fund-raiser to make an immigrant feel at home.

A staffer brought a crumpled wad of black cloth up to Carville. Maybe altered presidential tuxedo pants from the post–broken leg recovery period?

"You know how much people spent on just one of Princess Diana's gowns? Well, I expect we're gonna top that right now." Carville held up the rumpled mass of fabric. "This is a dress worn by a certain White House intern during a 'private meeting,' so to speak. That's right, it's the stained dress you've all heard so much about."

The audience oohed and aahed.

A man stood up. "Has it been laundered?"

"Aw, you must be from Kenneth Starr's office. Now, come on, you know we don't launder nothin' here," Carville reproved him.

The audience chuckled.

"Do I hear one hundred thousand? Two hundred over there, do I hear three?"

"Five hundred thousand!" said the man who'd stood up. "I am Billy Ray Wing. My family has been in the laundry business for fifty years," he said proudly. "We will launder the dress with a special environmentally friendly process approved by Vice-President Gore and put it in our shop window. The dress will be like a royal warrant to do the President's dirty laundry. Like Alfred Dunhill—'By Appointment to Her Majesty.'"

"I wish you hadn't brought up that whole tobacco mess, but I appreciate the sentiment. Sold!" said Carville. He looked at his staffer. "Are we ready for the grand finale?" The staffer shrugged uncomfortably.

"Well, why don't you just get your bony little butt down the hall and find out? Let's git it on, mama!

"Dum-de-dum, dum-de-dum, dum-de-dum," Carville intoned, as two young staffers carried out a large, heavy wooden box in pallbearer style. As the coffinlike box passed me, I saw that it read "Trust" in large white letters. Also attached was the presidential seal, with the eagle clutching the arrows of war and the olive branch of peace, and bearing the motto *E Pluribus Unum.*

Carville leaned into the microphone, "Ladies and gentlemen, one of the most valuable things in the possession of any President is not something that you can hold in your hand, link your cuffs with, or eat off of. You can't see it, feel it, taste it, smell it, or wear it. No, it's not that silent killer, carbon monoxide. But, like the finest china, it takes a long time to make and much less time to shatter.

"Trust. Trust!" he repeated. "It is worth far more than everything else in this room. But we will let you have it for a steal. Do I hear $500,000?"

Silence from the audience. Carville angrily pounded the podium with his fist.

"Goddammit! We need more money! If the Republicans get elected, old people will be dying in the streets!!!"

A man in a perfectly cut Savile Row suit in the front row shrugged.

Carville looked desperately around the room. Beads of sweat rolled down his shiny pate. His tie was limp and loose, and his collar was shriveled around his neck.

He finally realized what the problem was. He came out in front of the podium to remonstrate with the reluctant audience in a low, urgent voice.

"Guys, I know what ya thinkin'. That this ain't for real, that I'm just full of good ol' Louisiana 'gator shit.

"No!" he thundered so hard that he nearly lost his balance.

"This thing is legit!" he pointed to the coffinlike box. "It's got the presidential seal! It's dark blue, and see the eagle? It says *E Pluribus Unum,* which, as some of you may not know, means 'Don't Stop Thinkin' About Tomorrow.' It's real! Trust me. You have my word on this as a campaign consultant.

"And look! You also have the word of the President of the United States." Carville walked over, took a piece of paper from a staffer, and waved it in the air.

"The President cares about the people of America. He will do anything to help them. But it takes money, big money, to fight all those huge corporate PACs. Or they will destroy us!"

He took off his watch and held it high. "Look. The time is ticking away. Tick, tick! Chop, chop, *capisce*?! We need money for television ads in every major state. And we need it now!"

Finally, a man raised his hand.

"Five hundred," he said.

Carville was delighted. "Five hundred thousand from Eli Lilly."

"Do I hear six hundred?"

"Six hundred from the Lippo group!"

The dam burst. "Seven hundred! Nine hundred! One million!"

"Sold, for one million dollars, to Archer-Daniels-Midland!"

As I stepped out, another coffinlike box was being wheeled onto the stage. I could hear Carville bellow in the distance. "Moral Leadership! How much am I bid? This should be of particular interest to our friends in the entertainment business! David, Steven, Lew, are y'all here? Edgar Bronfman? How much am I bid for Moral Leadership?"

I sat down in a little chair in the hallway. Socks jumped onto my lap and started licking my hand.

26
The Ghosts of Kennedy's Pass

☆ ☆ ☆

As I finished packing my bags, I took a moment to lock out the window one last time. The day was beautiful, the sun was shining, the temperature was chilly and crisp. It was perfect football weather. In my mind's eye, I could imagine collegiate couples strolling across the White House lawn, arm in arm, as horny as, well, collegiate couples, and alums in porkpie hats and antique letter sweaters serving sandwiches and hot coffee (or maybe something stronger) from the open tailgates of their Country Squires. I was overcome with nostalgia for a mythic American past, although I'd never actually known it myself. Before me an imagined panorama of stock images, almost kitsch, unfolded. Kids joyously rolling around with puppies, courtly grandpas pushing well-preserved grandmas on playground swings, young lovers squirting each other with the garden hose as an attempt to wash the car turns into a wet, wild sexual roundelay: all these clichéd images and a thousand others like them straight out of the sketchbook of a journeyman advertising copywriter were spread out before me.

And still I was moved.

Although the cynic in me rebelled—I had, of course, paid to stay in the White House—the fantasy America I saw was charged with potent evocative energy. In it, I saw both America's eternal optimism and its vanished vigor: the nation that saw itself forever young and yet, after a mere blink of an eye on the stage of human history, was already showing its age. How had America gotten so old so quickly? I wondered. How had the corrupt ethics of the bad Old World, of the Borgia popes and the Medici dukes, of sybaritic Roman emperors, vain and weak French and English kings, and unimaginably cruel czars and sultans—how had these decadent seeds found such fertile soil here on the shores of our new Jerusalem? Did the fantasy America of mom-and-pop values have totemic power against the timeless evils of corruption and vanity?

I sure hoped so.

As I watched, Bill Clinton loped into the center of the tableau of Americana. Although he was apparently unable to see the Norman Rockwell scenes around him, he was holding a football, which seemed to place him in the larger picture.

"Come on! I know you're there. Come on out and play!"

The images in the scenes nearest the President solidified somewhat, and the people within them took some small notice of him.

"Let's go! Bobby, Jack! I brought the ball! You guys choose up teams."

And there they were. Striding out from among the scenes in this homespun tapestry were the Kennedy boys, followed closely by lesser relatives and assorted hangers-on. They were slightly translucent, as though stuck in the twilight zone between this world and the next. Clinton squinted, trying to make them out more clearly.

"You guys ready to play or not?! Here, Bobby, catch!"

Clinton tossed a pass at the ghost of Bobby Kennedy. Bobby appeared to raise his hands to catch it, but in slow motion and too late. The football passed through empty air and fell to the ground. I could see that the connection between Clinton's world and theirs was tenuous at best. The President was disappointed.

"Aw, man! I've been waiting all week for this. Look . . ."

He indicated a nearby knot of spectral spectators.

"Jackie's here! And Marilyn! And Sam Giancana! And Lem Billings! Everyone's here to see us play, so let's go! I want to play with you guys!"

Jack Kennedy reached down and picked up the football, which grew ghostly and insubstantial in his hands. The pigskin had passed over to the spirit realm.

Bill Clinton went out for a pass.

"Here, Jack! Hit me, I'm open!"

Kennedy cocked his arm and threw a long bomb that sailed through the air in a perfect spiral, heading straight for Clinton's outstretched arms.

The ball passed right through his hands. He wasn't able to even touch it. Kennedy's ghost looked momentarily puzzled. Clinton was crestfallen.

"Why? Why? Every week the same thing happens? It's like a bad dream!"

Sargent Shriver picked up the ball and threw it back to Jack. Sides formed, and a vigorous touch football game began. Jack's team against Bobby's. Clinton watched dejectedly from the sidelines in the world of the living.

Ivy League trash talk reached me as if from a great distance.

"Yee-ah, Baah-bee, yew, uh, yew throw like a, like a gurl-a."

"Jee-ack, we are, ah, going to, ah, turn you-or team intoo chowda."

The game continued with the legendary Kennedy vigor in full display. At one point, Clinton, seeing a pass come near him, couldn't resist and sprinted out to catch it. He ran straight through the play, and as he did so, he tripped over a small shrub and fell face first into the mud. As he picked himself up, the tableau began to fade along with all the other scenes from the collective fantasy past, until only Bill Clinton was left, a small, muddied figure on an empty lawn.

27
Greatly Emancipated
☆ ☆ ☆

Whenever I stay in a new place, it always surprises me how strong is our urge to domesticate our surroundings, and how quickly we humans make a place our own. Two or three days are all it takes to super-impose one's own little personal habits on a new environment—"This table is where I like to read the paper in the morning, over there is where I like to keep my toiletries; my clothes I hang up in this closet, not that one." Granted, hotel rooms—and I think it's safe to include the Lincoln Bedroom—are set up for this, but I always feel a twinge of sadness at leaving my new routines behind.

Also, Bill Clinton's Achilles penis had filled the place with a sense of foreboding, disappointment, and melancholy that were proving infec-tious. And then there was the glum difference between what my tempo-rary residence once was and what it is now. And the thought of leaving Socks.

I hated the idea of ending my stay on such a sour note. There had to be some good here, I told myself, something worth salvaging, worth tak-ing home other than, of course, towels, monogrammed robe, stationery, and presidential soap-on-a-rope. So, after packing up, I decided to take a final walk through the building, to say good-bye to the people and places I had visited, or at least thought I had visited, these past two days.

The halls were utterly empty; not a soul paced their carpeted lengths. I tried a few doors. They were unlocked, the offices and rooms devoid of life. I even opened the interns' supply closet to look for anyone hiding, but all I saw was a beautifully appointed table for two complete with a rose and a bucket of champagne.

It was spooky.

I saw what looked like a door artfully half-concealed in the wall of a reception area. I gave it a push and found myself in the Oval Office. Empty, of course, but what a chance to look around. I browsed the bookshelves. The collection was varied and intriguing: *The Silver Chalice, The Last of the Mohicans, Leaves of Grass, One Hundred Years of Solitude, The Prince of Tides, The Kama Sutra, Disraeli, The Autobiography of Traci Lords, They Only Look Dead.* Then, after listening carefully to make sure that no one was coming, I sat down at the President's desk.

The desk had the usual executive baubles on it: fancy pen set and inkstand, Magic 8-Ball, crystal obelisk, Chinese-English dictionary, "World's Greatest Dad" nameplate. Plus, there were some items that were distinctly Clinton: a bottle of all-purpose stain remover, kneepads, and an Official Breast Inspector card. I leaned back in his chair and stretched, trying to gain an insight into what it must be like to be President Bill Clinton.

Nothing. The lights were on, but nobody was home.

Like many a grand jury, I wondered what he had in his drawers. Spanish fly? A Happy Meal? A billion yuan? A dog whistle audible to only the eagerest of interns? Feeling very sneaky, I began to slide his top drawer open when I heard a noise.

Suddenly, Bill Clinton burst into the room.

He was muddy from his failed attempt to get in the Kennedys' football game, and seemed still preoccupied with having dropped the pass from JFK. I thought at first that he didn't see me. He bent down to tie a shoelace, and then, with his back to me, he said, "You know, Arianna, if you want to find out what's in my desk, all you have to do is ask."

He walked over to where I was sitting.

"We've got no secrets from you. Hell, we *like* you, Arianna."

He leaned over and put his arm around me.

"We like you *soooo* much that we want you to join us. Come on, Arianna, join us."

He began to squeeze.

"Join us. You'll love it. No worries, no guilt, no goddam conscience telling you what to do all the time . . ."

His grip was starting to hurt.

"You can do whatever you want once you join us, Arianna. Whatever you feel like doing, it's okay with us. Come on, think about it; you're here, you're looking through my desk, hell, you're halfway there already! Join us . . ."

He squeezed harder.

"One of us, one of us, one of us . . ."

I gathered all my strength and broke his grip.

"Nooooooo!" I screamed. I turned and ran out the door I'd entered through. The empty halls and room were now full of people. They all turned to stare at me, a vacant, zombielike look in their eyes.

"One of us, one of us," they repeated in a robotic monotone. "Join us. Join us." The crowd surged toward me.

I pushed past the two nearest drones and ran back toward my room. The crowd followed. I looked back and saw a mass of people joining the mob from various rooms along the hallway. The Thomasons were there. So were Carville, Blumenthal, and Begala. Kent popped out of a door and fell in with my pursuers. Even Tony Robbins was among them, rehabilitated by total immersion in group-think.

Gloria All-in-red howled like a harpy. Madonna, Madeleine Albright, Janet Reno, the other ladies from the tea joined her chorus. The guests from dinner were chasing me as well. A faceless mass of dinner-jacketed dignitaries.

"One of us, one of us!"

I ran up a flight of stairs. They were right on my heels. Strobe, Webb, and Jack, wearing bathing suits and dripping from the hot tub, joined the throng. Here was Newt Gingrich, rolling after me like the giant stone ball from *Raiders of the Lost Ark,* with Haley Barbour and Mitch McConnell tumbling along beside him. There were Vernon Jordan and Bill Richardson, actually managing to fly by flapping great sheaves of politically motivated job acceptance letters. There was Bonnie the Tour Guide, providing a running commentary for the heedless horde. A second Clinton appeared—either Bill Clinton Number Two or the real thing. The hideous Bipartisan was in the midst of the riot, his tentacles and drooling maw sometimes visible above the seething multitude.

The Al Gore statue staggered out of a doorway and took up a position at the head of the pack. A front-runner—for now, at least. He lumbered forward with his arms outstretched, looking like Frankenstein's monster.

"One of us, one of us!" Gore intoned, his voice merging with the general fray.

Hillary, all in pink, swooped down from some unseen hiding place, caterwauling like a banshee. "One of us!" she shrieked, whipping the mob into an even greater frenzy.

The walls themselves seemed to close in around me. My pursuers were almost upon me. My legs ached, my lungs burned. I was seconds away from being absorbed. Milliseconds.

Up ahead, Walter materialized. I was doomed. Walter had been my last hope, and now he was cutting off my only avenue of escape. I resolved to sit down and let the riot wash over me. It was all over.

Then Walter looked me in the eye. I knew at once that he was not one of them. He flung open the door of the Lincoln Bedroom and waved me inside.

"Hurry, Mrs. Huffington! Come on! They're right behind you!"

I raced into the Lincoln Bedroom as the hands of the first wave plucked at my clothes. Walter jumped in behind me and slammed the door. I could hear the noise of the mob as it went by the door, and then, gradually, it faded into silence.

I was safe.

"No one will bother you in here, ma'am. Not while *he's* here. They wouldn't dare."

He nodded toward the window. I looked and beheld a tall figure, dressed in black, seated in the rocking chair. Socks was on his lap, purring.

Was it really Abraham Lincoln?

"Hello, Mrs. Huffington. Please excuse me for not getting up. The cat seems so comfortable."

"Mr. Lincoln, Mr. President," I stammered, "am I *glad* to see you, sir."

"Sit down, sit down. You look like you've had an awful scare."

"The mob, sir, the President, and the Speaker, and the Bipartisan and their friends, they wanted me to become one of them. And, when I refused, they started chasing me. It was horrible, sir. Horrible."

I buried my head in my hands. Lincoln stood up, gently moving Socks to a nearby cushion next to Buddy. Lincoln's presence had brought about a ceasefire between those two. He came over and put a comforting hand on my shoulder.

"You don't have to worry about them anymore. You did the right thing. And you're with me now. Everything is going to be all right."

"But it's not just the mob and being chased, sir," I said, trying to settle down. "And it's not just this bunch of liars, philanderers, enablers, perjurers, and suborners who sully the White House. It's the whole thing. It's all so hopeless! The whole system is morally bankrupt, both sides completely corrupt. The only reaction a sensible person can have is to give in to utter despair."

Lincoln's eyes met mine.

"Don't say that. It isn't true. There's always hope. Believe me, I know. I know a little bit about despair."

He returned to the rocker and continued reflectively.

"As you probably know, this room didn't use to be a bedroom. It was my office. I called it 'the shop.' Back in those days, the President was more accessible than he is now. I used to receive visitors here. Ordinary people who just wanted to ask a favor or give me a piece of their mind. I liked it. Kept me in touch. Of course there were a few crackpots now and again, but if they abused the privilege of appealing directly to their President, well, I'd just take 'em by the collar and throw them out."

Lincoln looked as though he could handle just about any size crackpot.

"Bill Clinton should give it a try. Instead of selling photo opportunities and giving in to his baser instincts, he should tend to his soul more and open the door from time to time and see what some real people think. Not by polling, not by putting every decision up for statistical grabs, but face to face."

"What are you saying, sir?" I asked. "That character counts? Or that politicians should pay less attention to polls?"

"Both. I'm a big believer in the American people. This country belongs to the people who inhabit it. Its government exists to secure their rights, the equal rights of all citizens. I never forget that. But that's only a part of it. No, the solution, Arianna, simply put, is *leadership*—real leadership, with real leaders who know what is right and stand up for it, and who aren't afraid to make a difficult and unpopular decision even when the opinion polls and the consultants are all against them. Dick Morris told me I'd lose twenty points off my favorability rating for signing the Emancipation Proclamation. Told me it would be a disaster."

"He was around even then?"

"Deal with the devil."

"Explains a lot."

"You see, leadership is a risky business, Arianna. Not everyone has the stomach for all that it entails. And, despite what everyone says these days, real leadership is inseparable from character. A man who cannot govern himself cannot govern a nation. While things are good, while peace and prosperity reign, the people are forgiving. But George Washington warned us that 'morality is a necessary spring of popular government.' And it is nonsense to believe that corruption and dissolution in our leaders ought to be things of indifference to the people they lead."

"Is there anyone out there, sir? Anyone now living who has the character to be a great leader?"

"Oh, I'm sure there is, Arianna. I'm sure there is. Human nature doesn't change that much. But the arrangement you've got now for choosing your leaders, well, it just about *guarantees* that the cream won't rise to the top. Can you imagine Bill Clinton or Newt Gingrich or Al Gore or any of that lot having the moral fortitude to see a bloody war through to a just conclusion in order to preserve the principles upon which our nation was founded? That is, without some *Wag the Dog* imperative of distracting the nation from the latest Lewinsky?"

"You saw *Wag the Dog*?"

"Anything with Hoffman and De Niro. Anyway, you've got to start picking people to lead you who realize that leadership is about moving a people from where it is to where it has never been—but ought to be. You need to create a new consensus around the matter—to challenge the people's complacency, awaken the better angels of their nature. It's hard work. It requires wisdom, courage, and fortitude—all of which are attributes of character.

"Some say politicians now are out of touch. But that's not the problem. They're much too *in touch* with people's desires. They're out of touch with people's *needs*. The two don't always mean the same thing."

"But how are we to start? Where should we look?"

Lincoln laughed. "Well, not in the ranks of the bipartisans, who believe in nothing but staying in power. My creed is different: Stand with anybody that stands *right*. Stand with him while he is right and *part* with him when he goes wrong. But then you have to be able to tell the difference.

"Bipartisanship today is quite simply protecting the status quo. Things have gotten pretty ugly since I've been gone, especially in the last few years. Politics isn't about improving things for ordinary people anymore. It's about big donors playing both parties like hooked fish and both parties catering to their big donors. It's about incumbents protecting incumbents, both in politics and commerce. It's even about a bipartisan consensus on oral sex and adultery. And—above all—it's about ignoring the squalor and the pain of those left behind. You'll recognize the leaders who will save America. They're the ones who will fire their pollsters and their consultants and tell people what they may not want to hear. In my day, millions didn't want to hear that all men are created equal. Today, millions don't want to hear that we are again a house divided. We have become two nations between whom there is no sympathy, as if they were inhabitants of different planets. The new leaders will strike again the mystic chords of memory, and awaken in every living heart the impulse to care for the least among us."

Lincoln stood and put his stovepipe hat on his head. Socks roused himself from his pillow and sat, respectful and attentive.

The tall man with the sad, craggy face gripped my hand reassuringly. Then he walked toward the door. Walter opened it with his left hand and put his right over his heart. The Great Emancipator passed through the door and was gone.

A little while later, after giving Socks a farewell scratch—and my hair scrunchie—I walked out of the big doors on the North Portico. Walter trailed me with my bags. The parking valet had my car waiting for me. Walter put my bags in the trunk. I shook his hand wordlessly. He turned and walked back into the White House.

I got into the car and headed down the drive, immaculately swept clean of litter by Ted Danson and Mary Steenburger or their designated representatives. Behind me I heard a small voice crying, "Mrs. Huffington! Mrs. Huffington!" I looked in the rearview mirror.

It was Kent. He was running, holding the video camera to his eye at the same time.

My first instinct was to stomp on the accelerator. But he was waving a piece of paper. I slowed down.

Kent reached the window. I rolled it down a crack.

"Oh, hey, I'm glad I caught you, Mrs. Huffington. You almost left without your bill, and you didn't fill out the express checkout form for us to mail it to you."

He handed me a long itemized document. The total amount due at the bottom read $114,756.

I perused it quickly. "Hey, I didn't use the intern!"

"Oh, I'm sorry. We'll just subtract $200."

"Look, Kent, I don't really have much cash with me . . ."

"Oh, you don't have to settle it up right now. We've got your credit card number. It's all part of your FBI file, of course. Bye!"

I drove the car through the gates, past Lance, who gave me a lackadaisical wave, and out into the bright afternoon sunshine. The fresh air felt clean and invigorating, and a gentle, warm breeze brought a hint of change to come.

INTERLUDE IN BEIJING

 The Third Secretary looked out of his window in the Ministry and reflected. He had a problem. A big problem. "Operation Bubba" had been his idea. His baby. His ticket to the big time. It had seemed like a perfect plan. The Third Secretary had always read the American papers religiously. Others in the Party leadership had scoffed; now that China had so much day-to-day contact with the West, and Hong Kong was Chinese again, the value of such crude intelligence-gathering methods seemed to them to be negligible.

But the American newspapers had told the Third Secretary something that everyone else had missed: The President of America—the most powerful man in the world, the leader of the richest country on earth—needed money. The op-ed pages, by decrying it from all sides, had revealed the fact that in America elections were won by the candidate with the most money— money gathered with few questions asked. And in return, favors were granted. The quid pro quo was clearly understood. A little disapproving head-shaking was obligatory, of course; the business was not done entirely in the open. But the important thing was that you didn't have to beat around the bush with a lot of covert nonsense. You could simply buy as much influence as you wanted. It was better than Nigeria.

Naturally, some of his colleagues in the Party leadership had disapproved, at least at first. It was too simple for them. And it made all their elaborate webs of deceit obsolete overnight. But when the operatives started falling into their laps—Americans with connections to the President from Arkansas or through the American Democratic Party—it became too good an opportunity to pass up. The expenditure of vast sums of money was authorized. The Third Secretary was placed in charge. It was a triumph. His finest hour.

And now . . .

And now it was falling apart. The operatives, both the knowing proxies and the naive patsies, were under siege. Some had fled, some had been subpoenaed, some were even going to testify. Operation Bubba had become a nightmare.

The American President was having troubles—something about one of his mistresses having a fight with his wife or something. It was all very confusing to the Third Secretary, all somehow uniquely American. Why couldn't the President simply discipline his mistresses properly? How did the old proverb go? "If a cock will be master in the barnyard, he must first keep order in the henhouse"? That was a good one. He must jot that one down.

And the higher-ups, the senior mandarins of the Party who had been so quick to claim credit for the Third Secretary's scheme. were disavowing the plan. Now they were calling it "Operation That Has Brought Disgrace to Our Long-Dead Ancestors." Someone would have to be blamed, someone would have to take the fall, someone—he shivered—might have to be punished.

The Third Secretary thought for a moment. He tried to let his mind go blank. And then . . . he had an idea. A brilliant idea.

He lit a cigarette (contraband Marlboro Reds—he could still afford a few indulgences). The coffers had been refilled. It was time to start anew. This time he would do it right.

As he reflected on the matter, the Third Secretary decided that America's Chinese policy was right where the Great Leaders wanted it to be. The Chinese economy was booming, their arsenal was being modernized, courtesy of American technology, and all that international bellyaching about Tiananmen Square had finally subsided. And there was the President's triumphant visit complete with a formal state dinner and a performance by Mark Russell. Sure, the Third Secretary's plan had come a bit unraveled at the end, with the Senate hearings and such business. But still—he had discovered America's fatal flaw. Like delicate flowers, its political leaders could flourish only when covered by a thick layer of financial manure.

The Third Secretary would proceed more carefully this time. He'd hang back, watching, waiting. He'd look busy, he'd claim credit when appropriate. And when the time was ripe, he'd strike.

The Democrats had limited utility. Not realizing that had been a mistake. Despite their rapacious appetite for cash, their embarrassment threshold for big-time giving was still too low. They still hung on to their image as the party of the working stiff, the little guy, the honest citizen saved from the abyss by the sturdy webbing of the social welfare safety net. They were still hard-core Marxists. But the Republicans! They were a different matter. Everyone knew they loved big bucks. They were proud of it. These were the kind of people the Third Secretary could do business with.

And with two of their party leaders, Mitch McConnell and Trent Lott, committed to keeping the pipeline open, the new Third Secretary knew that this would be the beginning of a long and fruitful relationship. And the beautiful part was that it was easier to do legally than illegally.

Yes, he'd get it right the second time. In a way, he was grateful for his little setback. It had illuminated the way. Bright idea, not broad enough scope. The Third Secretary would spread the fertilizing manure of soft money evenly to both parties. And that way, no matter who got caught with their pants down, the People's Republic would still come out a winner.

He exhaled the smoke from his cigarette, looked out of his window, and smiled.

Epilogue

Phone Log

I Arianna Huffington and Vernon Jordan, March 3, 2:32 P.M., PST

"Hello?"

"May I please speak to Arianna Huffington?"

"This is Arianna."

"Arianna, this is Vernon Jordan."

"Okay."

"I understand you recently visited the White House."

"That's true."

"And how was it?"

"Quite stimulating."

"Stimulating? How do you mean?"

"You know, interesting. It was very interesting."

"So nothing happened . . . to make you feel . . . unhappy? There were no miscommunications . . . that led to any . . . potential ill will or . . . conflict?"

"No, I'm fine, Vernon. I don't think I need a forensics expert, if that's what you mean."

"Mean? I don't mean anything. I'm just calling to make sure . . . everything is . . . fine."

"We're all fine here."

"So we're all . . . fine."

"Yep. Fine is what we are."

"So you're fine, I'm fine, your trip was fine, everything is . . ."

"Fine."

"Fine, that s good . . . fine."

"To put your lawyerly mind at rest, Vernon, if I were to make a list entitled Things I Am, fine would definitely be one of the things."

"Good, good. That's very good. Although I'd like to make it clear that I never asked you to make such a list."

"It was purely my own suggestion, Vernon."

"Well, that's why I was calling, to make sure we're all . . . fine."

"Well, it looks like we've put this one to bed then, Vernon."

"Yes, it appears so . . ."

"Vernon?"

"Yes?"

"Is that all you wanted?"

"Yes."

"Would you mind terribly if we ended our conversation?"

"That would be fine."

"Okay, then I'm ending it . . . I'm putting the phone down, Vernon . . . I'm hanging up."

"Fine."

Phone Log

II Arianna Huffington and Webb Hubbell, March 5, 9:53 A.M., PST

"Hello?"

"Hello."

"Hello?"

" . . . "

"Hello?"

"Hello, Arianna . . . (sigh) . . . it's Webb Hubbell."

"Webb! What's up? You sound depressed."

"That's putting it mildly."

"What happened? Another grand jury?"

"No. Look, Arianna, this is damned awkward . . ."

"What? What is it, Webb?"

"Arianna, I just came back from my doctor and he said . . ."

"Your doctor?"

"Do you remember sharing a hot tub with me and a few other people about, oh, two to four weeks ago?"

"Yes, of course."

"Look, Arianna, the, uh, the reason I called is that . . . do you know what scabies are?"

"Scabies? Weren't they the real-estate couple from Texas at the State Dinner? They were very nice, as I recall."

"No. It's a skin infection. It's caused by a mite. It itches like hell and I'm apparently very contagious. Anyway, my doctor says I have a bad case of scabies and that I could have passed it on to other people . . ."

"Oh, dear. Well, don't worry about me, Webb, I don't feel unusually itchy, I'm happy to say."

"Oh, good! That's a relief. Because the White House called and apparently the President has been scratching like a coon dog. White House aides are already calling it Scabies Gate. Anyway, my doctor recommended a topical insecticide lotion for both him and the woman in question."

"Women . . . what?"

"Figure of speech."

"Is that what you told the grand jury?"

"Scabies is a personal matter. I thought it best not to go into it."

"Well, Webb, I hope you feel better."

"Thanks, Arianna, it's not life-threatening. See, at first it's just tiny, gray, scaly swellings between your fingers, in your armpits, on your wrists, and on your genitals. After a week or so, the bites turn red and start to swell up more . . ."

"It's like you're a painter with words, Webb. I think I get the picture."

"Painter?"

"Figure of speech."

"Oh."

"You stay out of trouble, you hear?"

(Laughter.)

"Bye, now!"

(Laughter.)

"Bye!"

Phone Log

III Arianna Huffington and Newt Gingrich, March 9, 4:23 A.M., PST

"Hello?"

"Arianna! Hi, it's Newt Gingrich!"

"Newt, my God, what time is it?"

"It's just before five. Up and at 'em, sleepyhead!"

"And I thought I was an early riser! What is that noise?"

"That's my Exercycle. I'm up to fifteen miles a day."

"Newt, I have to confess that I didn't expect to be hearing from you, now that I'm not so conveniently located, I mean . . ."

"Arianna, didn't the President tell you? We're all on the same team, working together now—you know, going about the nation's business, not dealing with all those personal things. This is the new Newt calling you, Arianna. The old Newt, the vindictive, backbiting, right-wing conspiring political intriguer, he's been put to rest. This is the new Newt . . . Get it? New Newt."

"Yeah, New Newt. I got it."

"New Newt."

"I'm going back to sleep, New Newt."

"Arianna, did you know that if you have a glass filled with dirty water and you begin filling it with clean water, then eventually the glass will only contain clean water? Isn't that the most wonderful thing you ever heard?"

"I'm stunned."

"Actually, Arianna, first and foremost, I called to say thank you."

"You're welcome. But for what?"

"For inspiring me to take a long hard look at myself."

"So what did you see?"

"I took a long, hard look at myself, and you know what, Arianna?"

"What, New Newt?"

"I was a big load."

"Welcome to earth."

"And you know what made me change?"

"Almighty God?"

"No, but I'm sure she had a hand in it."

"She?"

"It's hurtful when we exclude any gender or race from envisioning themselves as the Godhead."

"I'm back to being stunned."

"Actually, Arianna, it was when you wrote in your column that 'sometimes the highest form of leadership involves retreat' and that there is a 'higher loyalty—to ideas rather than leaders.'"

"I'm delighted that you took it so well."

"It's more than that, Arianna. I'm a new man. You see, being Speaker was fun and all, but it really cut into my private time. I was spending so many hours shepherding key legislation, fighting charges of ethical violations, spearheading the Contract with America, and then the Contract with Corporate America. By the way, I want to thank you for your terrific feedback on that. You're a damn fine sounding board, Arianna."

"Newt, I really didn't—"

"Where was I? Oh yeah . . . The new me. So I realized I was spending so much time on all that political stuff that I had nothing left over for the other me. And then the President really showed me that it's possible to have a lively and fulfilling private life and still be effective publicly. So I decided to start working for the most important constituency: me, the Inner Newt, the little Speaker that's buried deep down in my psyche. Inner New Newt was crying out—"

"I think it would just be 'Inner Newt.' <u>You're</u> New Newt. Inner Newt was inside Old Newt."

"Right, right. Inner Newt. I'm still getting all this worked out."

"Sorry to interrupt."

"No, no, quite all right. Anyway, Inner Newt was crying out for some attention, and that manifested itself in various inappropriate ways. Like when I made Paxon fall on his sword. Pure childishness! Am I right?"

"You said it—not me."

"Anyway, in the course of trying to improve my image, I started working out, eating better, taking more care with my personal appearance. A Pentagon intern even got me on that 'Zone' diet . . . And guess what?"

"You're not a big load anymore?"

"I love it! I wince when I look at those old photos, I really do. I looked fat and slobby—like an unmade bed. It was gross! I was a disgusting pig. I was a glass of dirty water, but you know what I didn't have?"

"Clean water?"

"Exactly, Ari!"

"Please don't call me Ari."

"Sorry. New Newt is still finding the right tone."

"Wish him luck for me."

"Will do, Arianna. Anyway, I have to catch the eight-thirty shuttle. Louis Licari is doing my roots and then Frédéric Fekkai is going to try and deal with this mop on my head. But I just wanted to say, on behalf of Little Newt—I mean New Newt—the real me, who was struggling to break out of my bloated, obnoxious exterior Old Newt shell, how much I appreciate your unrelenting animosity. By the way, I'm back in town next week to help that unhappy Ken Starr self-actualize and grant his inner prosecutor a little immunity—you know, release the guilt. So how about lunch? I know a great macrobiotic place in Adams-Morgan."

"Well, I have to check my schedule . . . ."

"Come on! I bet you got tired of eating Chinese food night after night in the White House."

"All right, New Newt, as long as you promise me one thing."

"Sure. What's that?"

"Just promise that you're not lying to me about turning over a new leaf and actually planning to lure me to an out-of-the-way location, kill me, and bury me in a shallow grave somewhere."

"Scout's honor, Arianna. The only thing I have planned is some really good tofu and some hot stinging-nettle tea."

"Stinging-nettle tea?"

"Andrew Weil."

"Ah . . . But just to be safe, I'm going to leave a letter with my lawyer implicating you if anything happens to me."

"That's completely understandable in light of my past behavior, Arianna. I want you to know that New Newt's not offended in the least. See you next week, then."

"Bye, New Newt."

"Bye."

Phone Log

IV Answering Machine Message from Don Fowler, March 12, 11:22 P.M., PST

"Hello. I'm not in right now, but if you'd like to leave a message, please do so after the tone."

(Beep)

"Hello . . . Arianna? Hello? Are you there, Arianna? Arianna? It's me, Don. Don Fowler. Though how many Dons would you really know, you know? But I guess you could know more than one. Let me see, there's Don Sipple, there's Don Rickles. He really makes me laugh. You hockey puck! Not you, Arianna. That's just what Don says. Don Rickles . . . Are you there? If you are, pick up. Pick up, pick up, pick up. I know you're there . . . Okay, I guess you're not there. Are you? If you are, pick up. Okay, maybe you're really not there. Anyhoo—I'm just wondering what you're doing for Independence Day. You know, that's our nation's birthday. I don't know what they do in Turkey or Crete or wherever you're from, but it's a pretty big deal here. And we've come up with an amazing new concept that we'd like you to be a part of. It's an elite group type of a thing limited to the number that can be seated in the State Dining Room, called Team Happy Birthday America. Team Happy Birthday America will be composed of business leaders, decision-makers, opinion-makers, opinion leaders, decision leaders. The <u>crème de la crème</u>. Are you there? Pick up, if you are . . . Okay, anyway, I'm reading now: 'Team Happy Birthday America will gather in the White House on Independence Day, popularly known as July the Fourth, for a special all-American barbeque with the First Family and their special, invited American and nor-American-but-America-loving foreign guests. They will take part in a celebration of all that is uniquely American, especially the exercise of free speech through political donations and, of course, the passing on of a small tax-deductible donation to those who can't exercise as much free speech. Roger Clinton will perform.' Anyway, Arianna, I'm sure an old fund-raising hand such as yourself will recognize a once-in-a-lifetime—"

"You have thirty seconds."

"—a once-in-a-lifetime opportunity to rub elbows with some of . . . uh, I guess I'm running out of time here . . . so I'm just gonna send you all the stuff. There's a million special benefits to being a member of Team Happy Birthday America, not to mention the fireworks and beer and stuff. My favorites are the sparklers. I like to write my name with them. You can write whatever you want with yours. Anyway, Arianna, I know you'd just love being back in the White House again and seeing all your old friends, you know. do the reacquaintanceship thing, you know? So I hope to see you there—you know, if I'm not indicted or anything. All I can say is, lie, Charlie Trie, lie! Not that I'm encouraging or in any way suborning perjury. In fact, for everybody listening—and these days, God knows who is, am I right, Arianna?—I, Don Fowler, outwardly and officially urge Charlie Trie to tell the truth. Anyway, see you on America's birthday, hockey puck! Just kidding—that's what I would say if I were Don Rickles instead of Don Fowler . . . Are you there? Arianna? Pick up if you are—"

(Beep)

(Click)

Phone Log

V Answering Machine Message from Bill Clinton, March 12, 11:27 P.M., PST

"Monica, are you there? It's the 'Principal.' Got your message. Memorized your number and ate it. 310 area code. You must have called from your dad's house? But what's with that Greek accent on your machine? Practicing for your anthropology class? I always liked that subject myself—only class you got to see topless women. I guess you're probably studying now. Got to keep up those good grades. Anyway, if you happen to get this, Mr. Lewinsky, your daughter was a fine part of our team. She put in crazy hours at the White House. Uhhhh.. While I have you on the phone, Mr. Lewinsky, you think I could get you to help finance a bridge to the twenty-first century? And, by the way, if you're a Republican, I'm calling from a pay phone at a Stop 'N' Shop near Dupont Circle. Oh yeah, Monica, I'm going to be in L.A. next week and if you're still there, I'm going to need some filing done at our office in the Santa Monica Sheraton. A lot of filing.

You know, for old times' sake. Could go all night. But hey, that's why we pay you interns the big bucks." (Beep. End of call.)

𝒫𝒽𝑜𝓃𝑒 𝐿𝑜𝑔

VI Arianna Huffington, Jack Quinn, and Al Gore, March 16, 1:53 P.M., PST

"Hello, Republican National Committee."

"Uh, hello, uh . . . I'm sorry, I must have the wrong number."

"No, no, I'm just kidding. Who were you calling for?"

"Well, I was looking for Arianna Huffington."

"That's me."

"Arianna, it's Jack Quinn!"

"Oh, hi, Jack. How's the weather inside the Beltway?"

"It always looks sunny from my perspective, Arianna. Not a cloud on the horizon."

"That's nice, Jack."

"When I see a glass that's half full, I say 'why?' and when I see a glass that's half empty . . . I . . ."

"Maybe you should keep working on that one, Jack. You know, this is a terrible connection. I can barely hear you."

"Yeah, I'm sorry, I have to route the calls through Luxembourg in order to be, you know, fully in compliance with the letter and spirit of the campaign finance laws yadda, yadda, yadda . . . anyway, I'm just checking in, seeing how you're doing . . ."

"I'm fine. No lawsuits, no scabies."

"So you talked to Vernon and Webb. Poor guy, Webb. He just <u>cannot</u> get a break. Guess you're glad you can't get pregnant from a hot tub . . ."

"What? What are you talking about?"

"Just kidding. You know, because, hey, at least it's still okay to make dirty jokes from <u>any</u> phone, am I right?"

"If it's okay with the President, I guess it's okay with me."

"Actually, the reason I'm calling is to say thanks and . . . You know what, let me put Al on for a second."

(Crash)

"Sorry, Arianna. I dropped the phone. Wait, let me hold it up to his ear here."

"Hello, Al? Al, can you hear me?"

"Hello, Arianna. Arianna, thank you very much for your commitment to the party and . . ."

"Al, are you calling me from the basement?"

"Yes, I'm still here, Arianna. But things have gotten a bit better. Begala and Blumenthal are here all the time now, shining me up for 2000. And Marty, of course."

"I hope you've picked out your inaugural music."

"I was thinking about that 'You Can Call Me Al' song. I'll sing a few bars, see what you think."

"That's okay. I trust you. So, have you been out pressing the flesh, meeting some real people?"

"Oh yes, most definitely. As a matter of fact, the chairman of Occidental Petroleum, Ray Irani, came by to see me last week. And someone from the National Association of Trial Lawyers dropped in yesterday. And just this morning, the President of the Teamsters! I strained my neck nodding."

"It's good to keep up with ordinary Americans."

"You're darn right. Speaking of which, I'm seeing a lot more of the President lately, too. He comes down himself from time to time and grooms me. I'm part of his legacy, you see . . ."

"I'm getting misty. But you're not leaving the basement?"

"Not yet. I was gonna go to Lake Tahoe for an environmental thing, but the Secret Service was afraid I'd fall in and sink."

"That would have been almost as much of a public-relations disaster as that Buddhist temple."

"And at this one, I wouldn't have gotten any soft money. Speaking of public relations, Arianna, let me run a few slogans by you for 2000. You're a media person. Give me your honest opinion."

"Okay. Shoot."

"'You Can Call Me Al.'"

"No."

"Okay, how about 'Gore: A Guy in a Suit.'"

"No."

"No? All right, what about 'Gore: 100% Backbone.'"

"No."

"Really, not that one either? What about 'Gore: Just Look at Him.'"

"No."

"Okay, what about 'Gore: He Can't Comment on the Lewinsky Affair Because There Is an Ongoing Investigation.'"

"Feels like I've heard that one before."

"You're pretty tough. How do you like this: 'Gore: He's a Big Tipper, Which Is Also His Wife's Name.'"

"That's the best one so far."

"Okay, this one's good. 'Al Gore: Because People This Stiff Are Usually Quite Honest.'"

"No."

"One more . . . 'Gore: I went to St. Albans and Harvard and It's My Turn.'"

"Maybe."

"Okay, what about 'You Can Call Me Al'?"

"Maybe."

"What about 'Vote for Al Gore'?"

"Bingo. By the way, Al, has Dick Morris been helping you with these?"

"How did you guess?"

"It doesn't seem like his best work."

"He's very busy. We're just getting started anyway, I—"

"Arianna, it's Jack Quinn again. I hate to interrupt, but my arm is getting really tired. Holding the phone next to Al's head all day is murder on my tennis elbow."

"Have you thought about Super-Gluing the phone to his ear?"

"Heh-heh, great, yeah. So, we've got quite a few more calls to make . . ."

"Sure, of course."

"It's one thing to get these bigwigs to make a pledge, but collecting on it is a whole 'nother ball game."

"Right, I understand."

"Particularly in some of these countries where they have an entirely different understanding of the concept of being a promise keeper."

"Uh-huh."

"But if they give me any trouble, I just put 'em on the phone with Al here. I call him 'The Enforcer'—that's our private joke. He shakes them down and they pay up right away, ninety-nine times out of a hundred."

"Well, maybe that's a good, forceful slogan for Al in 2000. 'Gore: The Enforcer.'"

"Hey, I like it, Arianna. I really do. I'll run it by Dick."

"Great, Jack. And you don't have to tell Dick Morris you got the idea from me. You go on and take all the credit."

"Are you encouraging me to lie, Arianna? If so, for the record I'd like to state that I, JACK QUINN, DO CAT-EGORICALLY REJECT ARIANNA HUFFINGTON'S SUGGESTION THAT I UNTRUTHFULLY CHARACTERIZE THE ORIGIN OF THE SLOGAN 'GORE: THE ENFORCER.'"

"You know, you were a lot more fun before this whole thing."

"So was Susan McDougal. Anyway, Arianna, thanks for your help. Who says you Republicans aren't generous? Am I right? See you on Team Happy Birthday America. Okay, good-bye."

"Bye, Jack."

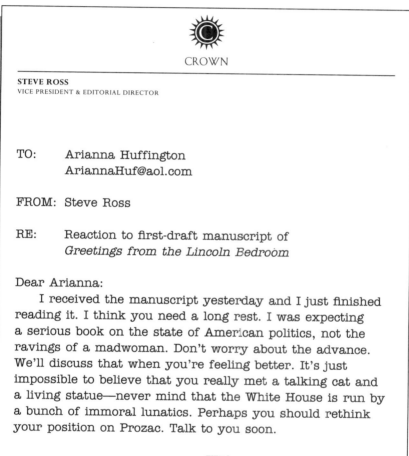

⊙

CROWN

STEVE ROSS
VICE PRESIDENT & EDITORIAL DIRECTOR

TO: Arianna Huffington
         AriannaHuf@aol.com

FROM: Steve Ross

RE: Reaction to first-draft manuscript of
         Greetings from the Lincoln Bedroom

Dear Arianna:

I received the manuscript yesterday and I just finished reading it. I think you need a long rest. I was expecting a serious book on the state of American politics, not the ravings of a madwoman. Don't worry about the advance. We'll discuss that when you're feeling better. It's just impossible to believe that you really met a talking cat and a living statue—never mind that the White House is run by a bunch of immoral lunatics. Perhaps you should rethink your position on Prozac. Talk to you soon.

                                    With concern,

                                    Steve Ross

                                    Steve Ross

P.S. Just thought I should give you a heads-up. When your manuscript started coming in, I got a little worried, so I started taping our conversations. Just to protect myself, of course. And also, I'm turning the tapes over to the Justice Department.

P.P.S. Things are really crazy around here—do you happen to know of a good intern? Or maybe you can get me Mr. Jordan's phone number so I can contact Vernon directly?

201 EAST 50TH STREET · NEW YORK, NY 10022 · 212.572.6176 · [FAX] 212.572.6192 · EMAIL: SROSS@RANDOMHOUSE.COM

Appendices

Dramatis Personae

☆ ☆ ☆

NAME: HALEY BARBOUR

RESIDENCE: Yazoo City, Mississippi, and Washington, D.C.

CLINTON CONNECTION: As RNC chief during the President's first term, was always available to provide biting critiques of the White House. Responsible for raising at least $165 million in soft money alone.

WHO IS HE REALLY?: Lawyer. Represents tobacco companies. Former head of the RNC. Set up a think tank called the National Policy Forum that received a $2.1 million loan guarantee from Hong Kong businessman Ambrous Tung Young. NPF passed on $1.6 million to the RNC, just before the 1994 elections. Under investigation by the Justice Department.

QUOTABLE QUOTE: "We spent enough money to burn a wet mule."

FUN FACT: Barbour's RNC farewell party, attended by many Republican lawmakers, was described by the RNC as "a thank-you to our longtime donors," like Chevron, Coca-Cola, Pfizer, and Bristol-Meyers Squibb.

NAME: LINDA BLOODWORTH-THOMASON

RESIDENCE: Santa Barbara and Encino, California

CLINTON CONNECTION: Old and dear friend of the Clintons. Not a big money donor, but gives the Clintons plenty of her time and creativity.

WHO IS SHE REALLY?: In the late seventies, while a writer for the television show *M*A*S*H*, met future husband Harry Thomason (see his entry) on the Columbia lot. The two went on to produce a string of television shows, including *Designing Women, Evening Shade, Hearts Afire,* and *Women of the House.* The Thomasons gave Bill's half-brother Roger a job as a production assistant upon his release from prison. Linda directed the Bill Clinton bio-film, *The Man from Hope,* for the '92 convention.

QUOTABLE QUOTE: On the Los Angeles riots: "I'm no longer a bleeding-heart liberal—just a brokenhearted one."

FUN FACT: Started her career as a teacher in Watts, California.

NAME: JOHNNY CHUNG

RESIDENCE: Torrance, California

CLINTON CONNECTION: Personally escorted many Chinese businesspeople and government representatives to meet with the President. And gave $366,000 to the Democrats, all of which was given back.

WHO IS HE REALLY?: A California entrepreneur and money launderer. His many accomplishments include the following: (1) Handing Maggie Williams, Hillary Clinton's chief of staff, a $50,000 check in the White House (both unethical and of questionable legality), in return for which six Chinese men got ringside seats at a Clinton radio address, complete with photo op. (2) Donating $25,000 to AfriCare, Energy Secretary Hazel O'Leary's favorite charity. Chung's Chinese friends then got a meeting with her, and were able to meet the President at an AfriCare dinner. (3) Giving $25,000 to an anti-Whitewater investigation group to bring about a meeting with the U.S. ambassador to China. (4) Using a photo of himself with Hillary and a handwritten note from her to spice up a brochure for his business.

QUOTABLE QUOTE: "The White House is like a subway. You have to put in coins to open the gates."

FUN FACT: Has made fifty-one visits to the White House.

NAME: BILL CLINTON

RESIDENCE: 1600 Pennsylvania Avenue, NW, Washington, D.C. 20500

CLINTON CONNECTION: Is Bill Clinton.

WHO IS HE REALLY?: President of the United States of America. At the center of fund-raising and sexual scandals. Thought up the idea of giving big donors overnight stays in the White House. Has said he doesn't recall phoning big donors, despite memos confirming that he did. After Harold Ickes (see his entry) refreshed his memory, he remembered. Has been denying stories of extramarital affairs since he first entered politics. Sued by Paula Jones for sexual harassment while simultaneously denying reports that he had an affair with Monica Lewinsky, a White House intern thirty years his junior.

QUOTABLE QUOTE: On Monica Lewinsky: "I did not have sexual relations with that woman."

FUN FACT: According to Lewinsky, Gennifer Flowers, and an Arkansas State Trooper, Clinton has allegedly said that according to the Bible, oral sex does not constitute adultery.

NAME: HILLARY RODHAM CLINTON

RESIDENCE: 1600 Pennsylvania Avenue, NW, Washington, D.C. 20500

CLINTON CONNECTION: Is Bill Clinton's wife, fund-raising helpmate, and defender against allegations of sexual impropriety.

WHO IS SHE REALLY?: The First Lady of the United States. Has stood by her husband throughout the sex scandals that have plagued his political career. Longtime Clinton aide Bruce Lindsey said in 1992 that such "bimbo eruptions" would sink Clinton only "when Hillary says it's too much." Blames Monica Lewinsky scandal on a "vast right-wing conspiracy." Was asked by the DNC to make fund-raising calls to potential big donors. Now can't recall doing so. Soon after her visit to Guam, its Governor and several Guam businessmen gave $132,000 to Clinton-Gore '96 and $510,000 to the DNC. The President subsequently supported more autonomy for Guam. Hillary was also instrumental in placing Craig Livingstone (see his entry) in his White House job.

QUOTABLE QUOTE: Defending her "gregarious and truly outgoing" husband's desire to share the White House with "as many people as possible": "We knew everybody who was invited. We may not have been the best of friends with everybody. We may not have known everybody for thirty or forty years, but we knew everybody who was invited."

FUN FACT: Was valedictorian of Wellesley's Class of 1969. In her commencement address, she said: "We're searching for more immediate, ecstatic, and penetrating modes of living." Might have been describing her future husband.

NAME: SOCKS (CLINTON)

RESIDENCE: 1600 Pennsylvania Avenue, NW, Washington, D.C. 20500

CLINTON CONNECTION: The Clintons' family pet and a jaundiced observer of the presidency.

WHO IS HE REALLY?: Formerly an only pet. Now surly and suspicious stepbrother to lovable First Dog.

QUOTABLE QUOTE: "Can you toss me your hair scrunchie?"

FUN FACT: Was on the cover of the January '93 *Cats Magazine*.

NAME: RAHM EMANUEL

RESIDENCE: Washington, D.C.

CLINTON CONNECTION: Longtime Clinton aide and fund-raiser. Raised $3 million in twenty days for Clinton in 1991. Raised a total of $20.3 million for Clinton during the 1992 campaign.

WHO IS HE REALLY?: Senior Adviser to the President for Policy and Strategy (George Stephanopoulos's former title). Emanuel also insisted on Stephanopoulos's former office with direct access to the Oval Office. Currently helping the President stonewall the press. During the Gulf War, he volunteered for an Israeli Army program that offered recruits cut-rate travel and lodging in exchange for civilian work. Spent his service rust-proofing brakes.

QUOTABLE QUOTE: On receiving a check for an amount he deemed not up to the donor's potential: "This is an insult! Five thousand is an insult! You are a $25,000 person! I won't take it. It is beneath you! I am sending the check back."

FUN FACT: Takes ballet lessons on Saturdays and Sundays.

NAME: GENNIFER FLOWERS

RESIDENCE: Dallas, Texas

CLINTON CONNECTION: Had twelve-year extramarital relationship with Bill Clinton. Nearly derailed his 1992 presidential campaign by revealing their affair.

WHO IS SHE REALLY?: Variously a singer, reporter, Arkansas state employee; most recently an author. Was a local television reporter when she met Clinton at a press conference in the 1970s and their affair began. In 1992, Flowers produced taped phone conversations in which Clinton seemed to urge her to cover up their relationship. Said Clinton had helped her obtain a state job and claimed she had aborted their child. Clinton denied her story in a dramatic interview on *60 Minutes;* Flowers subsequently wrote an excruciatingly detailed book about their sex life. In 1998, while testifying during the Paula Jones proceedings, Clinton reportedly conceded that he had after all had sexual relations with Flowers; he subsequently denied admitting it.

QUOTABLE QUOTE: "I am not a bimbo!"

FUN FACT: On *Larry King,* Flowers attributed the health of the American economy to Alan Greenspan, not Bill Clinton.

NAME: DON FOWLER

RESIDENCE: Columbia, South Carolina

CLINTON CONNECTION: Ardent practitioner and defender of Democratic fundraising during the President's first term.

WHO IS HE REALLY?: Former Chairman of the Democratic Party. Well known within the executive branch for getting access for big donors, to the frustration of career Clinton administration officials. Contacted the CIA in an effort to gain White House entrée for Roger Tamraz (see his entry). Had no recollection of doing so. Obtained White House audience for Hong Kong billionaire Eric Hotung because "Mr. Hotung has several policy options he would like to suggest for consideration." Hotung is not an American citizen, but his wife contributed $100,000. Also helped several American Indian tribes, which were big Democratic donors, to block a proposed new casino in Wisconsin. The casino was being pushed by Republican-supporting tribes. But through a memo to Harold Ickes and a call to the Department of the Interior, Fowler and his donor tribes prevailed, and the rival casino was squashed. Was told not to call government officials on behalf of donors by Treasury Secretary Robert Rubin, then-Trade Representative Mickey Kantor, and White House Political Director Doug Sosnik. Continued to call government officials on behalf of donors.

QUOTABLE QUOTE: "I have in the middle of the night, at high noon, late in the afternoon, early in the morning—at every hour of the day for months now searched my memory about conversations with the CIA, and I have no memory—no memory of any conversations with the CIA."

FUN FACT: Has taught political science at the University of South Carolina since 1964.

NAME: NEWT GINGRICH

RESIDENCE: Marietta, Georgia, and Washington, D.C.

CLINTON CONNECTION: Clinton's Republican doppelganger: both are smart, formerly overweight Southern politicians with an interesting attitude toward infidelity (see below). Raised $1,810,000 for himself in the first six months of 1997.

WHO IS HE REALLY?: Republican Congressman from Georgia. Speaker of the U.S. House of Representatives. Spearheaded the Contract with America. Had his picture taken with suspected Chinese agent Ted Sioeng (see his entry), but claims not to know Sioeng. The photo op came after Gingrich adviser Joe Gaylord asked Sioeng for a $50,000 donation to the National Policy Forum, a Republican money-raising front. Sioeng obliged.

QUOTABLE QUOTE: "I have an enormous personal ambition. I want to shift the entire planet. And I'm doing it."

FUN FACT: A former Gingrich lover was quoted in *Vanity Fair* as saying: "We had oral sex. He prefers that modus operandi because then he can say, 'I never slept with her.'"

NAME: AL GORE

RESIDENCE: Vice-Presidential Mansion, United States Naval Observatory, 3450 Massachusetts Avenue, NW, Washington, D.C. 20392

CLINTON CONNECTION: Was rescued from political decline when Clinton chose him as vice-presidential candidate in 1992. Made eighty-six fund-raising calls from the White House, which are estimated to have brought in $3.7 million.

WHO IS HE REALLY?: Vice-President of the United States of America. Claimed to have used his DNC credit card when making his fund-raising calls from his White House office. Many of the calls were found to have been billed to the government. May have been aware of the diversion of DNC "soft" money into "hard" accounts (thus placing a few big donors in violation of federal law), which caused even Attorney General Janet Reno to sit up and take notice. Wrote to the Indonesian Vice-President on behalf of Ellicott Machine Corporation. Ellicott got a $20 million deal from Indonesia and donated $15,000 to the DNC. Attended an event at a Buddhist temple that illegally raised over $100,000 (see John Huang entry). Claims he didn't know the event was a fund-raiser, even though his aides did.

QUOTABLE QUOTE: "No controlling legal authority." Repeated seven times during his March 3, 1997, press conference.

FUN FACT: Was a roommate of *Men in Black* star Tommy Lee Jones at Harvard, and falsely claimed that *Love Story* was based on his life as a Harvard student.

NAME: JOHN HUANG

RESIDENCE: Glendale, California

CLINTON CONNECTION: Raised $3.4 million for the DNC. Roughly half was returned.

WHO IS HE REALLY?: Has known the Clintons since 1985, when he was an official with the Worthen Bank in Little Rock. Approved a crucial loan during Clinton's 1992 campaign. Left a $205,000-a-year job as head of the Lippo Group's U.S. operations (see Mochtar Riady entry) for a midlevel Commerce Department job at $119,000, then moved to an even lower-paying job ($60,000) as vice-chairman of finance at the DNC. Received a top-level security clearance five months before he went to work at Commerce, and kept it after he went to the DNC. Was briefed numerous times on Chinese affairs. Maintained close contact with the Riadys while at Commerce and the DNC. Used his Commerce post to push for resuming diplomatic relations with Vietnam and delinking China's trade status from human rights violations. Clinton reversed his earlier stand and resumed diplomatic relations with Vietnam and formally delinked China's trade status from human-rights violations. The Lippo Group stood to benefit hugely from both decisions. Some highlights of Huang's fund-raising career: $250,000 from a South Korean company; $250,000 from Thai lobbyist Pauline Kanchanalak (see her entry); $450,000 from Arief Wiriadinata, landscaper, who'd gotten the money from the Riadys (see Mochtar Riady entry). Also, organized the notorious Buddhist temple fund-raiser attended by Vice-President Gore (see his entry).

QUOTABLE QUOTE: Asked why he ducked a subpoena and disappeared: "It's been a really confusing period of time for me."

FUN FACT: Has visited the White House 164 times.

NAME: WEBSTER HUBBELL

RESIDENCE: Washington, D.C.

CLINTON CONNECTION: Old friend of Bill and Hillary Clinton's. Recipient of several big favors by Vernon Jordan and other big donors (see below).

WHO IS HE REALLY?: Former Associate Attorney General. Convicted felon. Got into trouble because of his questionable business practices at the Rose Law Firm in Little Rock. Top Clinton aides Mack McLarty, Erskine Bowles, and Mickey Kantor helped out Hubbell by lining up several high-paying cases so he could pay his legal bills and several high-paying jobs—for which he apparently did no work—with Dick Batchelor, Truman Arnold, Eli Broad, and the Riadys (see Mochtar Riady entry; see Overnight White House Guests). Hubbell subsequently refused to cooperate with Whitewater investigators.

QUOTABLE QUOTE: On his bad press: "You piece together this and that, and you make this grand conspiracy. But is it some grand conspiracy or is it Arkansas?"

FUN FACT: Spent eighteen months in prison for embezzlement.

NAME: ARIANNA HUFFINGTON

RESIDENCE: Los Angeles, California, and Washington, D.C.

CLINTON CONNECTION: A student of fund-raising practices of both parties.

WHO IS SHE REALLY?: Syndicated columnist, author of *Greetings from the Lincoln Bedroom,* and mother of Christina, age 8, and Isabela, age 6.

QUOTABLE QUOTE: "Isabella! Christina! Take the dress off Snowflake—the cat is not a doll!"

FUN FACT: Isabella was utterly charmed by President Clinton during the Renaissance Weekend at Hilton Head. Regularly admonishes her mother: "Mommy, you're not writing anything bad about that nice Mr. Clinton, are you?"

NAME: HAROLD ICKES

RESIDENCE: New York City

CLINTON CONNECTION: Long-standing political ties to Clinton finally resulted in White House job. Discarded by Clinton after '96 fund-raising abuses came to light. Taken back into the Clinton fold after the Monica Lewinsky story broke.

WHO IS HE REALLY?: Former White House Deputy Chief of Staff. Was the reluctant dark lord of Clinton fund-raising. Blamed by former DNC Chairman Don Fowler for much of the fund-raising scandal. Is reported to use extremely colorful language. Has said he had to practically beg Clinton to make fund-raising calls. Confirmed that Clinton did indeed make such calls from the White House, though not from the Oval Office. Representative Ickes anecdote: When wealthy businessman William Morgan wanted access to the Federal Reserve to help smooth a proposed bond deal, he offered, through his intermediary Warren Meddoff, to donate $55 million to the DNC. Morgan also wanted a tax deduction for his contribution. Ickes advised Meddoff on how to take deductions by giving the money to nonprofit organizations allied with the Democratic Party. Ickes then supplied the bank account numbers of these organizations. When Ickes realized this was illegal, he asked Meddoff to shred the incriminating fax. Meddoff refused.

QUOTABLE QUOTE: "Who is John Huang?" he asked a year after he'd recommended Huang for a job with the DNC.

FUN FACT: His father quit as President Truman's Interior Secretary after Truman criticized him for telling the truth about a fund-raising scandal.

NAME: PAULA JONES

RESIDENCE: Los Angeles, California

CLINTON CONNECTION: Alleges that Bill Clinton sexually harassed her in 1991; her lawsuit against him seeks $2 million and an apology.

WHO IS SHE REALLY?: Former Arkansas state employee. Claims that, in 1991, Clinton had a state trooper bring her to his hotel room and that Clinton then dropped his trousers and urged her to "kiss it." Filed suit in 1994 claiming sexual harassment. Her suit describes Clinton's penis as being five inches long, the diameter of a quarter, and having a pronounced bend to the left. Her attorneys have subpoenaed Monica Lewinsky, Kathleen Willey, Gennifer Flowers (see their entries), Shelia Lawrence, and several other women. The suit goes to trial in May 1998.

QUOTABLE QUOTE: On Clinton's seduction technique: "He proceeded to take my hand, pull me over, and slide his hand up my leg."

FUN FACT: To update her image, Jones has changed her hairstyle, hair color, clothes, teeth, and lipstick shade. Columnist Mary McGrory pointed out that Clinton could truthfully testify that he does not recall meeting anyone who looks like her.

NAME: VERNON JORDAN

RESIDENCE: Washington, D.C.

CLINTON CONNECTION: Democratic power-broker, Clinton golf partner, and all-purpose aide and adviser.

WHO IS HE REALLY?: Lawyer and lobbyist. Serves on several corporate boards. Former executive director of the Urban League. Regarding off-color banter while golfing with Clinton, Jordan has said, "Nothing wrong with a little locker room talk." Fond of quoting the Bible at board meetings. While having lunch with Zoe Baird, then-nominee for attorney general, received call from Clinton who said, "You're having lunch with a very pretty woman and I'm working." At a state dinner in 1995, regarding a blond woman sitting next to him, was told by Clinton, "I saw her first, Vernon." Helped Monica Lewinsky (see her entry) find a job at Revlon after she was exiled from the White House. The job offer was rescinded when current scandal broke.

QUOTABLE QUOTE: Explaining why he met personally with Lewinsky and escorted her to a lawyer's office after she had been subpoenaed in the Paula Jones case: "I believe to whom much is given, much is required."

FUN FACT: Jordan also arranged a $63,000 no-show job with Revlon for convicted Clinton friend Webster Hubbell.

NAME: PAULINE KANCHANALAK

RESIDENCE: Bangkok, Thailand

CLINTON CONNECTION: Gave $250,000, which was all returned. Her family members gave a total of $526,000, most of which was returned.

WHO IS SHE REALLY?: Prior to fleeing the United States, she lobbied on behalf of Charoen Pokphand, a Thai conglomerate. At the behest of John Huang, she illegally donated $250,000 and accompanied several Charoen Pokphand executives to a White House coffee.

QUOTABLE QUOTE: On her donations and White House meetings: "The incidents took place in such a way that this has the appearance of impropriety or something sinister. But I can assure you there is no impropriety."

FUN FACT: Has visited the White House twenty-six times

NAME: MONICA LEWINSKY

RESIDENCE: The Watergate apartments in Washington, D.C.

CLINTON CONNECTION: Her intern job at the White House was arranged by Walter Kaye (see Overnight White House Guests), big Clinton donor and close friend of Hillary Clinton. Lewinsky performed services for the President without compensation, both during and after hours.

WHO IS SHE REALLY?: Lewinsky was an unpaid intern in the White House from June 1995 to December 1995. Raised in Beverly Hills, California, Lewinsky graduated from Lewis and Clark College in Oregon in May 1995. After her White House service, she was transferred to the Pentagon Office of Public Affairs, where she became friends with former White House employee Linda Tripp (see her entry). Tripp surreptitiously taped twenty hours of conversations in which Lewinsky purported to have had a year-and-a-half affair with the President and also to have conspired with him and his close friend Vernon Jordan (see his entry) to cover up the relationship. Lewinsky was subpoenaed by Paula Jones's lawyers. The rest, as they say, is history.

QUOTABLE QUOTE: "Dear Schmucko, thank you for being. As my little nephew said, it was great to meet the Principal of the United States."

FUN FACT: Monica's mother, Marcia Lewis, wrote *The Private Lives of the Three Tenors*, a book about Luciano Pavarotti, Plácido Domingo, and José Carreras. It is alleged that she had an affair with Tenor Number Two.

NAME: CRAIG LIVINGSTONE

RESIDENCE: Orange County, California

CLINTON CONNECTION: Worked for Clinton-Gore campaign in '92.

WHO IS HE REALLY?: In 1993, was named Director of the White House Office of Personnel Security. Prior to that, was an advance man for Al Gore. Prior to that, was a bouncer. Is said to have gotten his White House job with the help of Hillary Rodham Clinton. Because it was a post of few responsibilities (the Secret Service handles presidential security), he kept himself busy looking through the FBI files of past Bush administration officials. The result was what the press termed "Filegate."

QUOTABLE QUOTE: "Basically, my job is to be invisible. If I'm around, something's wrong."

FUN FACT: Repeatedly threatened to beat up a neighbor woman whose dog barked too much.

NAME: MITCH MCCONNELL

RESIDENCE: Louisville, Kentucky, and Washington, D.C.

CLINTON CONNECTION: He promised to stop McCain-Feingold campaign finance reform bill backed by Clinton. Raised $2.1 million for the National Republican Senatorial Committee in the first six months of 1997.

WHO IS HE REALLY?: Republican Senator from Kentucky. Chairman of the National Republican Senatorial Committee. Believes that unregulated political contributions are equivalent to free speech. Has set new fund-raising records. Has promised to stop campaign finance reform. So far has kept his promise. Once received a campaign contribution from John Huang (see his entry).

QUOTABLE QUOTE: On the bargain that was the 1996 election cycle: "We spent per eligible voter $3.89—about the price of a McDonald's value meal."

FUN FACT: Elaine Chao, his wife, is the godmother of Isabella Huffington.

NAME: DICK MORRIS

RESIDENCE: Redding, Connecticut, and New York City

CLINTON CONNECTION: Has played an on-again, off-again role as political consultant and adviser to Clinton since the early 1980s. Provided the catalyst for the Clinton campaign's fund-raising frenzy with his demand that millions be raised to pay for early Clinton television commercials.

WHO IS HE REALLY?: Former top Clinton consultant who resigned in disgrace when, during the 1996 Democratic Convention in Chicago, *The Star* published photos of him with a prostitute. When the Monica Lewinsky story broke, according to Morris he was hastily brought back; according to the White House he faxed unsolicited advice. His role as political consultant became off-again after a Los Angeles radio interview in which he discussed the possibility that Hillary Clinton is a lesbian. Was also consultant for Trent Lott, Jesse Helms, William Weld, and George Bush.

QUOTABLE QUOTE: "I'm two people," he told Judith Regan. "An asshole who fucks hookers and a political genius who elects Presidents."

FUN FACT: Is convinced that Al Gore will be the next President.

NAME: DON NICKLES

RESIDENCE: Ponca City, Oklahoma, and Washington, D.C.

CLINTON CONNECTION: On the Thompson Committee investigating Clinton's 1996 fund-raising. In addition to raising money for his own campaigns, Nickles used to peddle dinners with top Republicans and a reception at the White House.

WHO IS HE REALLY?: Republican Senator from Oklahoma. A member of the Senate Governmental Affairs Committee. Rails at Lincoln Bedroom sleepovers, despite his own history of selling access.

QUOTABLE QUOTE: To Don Fowler (see his entry), during campaign finance hearings: "There are some things that make me wonder whether you're really being truthful with this committee."

FUN FACT: Has difficulty pronouncing the name of Clinton aide Ira Magaziner. Own name rhymes with that of a well-known "insult" comedian.

NAME: JACK QUINN

RESIDENCE: Washington, D.C.

CLINTON CONNECTION: Ardent defender of Al Gore's fund-raising tactics.

WHO IS HE REALLY?: Former White House Counsel, now in private practice. Dogged defender of the Clinton administration. In 1993, after writing three checks to the DNC for $15,000 apiece, John Huang sent Quinn a thank-you note, apparently in appreciation for being allowed to donate $45,000. Quinn also helped facilitate a meeting between Gore and Shen Jueren, Chairman of China Resources, owned by the Chinese government.

QUOTABLE QUOTE: "The Vice-President's actions—making fund-raising phone calls from his office—were legal. Not arguably legal, just plain legal."

FUN FACT: Photogenic addition to the drab lineup on the Sunday talk shows.

NAME: JANET RENO

RESIDENCE: Washington, D.C.

CLINTON CONNECTION: Has refused to appoint an independent counsel to look into Clinton's and Gore's fund-raising practices. But has approved Kenneth Starr's request to expand the Whitewater investigation to include Monica Lewinsky.

WHO IS SHE REALLY?: Attorney General. Criticized by James Carville and George Stephanopoulos for being too quick to name independent counsels. Subsequently resisted looking into White House fund-raising despite having firsthand knowledge of questionable activities. Was reportedly asked by Don Fowler (see his entry) to help out with fund-raising. (There is no evidence that she did.) Was Clinton's third choice for attorney general.

QUOTABLE QUOTE: On whether to appoint an independent counsel to investigate Clinton and Gore: "I haven't felt any pressure from the White House whatsoever. But I haven't felt any pressure from Congress whatsoever. Or the press. If somebody wants to impeach me, then I'll face the issue at that point, but that won't be a factor in my consideration."

FUN FACT: Relaxes by paddling a "big fat canoe" on the Potomac.

NAME: MOCHTAR RIADY

RESIDENCE: Jakarta, Indonesia

CLINTON CONNECTION: Family and family-owned businesses gave $800,000 to the Democrats.

WHO IS HE REALLY?: Ethnic Chinese Indonesian businessman who controls the Lippo Group, a multibillion-dollar conglomerate. With his substantial business interests in China, he has a vested interest in the United States continuing China's Most Favored Nation trading status. Estimates of Lippo campaign contributions are extremely large, though it is hard to trace them. Lippo received U.S. backing for a $2 billion project in Fujian, China—and President Clinton has become one of the biggest champions of uninterrupted trade with China, despite its 40 percent tariffs on U.S. goods. Riady met with Clinton at least once and, like John Huang (see his entry), personally lobbied Clinton on MFN as well as on lifting trade restrictions with Vietnam.

QUOTABLE QUOTE: In a letter to Clinton, he wrote that expanding trade with China was "the best way to achieve political reform."

FUN FACT: Paid Webb Hubbell (see his entry) $100,000 at a time when he was facing criminal prosecution and needed cash.

NAME: DONNA SHALALA

RESIDENCE: Washington, D.C.

CLINTON CONNECTION: Defended the President in a press conference at the outbreak of the Monica Lewinsky scandal.

WHO IS SHE REALLY?: The Secretary of Health and Human Services. Has a unique ability to make friends with her political enemies. Author's favorite cabinet member to share a red-eye flight from Los Angeles to Washington with.

QUOTABLE QUOTE: On spinning the '96 debates: "What we do is embellish."

FUN FACT: Secret Service code name is "Spin Doctor."

NAME: TED SIOENG

RESIDENCE: Los Angeles, Hong Kong, Singapore, Beijing. Has a Belize passport.

CLINTON CONNECTION: Sioeng, his family, and his companies gave $412,500 to the DNC and $152,000 to Republicans.

WHO IS HE REALLY?: International businessman. Exports Chinese Red Pagoda Mountain cigarettes to the United States. Owns a pro-China newspaper in California. Sat next to Clinton at fund-raising dinner, and sat at Gore's table at the Buddhist temple event. Has also met with Newt Gingrich (see his entry). Donated money to California Republican Matt Fong because he got tired of Fong's nagging. The FBI and the CIA have said they have information indicating Sioeng was in fact acting for the Chinese government in its attempts to influence the U.S. elections. Sioeng denies this.

QUOTABLE QUOTE: An associate of Sioeng's on the source of his money: "Since he did a lot for Yunnan [province, in China], he got the cigarette franchise, and that's where he got the big money from."

FUN FACT: Loves the United States so much that he often wears Statue of Liberty ties.

NAME: KENNETH STARR

RESIDENCE: Washington, D.C., area

CLINTON CONNECTION: The independent counsel doggedly but so far unsuccessfully investigating dozens of alleged Clinton misdeeds, including whether he encouraged White House intern Monica Lewinsky to commit perjury.

WHO IS HE REALLY?: Formerly solicitor general under President Ronald Reagan, former federal judge. Lucrative private law practice with clients that include tobacco companies. Appointed in 1994 to investigate the Clintons' Whitewater land deal and the death of Vincent Foster. Obtained convictions of Arkansas Governor Jim Guy Tucker, former Clinton business partners Jim and Susan McDougal, and close Clinton friend and former Associate Attorney General Webb Hubbell (see his entry). In 1997, Starr announced he would become dean at Pepperdine University in Malibu, leaving the Whitewater investigation before its conclusion; public outcry caused him to change his mind. New avenues of investigation were opened by tapes of Lewinsky discussing an affair with President Clinton.

QUOTABLE QUOTE: A former federal prosecutor, on the mostly glacial pace of Starr's investigations: "There's a feeling among most observers that if we had $30 million, we could have indicted our mothers."

FUN FACT: Blames the Supreme Court's seeming obsession with obscenity and pornography cases on youthful law clerks who have too much influence over the docket.

NAME: ROGER TAMRAZ

RESIDENCE: New York City

CLINTON CONNECTION: Donated $300,000 to the DNC and the Virginia Democratic Party.

WHO IS HE REALLY?: Lebanese-American oilman. Claims to have been a CIA asset during the seventies and eighties. Bought oil concessions in Turkmenistan in the early nineties. Then tried to get U.S. political support for a pipeline deal to move the oil to Turkey—a project opposed by American oil companies. The National Security Council resisted his attempts to meet with Gore because of his shady reputation. After his contributions to the Democrats, however, he visited the White House four times. Personally pitched his pipeline to the President at a White House dinner. Clinton instructed his trusted aide Mack McLarty to see what could be done for Tamraz. Ultimately, because of resistance from the NSC, the United States declined to help.

QUOTABLE QUOTES: On whether his large donations were made in order to gain White House access: "The *only* reason [to donate] is to get access." When asked whether the access he got for $300,000 was worth it: "I think next time I'll give $600,000." On donating large amounts of money to get into the White House after he'd been barred by the National Security Council: "If they kick me away from the door, I come through the window."

FUN FACT: Was asked by the Russians to give $100 million to Boris Yeltsin's campaign.

NAME: HARRY THOMASON

RESIDENCE: Santa Barbara and Encino, California

CLINTON CONNECTION: Has given large quantities of his time and energy to the Clintons (see below), including, most recently, contributing to the White House's Lewinsky damage control.

WHO IS HE REALLY?: With his wife, created the television shows *Designing Women, Evening Shade, Hearts Afire,* and *Women of the House.* With Linda, met Bill and Hillary in 1981 and became close friends. At the peak of their professional success in 1991, they obtained access into Hollywood circles for Clinton, who was at the time seen as provincial. Harry was the "producer" of both the '92 convention and Clinton's first Inaugural. The furor over his company's attempted takeover of the White House Travel Office in 1993 damaged his political prospects within the Clinton administration.

QUOTABLE QUOTE: On his stays in the Lincoln Bedroom: "Nobody goes to bed before midnight. There's always a card game going on or somebody watching TV. You know, the President loves to talk to his Arkansas friends."

FUN FACT: Before he became a TV mogul, he was a high school football coach in Arkansas.

NAME: FRED THOMPSON

RESIDENCE: Nashville, Tennessee, and Washington, D.C.

CLINTON CONNECTION: Chaired Senate hearings investigating Clinton fundraising.

WHO IS HE REALLY?: Republican Senator from Tennessee and chairman of the Governmental Affairs committee looking into campaign finance scandals. Was a counsel to the Watergate Committee in 1973. Said to be a presidential contender. Former actor.

QUOTABLE QUOTE: "High-level Chinese Government officials crafted a plan to increase China's influence over the U.S. political process. Our investigations suggest that it affected the 1996 presidential race."

FUN FACT: His acting career includes a role as an admiral in *The Hunt for Red October.*

NAME: YAH LIN "CHARLIE" TRIE

RESIDENCE: Travel restricted by the Justice Department to Washington, D.C., Norfolk, Virginia Beach, and Arkansas

CLINTON CONNECTION: Met Clinton in the early 1980s while running Fu Lin, Clinton's favorite restaurant in Little Rock. Gave $789,000 to the Clinton defense fund and $100,000 to the DNC, all of which was returned.

WHO IS HE REALLY?: When Clinton was Governor, he appointed Trie to the Arkansas Fire Extinguisher Board. As a result of his large donations, visited the White House twenty-two times and received an appointment to the Commission on

Pacific Trade. Clinton expanded the number of seats on the commission to make room for Trie. This favor was granted even though Trie's Daihatsu International Trading Corporation never made any money. Trie's only real source of funds was Mr. Wu, a foreign businessman who was also the source of his defense fund and DNC donations (see Mr. Wu's entry). Like Johnny Chung (see his entry), Trie obtained a White House visit for Chinese arms smuggler Wang Jun. After fleeing to Asia in late 1996, Trie returned in February 1998 to face a fifteen-count indictment for funneling illegal foreign donations to the Democrats.

QUOTABLE QUOTE: On hiding out from Congressional investigators in China: "They'll never find me."

FUN FACT: Used to show up at the Clinton defense fund office with bags stuffed with checks and money orders.

NAME: LINDA TRIPP

RESIDENCE: Columbia, Maryland

CLINTON CONNECTION: Secretly recorded her conversations with Monica Lewinsky and handed over the tapes to Kenneth Starr.

WHO IS SHE REALLY?: Pentagon civil servant. Former White House employee under Presidents Bush and Clinton. In late 1993, she encountered Kathleen Willey (see her entry) in a West Wing hallway. Willey told her she had been groped by the President. Willey later confirmed the story in testimony before a grand jury. When Monica Lewinsky (see her entry) revealed to Tripp that she had had an affair with the President, Tripp taped their conversations, first at the prompting of a friend, and then for Kenneth Starr (see his entry). When the existence of these tapes was revealed, Clinton, for the second time, was forced to deny having an extramarital affair on national television.

QUOTABLE QUOTE: Tripp confidante Lucianne Goldberg, on Tripp's reaction to the Clinton team: "[She] was heartsick about this crowd that had taken over the White House. The carpets were getting dirty. People were eating at their desks."

FUN FACT: Ghostwrote articles for the Bush White House defending another public figure accused of sexual harassment, Clarence Thomas.

NAME: KATHLEEN WILLEY

RESIDENCE: Midlothian, Virginia

CLINTON CONNECTION: With her late husband, was a Democratic contributor and fund-raiser. Attended Clinton's election night party in Little Rock in 1992.

WHO IS SHE REALLY?: USO board member and former staffer in the White House counsel's office. After her husband was accused of embezzlement in 1993, she requested a meeting with the President to discuss a paying position (she was an unpaid volunteer at the time). Afterwards, she told a friend—Linda Tripp (see her entry)—she'd been kissed and fondled by the President. The body of Willey's husband, who had committed suicide, was discovered the next day. Shortly thereafter, Willey got the job in the counsel's office and later the USO appointment. Was subpoenaed by Paula Jones's legal team, and under oath corroborated Tripp's account of her meeting with the President, but has refused to talk about the "fondling" incident. Her lawyers claimed her case was not relevant.

QUOTABLE QUOTE: Linda Tripp said Willey emerged from her meeting with Clinton "disheveled. Her face was red and her lipstick was off. She was flustered, happy, and joyful."

FUN FACT: At taxpayer expense, Willey attended international conferences on social development and biodiversity. A State Department official said he was "kind of surprised" because Willey had no expertise in these areas, but "a good way to get yourself in a jam is to ask too many questions when someone comes from the White House."

NAME: NG LAP SENG (AKA MR. WU)

RESIDENCE: Macao

CLINTON CONNECTION: Illegally funneled $905,000 through Charlie Trie (see his entry). Personally, and illegally, donated $15,000 to the DNC.

WHO IS HE REALLY?: Beijing puppet, business tycoon, and "business partner" of Charlie Trie. Among their "business ventures" was an attempt to market inflatable stadium cushions sporting corporate logos. Trie managed to get his partner into the White House on ten separate occasions.

QUOTABLE QUOTE: FBI Special Agent Jerome Campane, who was assigned to investigate Charlie Trie's donations: "We attempted to interview Mr. Wu when our investigators traveled to Asia. He said he would refuse to submit to an interview for us."

FUN FACT: On at least one occasion, Wu opened up a suitcase full of cash and handed Charlie Trie $20,000.

Overnight White House Guests:

IT'S NOT WHO YOU KNOW, IT'S HOW MUCH YOU GIVE

☆ ☆ ☆

"It's a special way of saying 'Thank you for services rendered.'"
—White House Spokesman Mike McCurry, on White House overnight visits by donors

MERV AND THEA ADELSON: $145,000. He is chairman of East-West Capital Associates (venture capital) and founder of Lorimar Telepictures, which produced *Dallas*. Called by Al Gore, who asked for $125,000.

TRUMAN ARNOLD: $234,950. Chairman and CEO of Truman Arnold Petroleum and founder of the Roadrunner convenience store chain. Other businesses include construction, banking, and cattle. Was one of the big DNC contributors who gave Webb Hubbell a no-show job after Hubbell resigned from the Justice Department. DNC chief for five months in 1995. Admitted using the White House donor database to ensure that big givers got the appropriate perks, including nights in the Lincoln Bedroom. His companies often provided air transport for Clinton when he was Governor of Arkansas.

NORMA ASNES: $36,000. Writer. Friend of Hillary Clinton's. Her cook baked the cookies for a 1992 tea in her honor. Named by Clinton as a delegate to the 1995 White House Conference on Aging. Appointed to the Madison Council of the Library of Congress.

JOSEPH AND KATHLEEN BACZKO: $27,500. He is a private investor and former CEO of Blockbuster Video. Fired in 1993.

LEN BARRACK: $10,000. His law firm, Barrack Rodos & Bacine, gave $115,000 (see Dick Batchelor). On the intense and unwelcome scrutiny being given to big donors: "I'm a longtime supporter of the party. I'm happy to donate."

DICK BATCHELOR: $1,250. His law firm, Barrack Rodos & Bacine, gave $115,000 (see Len Barrack). Former Florida State Representative and early fund-raiser for Clinton. Spent his tenth anniversary in the White House. On his stay: "Jody Powell and Larry King were there, and we watched the movie *Rudy.*"

NANCY BEKAVAC: $2,500. President of Scripps College. Friend of the Clintons from Yale Law School. Appointed chair cf the White House Fellows program in 1993. On Clinton's appetite for finding out the details of people's lives: "If he were a novelist, he would be like Tolstoy." On Clinton's Yale days: "You could never view his performance in a totally positive way. You wondered, 'Is it real?' There were moments that were so genuine that there was no doubt about it, and moments when you wondered, 'Is this posture?'"

MARILYN BERGMAN: $1,000. Songwriter. Cofounder of the Hollywood Women's Political Committee, which recently disbanded because of members' disgust over constant fund-raising. Rewrote lyrics of her song "The Way We Were" for Barbra Streisand (see her entry) to sing at a 1996 Clinton fund-raiser.

WILLIAM BRANDT: $171,800 personally and from his company, Development Specialists, Inc. (corporate turnaround consulting). Also gave $100,000 for the 1996 Democratic National Convention. Major Clinton fund-raiser and DNC member, has raised over $2 million in the past two years. Attended Ireland state dinner. Senator Charles Grassley (R-Iowa) has asked the Justice Department to investigate a 1996 fund-raiser at Brandt's home attended by the Clintons, as well as Brady Williamson, head of the commission on reworking bankruptcy law. According to bankers who attended, Brandt told them the event would be a chance for them to influence bankruptcy laws. The event raised over $1 million. Also lied in court about receiving a Harvard degree and working for the CIA. On his Midas touch: "It's been kind of fun doing this. I've been told by the DNC that I was one of their largest donors and one of their biggest fund-raisers. But they probably tell that to a lot of people."

ELI BROAD: $187,500 personally and from his companies. Cofounder of Kaufman & Broad Home Corp., the largest home builder in California, and founder and chairman of SunAmerica, an investment firm, which also gave $30,000 to the GOP. Called by Al Gore, who asked for $50,000. SunAmerica gave Webb Hubbell a no-show job after the disgraced Assistant Attorney General had to resign from the Justice Department. Once used an American Express card to buy a $2.5 million painting so he'd get a frequent-flyer-mile bonus.

RON BURKLE: $285,000 personally and from his company, Food 4 Less Supermarkets. Hosted a $4 million fund-raiser for Clinton. Guests included Steven Spielberg, David Geffen, Lew Wasserman (see their entries), and Sharon Stone. Entertainment was provided by Tom Hanks, Barbra Streisand (see their entries), Don Henley, and Paula Poundstone. A minor crisis erupted when Clinton had to move: Aides feared that Clinton would be photographed next to Calvin Klein, who was facing heavy criticism for his ad campaign that some had called "kiddie porn," and Clinton had to switch seats. Made a last-minute donation that helped Representative Loretta Sanchez outspend and defeat Republican Congressman Bob Dornan. Has played golf with Clinton. On his tour of Air Force One with other donors: "There wasn't a napkin or box of M&Ms left."

IRIS CANTOR: $15,000. Widow of Gerald Cantor, arts patron, and founder of the Wall Street investment firm Cantor Fitzgerald. The Cantors received the National Medal of Arts in 1995.

JOHN CATSIMATIDIS: $82,000 personally and from his companies. Chairman of Red Apple Companies (supermarkets, etc.). Called from the White House by Gore, who left a message. Later hosted a New York fund-raiser featuring Gore. Once committed Red Apple stores to a boycott of California grapes to protest use of harmful pesticides. On the supermarket business: "When I open another store, and see the reaction my customers have to it . . . I'm happy again."

PAUL AND TRUDY CEJAS: $200,700. He is the former chairman of CareFlorida Health Systems. Chairman, Free Cuba Commission (advises Florida Governor). Enjoys fishing and ice hockey. Has been delinquent on his property taxes. On the business community's support for Clinton: "The [erroneous] assumption is that Republicans are for business and the Democrats are for the people."

CHEVY CHASE: $55,000. Actor. Cosponsored a $1,000-a-plate benefit in 1992 with Richard Dreyfuss (see his entry), producer Jon Peters, and Neil Simon (see his entry). Performed at many Democratic fund-raisers, including one in Little Rock that raised $3 million in 1992.

JOHN CONNELLY: $200,000. Owner of President Casino Corp. (riverboat gambling) and other businesses. Building a hotel for the Pope in Vatican City. On his night in the Lincoln Bedroom: "One of the highlights of my life."

ROBERT AND DENISE DANGREMOND: $2,000. He is a partner at Jay Alix & Associates (business turnaround specialists). She is a sometime Democratic volunteer who, during the 1996 convention, tried to confiscate flyers critical of Clinton from reporters and delegates.

SEAN DANIEL: $750. Movie producer. Former head of production at Universal Pictures, which is owned by MCA, Inc. (see Lew Wasserman). Produced, among other films, *Dazed and Confused,* whose characters inhale repeatedly. His father was blacklisted during anticommunist witch hunts in the 1950s. On the current lack of political moviemaking: "Political battles as played out on the news are so much a part of people's daily life that it's a difficult problem to capture something that they get so much exposure to." On the Hollywood Women's Political Caucus, which disbanded last year: "I can certainly understand their frustration with fundraising always dominating any other kind of political activity. But that's never going to change . . ."

TED DANSON: $10,000. Actor and producer. Married to actress Mary Steenburgen, an old friend of the Clintons from Arkansas. Wedding was attended by the First Couple. Member of Environmentalists for Clinton-Gore in 1996.

RONALD AND BETH DOZORETZ: $171,640. She raised over $2 million and was present at a White House coffee with John Huang (see Dramatis Personae). Told Senator Thompson's committee that Huang did not solicit funds at the coffee. She was appointed to the Holocaust Commission by Clinton. He was appointed to the board of the Kennedy Center. Bought their Washington home from author of *Greetings from the Lincoln Bedroom* in a completely aboveboard transaction.

RICHARD DREYFUSS: $2,500. Actor. Gave stump speeches during Clinton's '92 campaign bus tour. Has his own personal political adviser, Donna Bojarsky. Sponsored a fund-raising event with Chevy Chase (see his entry). On his night in the Lincoln Bedroom: "They let you call anywhere, so I called my kids from the Lincoln Bedroom. My daughter said, 'That's so cool! Steal something!'" Woken up by Clinton the next morning at 7:20 to discuss politics, the Constitution, the Middle East, and golf.

PATRICIA DUFF: $2,000. Stayed in the Lincoln Bedroom with then-husband, movie executive Mike Medavoy. Hosted Clinton in their home in 1992 and introduced him to many Hollywood people. With estranged husband Ron Perelman, Duff hosted a Palm Beach fund-raiser that raised $1 million. Perelman's Revlon Group has given $455,000. Now on the Library of Congress Trust Fund Board.

DANIEL DUTKO AND DEBORAH JOSPIN: $2,250 personally and from Dutko's company. He is CEO of Dutko Group (lobbying). Was national finance vice-chairman of Clinton-Gore '96. Solicited donations to the DNC from clients whom he still represented as a lobbyist. Got lobbying clients invited to White House coffees. Now raising money for the DNC for the '98 midterm elections. Considered a Gore ally. Once coordinated the Council for a Secure America, which united New York Jewish leaders and Texas oilmen to push for tax breaks for the oil industry and for support of Israel.

RICHARD FRIEDMAN: $10,000. Boston developer. Owns restaurants, hotels, and shopping centers. Owns a twenty-acre estate on Martha's Vineyard where the Clintons twice vacationed. Now calls it the "Clinton Cottage." The night he stayed in the Lincoln Bedroom, Clinton and others watched Oliver Stone's *Nixon*, but Friedman left early so he could spend more time in the historic room. On his taste in friends: "Highly successful people excite me. I love people who have a tremendous amount of creative energy—whether they are in Hollywood, business, or the White House."

ROY AND FRIEDA FURMAN: $260,000. He is cofounder and vice-chairman of Furman Selz (investment bank). White House stay was arranged by DNC fund-raiser Marvin Rosen in the hope that Furman would donate more money. Furman later wrote the DNC a check for $50,000.

JOHN AND PATRICIA GARAMENDI: $3,400 personally and from Garamendi for Governor. He is a former California insurance commissioner and current Deputy Secretary in the Interior Department responsible for Guam policy. Following Hillary Clinton's visit in 1996, several Guam businessmen donated over $600,000. Garamendi subsequently came out in support of more autonomy for Guam. He denied any connection to the donations. The autonomy was not granted. Also intervened with several federal agencies on behalf of Angelo Tsakopoulos (see his entry), a friend and major contributor.

DAVID GEFFEN: $425,127. Cofounder of DreamWorks SKG (movies, television, music). Major Democratic fund-raiser. In 1995, he cohosted with DreamWorks partners Jeffrey Katzenberg and Steven Spielberg (see his entry) an event that raised $2 million. On what he expects to gain from his fund-raising: "I have no active involvement in trying to influence legislation of any kind."

CHARLES AND FELICIA GERVAIS: $53,000. He is a partner in Gervais, Carew & Dick (real estate consulting). She is president of Leonard L. Farber, Inc. (shopping center development). Also gave $1,000 to the Clinton defense fund. Attended a state dinner for the President of France at which Michael Douglas switched places in the receiving line with Clinton. She was named chair of the Presidential Scholars program.

GARY DAVID GOLDBERG: $30,000. TV producer, head of UBU productions. Once a major Democratic contributor. But after a conflict with James Carville over the Clinton health care plan, his giving slowed to a trickle.

STEVEN GREEN: $11,000. Real estate developer and CEO of Astrum International, a billion-dollar company that owns Samsonite, among other things. Worth over $500 million. Clinton threw him a twenty-eighth-anniversary party at the White House, which included the Lincoln Bedroom stay. His foreign ventures, like those of Alan Patricof, have been subsidized by the Overseas Private Investment Corporation, a corporate welfare program. Received a $240 million government loan guarantee for projects in the former Soviet Union. Accompanied the late Commerce Secretary Ron Brown on numerous trade missions. Appointed to President's Export Council in 1995.

BRIAN GREENSPUN: $165,950 personally, from family members, and his business. President and publisher of the *Las Vegas Sun* newspaper. Clinton's roommate at Georgetown University. Introduced Clinton to contributors from the gambling industry. Hosted a $25,000-per-couple lunch with Clinton at his home. Half the money raised came from gaming interests. Appointed to the 1993 White House Conference on Small Business. On his two-night Lincoln Bedroom stay: "The greatest field trip of my life."

STEVEN AND BARBARA GROSSMAN $357,240. He is the president of the Massachusetts Envelope Co., and a former president of the American Israel Public Affairs Committee, a pro-Israel lobbying group. National Chairman of the DNC. Proposed raising money by issuing affinity credit cards to party members.

Now favors banning soft money. She was appointed to the National Council for the Arts.

PETER AND LYNDA GUBER: $103,000. He is the former head of Sony Pictures and current head of Mandalay Entertainment, a film production company. Also gave $100,000 to Republicans.

TOM HANKS AND RITA WILSON: $5,000. Actors. Hosted a 1995 fund-raiser at L.A.'s Century Plaza Hotel that raised over $1 million. Watched a screening of his movie *Apollo 13* the night he stayed in the Lincoln Bedroom. The next day he attended the presentation of the Medal of Honor to astronaut James Lovell, whom Hanks played in the film.

FRED HOCHBERG: $75,750. Former president of Lillian Vernon Corp., son of founder Lillian Vernon (see her entry). Now a gay-rights activist.

RAY IRANI: $105,000 personally and from his company. Chairman and CEO of Occidental Petroleum. Recently received a $95 million bonus for agreeing to stay in his job. Was a guest at a Bush state dinner for the President of Argentina.

NORMAN JEWISON: $1,350. Director. Films include *In the Heat of the Night* and *A Soldier's Story*.

STEVEN JOBS: $150,000. CEO, Apple Corp. Helped bring Silicon Valley execs into the Clinton camp in '96, despite their anger at Clinton's veto of a bill to discourage shareholder lawsuits. Just before a dinner with computer executives at Jobs's home, Clinton announced his opposition to a California law that would have made shareholder lawsuits easier to file.

ROGER AND JANICE JOHNSON: $6,100. Were moderate Republicans, but supported Clinton in 1992. He is now a Democrat. But when he was appointed head of the General Services Administration in 1992, he was the highest-ranking Republican in the Clinton administration.

ROBERT TRENT JONES, JR.: $62,450 personally and from his company, Robert Trent Jones, Inc. (golf course architects). Clinton is a member of the Jones golf club in Virginia, and he hired Jones to replace the artificial putting green at the White House with real grass. The $23,000 cost was covered by donations.

WALTER KAYE: $347,658. President of Kaye Insurance. In addition to his overnight stay, Kaye got invitations to a White House reception, the White House Christmas party, and other events. And he facilitated Monica Lewinsky's ill-fated internship at the White House.

LARRY AND SHELIA LAWRENCE: $200,000. He is the late owner of the famed Hotel del Coronado. Hosted the Clintons at their home when the President and First Lady were in San Diego. Donated over $10 million to the Democratic Party over a period of forty years. In 1994, he became Ambassador to Switzerland, and she became special envoy to the World Conservation Union. She donated $50,856 to DNC after her husband's death. On December 12, 1997, he was dug up from Arlington National Cemetery after confirmation that his World War II record as a merchant marine was fabricated.

IRA AND CYNTHIA LEESFIELD: $122,500 personally and from his firm, Leesfield, Leighton, & Rubio (law firm). Called by Gore, who asked for $50,000. Attended a White House coffee. Named head of the President's Council on Fitness.

ALAN LEVENTHAL: $180,000 personally and from his company. Managing partner of Beacon Properties Corp. His family and business associates also gave $140,000. Leventhal also gave $1,000 to the Clinton defense fund. Attended three White House coffees. With Fred Siegel, his business partner, raised $3 million. They were called the "Energizer bunnies" of fund-raising by Clinton. Their company, Energy Capital Partners, was chosen to run a new loan program for HUD, structured so that they could make a lot of money while being protected from loss by the government. Subpoenaed by the Senate Governmental Affairs Committee for his role in fund-raising.

CARL LINDNER: $315,000 personally and from his companies, which include Chiquita Brands International and American Financial Corp. Also gave $500,000 to the National Policy Forum, a front organization for Republican Party fund-raising, and $150,000 to a GOP congressional committee. Chiquita Brands successfully lobbied to have the European Union lift trade barriers on its bananas, angering U.S. allies in the Caribbean, whose bananas had benefited from the restrictions.

PETER AND LENI MAY: $432,250. He is president of Triarc Companies, which owns Arby's, Royal Crown Cola, and Snapple. Called by Al Gore, who asked for $50,000. On Triarc's Mistic beverages: "The rain-forest line appeals to people on an emotional level because it benefits rain forests."

RICHARD MAYS: $33,800 personally and from his law firm, Mays & Crutcher. Longtime friend of Clinton's. Appointed to the Arkansas Supreme Court in the early 1980s. He is also the lawyer for Eric Wynn, whom Mays recruited as a big Democratic donor. Wynn has been convicted of tax evasion and securities fraud and has ties to organized crime, but attended several events with the President. Mays was a key fund-raiser for Clinton in '92, and organized an event in Washington, D.C., that raised $500,000.

OLAN AND NORMA MILLS II: $121,000. He is chairman of Olan Mills, Inc. (portrait studios). Also attended a coffee. On why he gives: "The Democratic Party needs to raise enough money to be viable, and I guess that's the simplest explanation."

LESLIE MOONVES: $7,500. President of CBS Entertainment. Named by Clinton cochair of the Advisory Committee on Public Interest Obligations of Digital Television Broadcasters. The committee is to study ways of giving free airtime to federal candidates.

PETER AND EILEEN NORTON: $350,000. He is the founder of Norton Utilities, a software company. She is on the board of the Children's Defense Fund. He is now retired and devotes his time to the Norton Family Foundation, which supports cultural and humanitarian projects.

DEAN ORNISH: $500. Physician and best-selling author of *Eat More, Weigh Less.* Demonstrated that heart disease is reversible by changing diet and lifestyle. Introduced the Clintons to veggie burgers.

ALAN AND SUSAN PATRICOF: $90,250. He is the president of Patricof & Co. (venture capital). Brought many guests to coffees at the White House. Patricof executives donated $72,000. Chaired Clinton's 1995 White House Conference on Small Business. Helped line up business support for Clinton. Son's company designed the Clinton-Gore '96 Web site. Patricof & Co.'s foreign subsidiary has benefited from "corporate welfare" intended to promote U.S. exports (see Alan Leventhal). Company lost money on an investment in a new strain of lab mice. On Clinton: "This country should be proud to have such a brilliant man leading it."

WILLIAM AND PATRICIA PODLICH: $13,200. He is founder and co-CEO of Pacific Investment Management Co. Early Clinton supporter. Democrat from Orange County, California. On his first donation: "Finally Clinton . . . came out to California two years ago [in 1990], locked me in a room, twisted my arm, and I finally decided to [donate]. These are the kinds of things that are fun."

MORRIS PYNOOS: $1,000. P & M Realty Corp. Also gave $1,000 to the Clinton defense fund.

WILLIAM AND CAROLYN RAINER: $29,000. He is a cofounder of Greenwich Capital Markets, a bond-trading firm. A key '92 Wall Street supporter of Clinton. Lifelong Republican, but switched allegiance from Bush because he had "great confidence in Clinton's leadership." He and his company each loaned Clinton's inaugural committee $100,000. In 1994 was appointed chairman of the U.S. Enrichment Corp., which oversees the Energy Department's procurement of uranium.

BRUCE AND JULIE RATNER: $21,500. He is president of Forest City Ratner Companies (real estate). After Forest City donated to then-Governor Mario Cuomo, he was beneficiary of a deal to rent space to New York State agencies. Raised funds for former New York mayor David Dinkins. Now raises money for Republican mayor Rudy Giuliani.

STEVEN AND MAUREEN RATTNER: $189,000. He is Deputy CEO of Lazard Frères & Co. (investment bank). Raised over $750,000. The Rattners' White House stay included dinner in the Solarium with Clinton, a swim in the pool, and another dinner with Judy Collins and Liza Minnelli.

RENEE RING: $3,000. International lawyer. Friend of Hillary's. Contributed to Clinton's gubernatorial campaigns. Attends Renaissance Weekends with the Clintons.

WILLIAM ROLLNICK AND NANCY ELLISON: $501,300. He is a co-owner of Mattel. On staying in the Lincoln Bedroom: "For a kid from Cleveland, it was pretty heady stuff. It was major-league excitement . . . I could see a causal relationship between being invited to stay there and then giving . . . I guess I never did anything right; I was already giving."

LEWIS RUDIN: $75,000. President, Rudin Management (landlord). Like Bruce Ratner (see his entry), Rudin was a supporter of David Dinkins, but now raises money for Rudy Giuliani.

STANLEY AND BETTY SHEINBAUM: $17,000. He publishes *New Perspectives Quarterly*. She has two paintings hanging in the residence of Derek Shearer, U.S. Ambassador to Finland. Stanley's fondest wish: "That people will come to understand the effect on economic policy of the policymakers in Washington who are primarily supported by the wealthy."

SIDNEY AND LORRAINE SHEINBERG: $220,000. He was the president of MCA, Inc., under Lew Wasserman (see his entry). Now owns the Bubble Factory, a film production company. Was once thrown off a New Orleans bus for sitting in the back with blacks. On one of Bubble Factory's movies: "*McHale's Navy* was a disaster. I'm not pretending it wasn't a disaster."

STANLEY SHUMAN: $214,700. Executive vice-president and managing director of Allen & Co. (investment bank). Raised $750,000. Got a happy birthday call from Clinton. Attended a state dinner. Was appointed to the President's Foreign Intelligence Advisory Board, which grants members access to all categories of U.S. intelligence. Has no foreign policy experience.

NEIL SIMON: $31,000. Playwright. Frequent guest at big California fund-raisers such as Lew Wasserman's (see his entry). Has not announced any plans to write another of his hotel sex farces based on his overnight stay (perhaps called *White House Suite*).

ALAN SOLOMONT: $201,400 personally and from his former company, ADS Management, Inc. (nursing homes). Finance chairman, DNC. Jogged with Clinton and accompanied him on a trip to the Middle East. Subpoenaed by the Senate Governmental Affairs committee to testify about fund-raising. Had high-level access to the Clinton administration when officials were considering loosening rules on nursing homes. Now favors banning soft money. An old friend of Ira Magaziner. On his beginnings as a major donor and fund-raiser: "I never set out to be a heavy hitter." On fund-raising now: "It's a hard time to be a fund-raiser . . . We endure a lousy press, people asking if we are just influence peddlers."

ROY SPENCE: $27,000. Cofounder and president of GSD&M (advertising and public relations). His firm has been a paid consultant to Clinton's advertising team. Met Clinton while working on George McGovern's 1972 presidential campaign. Helped prepare Clinton for his '92 convention speech and the '95 State of the Union address. Well known in the White House for his oft-repeated admonition that Clinton needs to stay focused on "the heart of the heartland and not the belt of the Beltway."

STEVEN SPIELBERG AND KATE CAPSHAW: $436,023. He is cofounder of DreamWorks SKG (movies, television, music). Hosted a 1995 fund-raiser with his DreamWorks partners Jeffrey Katzenberg and David Geffen (see his entry) that raised $2 million. Afterward, Clinton stayed at their Pacific Palisades home.

CARL SPIELVOGEL AND BARBARALEE DIAMON-STEIN-SPIELVOGEL: $160,650. He is chairman of Carl Spielvogel Associates and former CEO of United Auto Group. She is an author and landmarks preservation expert. They stayed in the Lincoln Bedroom during Clinton's first term before the President's famous handwritten note: "Ready to begin overnights." He was named to the Broadcasting Board of Governors for the International Bureau of Broadcasting. She was named to the Commission on Fine Arts.

WARREN STEPHENS: $35,000. CEO of Stephens Inc., one of the largest brokerage houses outside Wall Street. Stephens Inc. is one of the biggest clients of the Rose Law Firm, Hillary Clinton's former employer. He and his late father, Witt, were longtime supporters of Bill Clinton, and their companies did substantial business with the state. Stephens Inc. illegally helped the notorious Bank of Credit and Commerce International gain entry into the United States. The Stephens family also owned a large part of Little Rock's Worthen Bank in 1992, when Worthen officer John Huang (see Dramatis Personae) approved a crucial loan to the Clinton campaign. The Riady family (see Dramatis Personae) also held a stake in Worthen at the time. On his stay in the Lincoln Bedroom: "It was really special—a thrill. I don't know exactly what gets you an invitation. I don't know why I got invited, but it was a damn nice honor."

BARBRA STREISAND: $85,000. Singer/director/actress/activist. Has a personal political adviser, Margery Tabankin. At a '96 fund-raiser at Lew Wasserman's house (see his entry), Streisand updated the words of "It Had to Be You" and sang it to Clinton.

ROSE STYRON: $1,000. Poet and journalist. Socializes with the Clintons on Martha's Vineyard.

ANGELO TSAKOPOULOS: $245,000 personally and from his family. Owns AKT Development Corp. Organized a 1994 fund-raiser at which Clinton was a guest. Attended a state dinner for the President of Greece and a coffee, at which he told Clinton that "bureaucrats are running wild" because his plans to develop vineyards on 8,000 acres that included wetlands were being blocked by the government. He began work on the development without permits. His old friend Deputy Secretary of the Interior John Garamendi (see his entry) intervened with federal agencies on his behalf.

LILLIAN VERNON: $239,000. Owns Lillian Vernon Corp., a mail-order business. Made several small but oddly useful stump speeches for Clinton.

ALICE WALTON: $162,500. Wal-Mart heiress. Her Llama investment company is named after her favorite animal. Held a crucial fund-raiser in New York the week before the 1992 primary. Friendly enough with the Clintons that Warren Christopher, in a speech in Buenos Aires, made a joke about running into her as she left the Oval Office.

LEW WASSERMAN: $335,000. Chairman emeritus of MCA, Inc. (movie and television production). An old California Democratic lion, but had a long relationship with Ronald Reagan, whom he helped make a star. Raised $1 million for Clinton at a party attended by Barbra Streisand (see her entry) and Republican Kevin Costner. In the late 1970s, single-handedly rescued the DNC from near bankruptcy with a large donation.

HUGH AND CAROLE WESTBROOK: $90,002 personally, from their sons, and from his company. He is CEO of Vitas Healthcare Corp. Their sons, Matthew and Stever, also stayed in the White House. Hugh was also the head of Vote Now '96, a nonprofit get-out-the-minority-vote organization allied with the Democrats. Harold Ickes (see Dramatis Personae) tried to funnel donations to Vote Now to help a contributor who wanted a tax deduction.

AUDREE WIRGINIS: $20,000. Owns the Gateway Clipper riverboat cruise fleet, which she purchased from her father, John Connelly (see his entry). Attended state dinner for German Chancellor Helmut Kohl. Had her picture taken with both Bill Clinton and the Pope. Amount tithed to the Pope, if any, is unknown.

DIRK ZIFF: $612,000. Chairman of Ziff Bros. Investments, which invests his and his brother's fortune. First-ever donation, in 1995: $300,000. Socializes with Clinton on Martha's Vineyard.

Acknowledgments

☆ ☆ ☆

This book is for me a departure, but also a coming home—to the journalism of my youth and to my life in England, where I learned the power of satire and invective the hard way, often at the receiving end during endless debates at the Cambridge Union. From Cambridge I moved to a London steeped in the culture of *Monty Python* and *That Was the Week That Was,* wrote satirical columns for *Punch* and the *Daily Mail,* and traveled around the country giving after-dinner speeches—the ritualized British version of standup.

Then I sobered up, wrote biographies and books on various states—of women, of political leadership, of our soul, and of the Greek gods—and moved to America. My journey back to the world of comedy and satire started in 1994 when I was asked to appear on a little-known cable show taping in New York called *Politically Incorrect.* On that *Politically Incorrect* I met Harry Shearer. Spending time with Harry—whether on TV, working on our media spoof *Eat the Press* or bonding at a Steve Forbes fund-raiser—has been a comedic education on which I drew in writing this book. Also, Scott Carter, *PI*'s executive producer, became a mentor and a friend on a strange path that led to my first satirical work in bed, a running segment for the 1996 conventions with Al Franken called, appropriately, *Strange Bedfellows.* For the record Al, it was the best political coverage from bed I've ever had.

Al, Harry, and Bill Maher all in their different ways taught me a lot, but bear no responsibility for what I haven't yet learned. Al also introduced me to Billy Kimball, who produced *Summit After Dark,* our light-hearted look at the Presidents' summit in Philadelphia, as well as a harrowing live hour of *Strange Bedfellows* in New York. I'm grateful to Billy for his help in structuring and shaping the book, as well as for steering me out of many blind alleys. I'm also grateful to Michael McCarthy for his imaginative contributions and Celtic disposition, and to Stephen Sherrill for bringing his biting wit to bear on the manuscript.

Mike Anton brought to the book skills ranging from his deep knowledge of Lincoln and the Founding Fathers to his editing through successive drafts. I'm thankful to Fleming Saunders, Geoff Rodke, Jon Hotchkiss, and Eric Fettman for their editorial suggestions; to Andrew Breitbart for his help with research; and to Francis Gasparini for ferreting out new facts and suggesting interesting twists.

I will always be grateful to my agent, Richard Pine, for suggesting that I write this book, for coming up with its name, and above all, for introducing me to Steve Ross, my editor at Crown. Steve not only instantly embraced the idea but guided me through every step, and encouraged me to take risks I would never have taken had he not been there to catch me. Although we had a few bargaining sessions, I grew to trust and depend on his judgment so much that around my office he's known as the Pope. My gratitude to Steve for the myriad ways in which he strengthened the book is compounded by how much of a pleasure it was to work with him. I'm also indebted to all at Crown who took part in that first brainstorming session and brought so much enthusiasm and creativity to the project. Special thanks go to Whitney Cookman for the jacket, to Harry Trumbore for the illustrations, to Alexia Brue for helping steer the book through all its different stages, and to Barbara Marks for helping make sure that the book not only was written but would also be read.

In the background of many editorial sessions were Christina and Isabella, to whom I'm grateful for putting up with Mommy working again, as well as for being the best thing I ever did. Isabella even provided me with two professional funny dads from her class, Seth Greenland and Billy Diamond, who were generous enough to read the first draft and offer many valuable suggestions. I'm also very thankful to Lynn Sweet, Washington Bureau Chief of the *Chicago Sun-Times*—who broke the first story on the selling of White House access back in 1995—for sharing her knowledge and checking mine.

Deep thanks go to all those who provided me with facts and first-hand accounts about the Lincoln Bedroom and life at the White House—Lisa Caputo, Beth Dozoretz, Phyllis George, Dick Morris, and his wife, Eileen McGann. They share no blame for the fantasy I built on their facts.

Keeping the kitchen, the love, and the support going through many long nights of writing was my mother, Elli Stassinopoulos, whose own journey began in Greece seventy-five years ago and whose breadth of appreciation ranges from stuffed grape leaves to jokes about the American President and the Speaker of the House.

And, of course, thanks to Bill Clinton, Newt Gingrich, Don Fowler, Haley Barbour, Mitch McConnell, Al Gore, and all the others whose tireless efforts to promote political participation and free speech provided the carbon and hydrogen for the elements herein. This entire cast freed me from that most difficult of the writer's tasks: creating unique, memorable characters. Thanks, guys, I couldn't have made you up.

And thanks to Monica Lewinsky, Paula Jones, Linda Tripp, Ken Starr, Vernon Jordan, and all the others whose tireless efforts to provide, promote, or interfere with sex in the White House dragged political satire into the gutter, turning a book that I would have proudly shown to my young daughters into one that I now have to keep locked and hidden.